Preparing people to lead extraordinary lives

LOYOLA UNIVERSITY CHICAGO

Born in Chicago

A History of Chicago's Jesuit University

Ellen Skerrett

Foreword by Andrew M. Greeley

LOYOLAPRESS.
A JESUIT MINISTRY
CHICAGO

LOYOLA PRESS.
A JESUIT MINISTRY
3441 N. ASHLAND AVENUE
CHICAGO, ILLINOIS 60657
(800) 621-1008
WWW.LOYOLAPRESS.ORG

Jacket and book design by Herman Adler
Front and back jacket photos by Mark Beane

Library of Congress Cataloging-in-Publication Data

Skerrett, Ellen.
  Born in Chicago : a history of Chicago's Jesuit university / Ellen Skerrett ; foreword by Andrew Greeley.
    p. cm.
  ISBN-13: 978-0-8294-2794-3
  ISBN-10: 0-8294-2794-5
  1. Loyola University of Chicago—History. I. Title.
  LD3131.L72S54 2008
  378.773'11—dc22
                                      2008015315

Printed in Malaysia for Imago
01 02 03 04 05 IMG 10 9 8 7 6 5 4 3 2 1

Contents

Introduction

The history of this great University began as an inspiration. Father Arnold Damen, S.J., an indefatigable man with a big vision, believed that the town of Chicago, emerging on the banks of the great Lake Michigan, would one day be home to a different kind of citizen. He sensed that the energy he found in the people who pioneered this new settlement would create something unique, and he knew they would need educational opportunities of a higher order to assist them. Father Damen started this University in fulfillment of the Jesuit intellectual mission so that the diverse talents of its community could be harnessed to benefit the city, the country, and the world.

Ever since then, Loyola University Chicago, through its alumni, has been a partner in building and sustaining this city. Chicago's fortunes have shaped the fortunes of the University from the earliest days, just as Loyolans have helped shape the city that gave them so much. Throughout its nearly 140 years, Loyola's graduates have taken their places in the halls of government, in hubs of industry and commerce, in churches, and in vital professions of all kinds. More than 120,000 alumni help shape their communities in nearly every part of this vast American continent and throughout the globe. Our alumni approach their careers and lives with the attitude that one must give back to one's community. Ultimately, Loyolans understand what the Jesuit educational tradition has always taught: that our lives and communities are sustained by God and that our aim must always be His greater glory.

Like the history of the University itself, this project was the result of hard work and collaboration. We are tremendously grateful to Ellen Skerrett for her meticulous research on all things Loyola. She has captured the University's rich history and, with it, the history of Chicago. In these pages, you'll encounter photographs and archival images that have never been seen before. The full revelation of Ellen's exhaustive effort was only possible due to the extraordinary contributions of a few key individuals. Sylvia Bace tirelessly edited the manuscript in its many versions. Beth Adler expertly wove together the text and hundreds of visual materials. Mark Beane contributed numerous awe-inspiring photographs—including the cover photograph—that capture the spirit of who we are as a University community. Father George Lane, S.J., and his colleagues at Loyola Press were enormously helpful in shepherding this project from beginning to end. We owe a debt of gratitude to these individuals and many others whose commitment to Loyola University Chicago and to the idea of sharing our story made this book a reality.

I hope that you will enjoy reading *Born in Chicago*. The book is an invitation to linger over all that reminds us of our proud heritage and keeps us looking toward an even more ambitious future.

Ad Majorem Dei Gloriam.

Michael J. Garanzini, S.J.
President, Loyola University Chicago

Foreword

To read this book is not merely to read a history of a great university; it is to read a history of a great city through the lens of a university. Loyola University Chicago has both shaped and been shaped by Chicago. From 12th Street to Lake Shore Drive; from Holy Family Church to the Madonna della Strada Chapel; from St. Ignatius College to Loyola University Chicago; from the "Playing Fields" to Rush Street; from Arnold Damen, S.J. to Michael Garanzini, S.J., Loyola has been wrapped up in the vibrant history of a city with constantly expanding expectations.

As I look out the window and view the campus which has sprung up and continues to grow around Lewis Towers, I realize that there seems to be a logic even greater than that which informed the pragmatic decisions of those who presided over this expansion in "Tower Town" (as "Water Tower" was called by an earlier generation). Perhaps it was the logic of seeing opportunities and seizing them or of taking the big risks with trust in God or of being open at just the right minute to hints from the Holy Spirit. Mistakes have been made, but on the whole, the empiricism of many University leaders has paid great dividends.

One of the great merits of the following narrative is that the author, Ellen Skerrett, sets the Loyola story against the backdrop of the frenetic growth of the Catholic Church in Chicago—something for which her studies of Catholic life in the city have uniquely qualified her. She conjures images of Jesuits extinguishing one firestorm of demands, only to realize that there was another storm heading their way—the survival of firestorms being familiar to both Loyola and the city of Chicago. My favorite storm, because it involved young people from my birth cohort, were the GIs who returned from the War (WWII) and demanded admission. The Jesuits responded and thereby justified the existence of the University and assured its future.

There were, of course, controversies from the time of Arnold Damen on. The Jesuits, it often seems to this outsider, don't shy away from controversies, but instead relish them. There is no need to seek secret archives for the "real" story. Ms. Skerrett is gently transparent about these controversies, even-handed in her treatment of them and non-judgmental in her conclusions, which is of course what the author of a book like this should be. I was around for some of these crises and have strong feelings about them. I am, after all, an alumnus (*honoris causa, autem*). But the proper stance for a foreword-writer is to follow Ms. Skerrett's good example. Dear God in Heaven, what a miracle it is that this institution, under your guidance, has survived and flourishes!

So I turn to eighty years of vivid memories:

My father talks to me about St. Ignatius College with respect for his contemporaries that went there, a hint perhaps of an alternative to Quigley Seminary (RIP!).

Young V-5 midshipmen pour out of Lewis Towers in funny hats and pea coats, and double-pace it over to Abbott Hall for classes. They will soon be officers and gentlemen and, in some sad cases, gold stars in their mothers' windows. As I enter Quigley on these cold winter mornings I know that not all of them will come home.

Some of my contemporaries, home safe from the war, tell me about the legendary Dean Finnegan who is getting them into Loyola.

One summer day, after swimming at Loyola beach (where it was licit for major seminarians to swim), I walk into Madonna della Strada for the first time and see Mr. Steinfels working on his astonishing frescos.

In my first assignment at Christ the King parish I am deputed to preside over the high club, a task for which I am monumentally unqualified. I am told by those who know (young women of course) that I will have no success unless I invite the St. Ignatius Melody Knights Dance Band to perform.

My young people dominate the St. Ignatius basketball team (they almost take city). I venture to St. Ignatius's crumbling gym, to which I must ascend on a dubious iron staircase. The team is coached by Ralph Hinger, the husband of a grammar-school classmate. They lose that game. I am decried as bad luck.

Hardly a Jesuit fan, I cannot escape the conclusion that the young men who have gone to St. Ignatius have received the best education of any young people in the neighborhood.

I am asked occasionally to lecture at Loyola. I am impressed by the young people and the few scholastics that are still around.

I am awarded an honorary degree from Loyola, and I claim the right to act like every other alum and tell them what I think.

John Costello, one of my ex-teens, becomes assistant to the President and establishes a Board of Regents to which I am invited. I at least feel guilty when I miss a meeting.

Every year I am feted at a Christmas dinner at Loyola (on which my father must look down from heaven with some bemusement) to meet a new crop of young Jesuits in scholarly training—all very impressive young men.

My nephew, Sean Durkin (Loyola Academy and Georgetown), tells his son Jack that he will go to St. Ignatius for high school and then he can choose his own college.

You let the Jesuits into your life and pretty soon they invade the whole neighborhood.

When one is in one's ninth decade, such a flood of disparate images brings tears—considering the imprint of an institution on one's life and of one's life on an institution. I am, however, all smiles again to agree with Ms. Skerrett's conclusion that Loyola is a great university, and becoming greater. Thanks be to God.

Andrew M. Greeley

Preface

While enjoying the splendor of the Cudahy Library nearly forty years ago, I had little inkling of its historical importance. Now, after researching and writing *Born in Chicago*, I have newfound appreciation for the genius of architect Andrew Rebori and artist John Warner Norton and admiration for the Jesuit community, which "made no little plans" for its university in Chicago.

Following the untimely death of author Richard J. Whittingham in 2005, Robert F. Ward (BA, 1965), then director of Alumni & Special Events, invited me to write the history of Loyola. Bob endorsed my idea of a social history that would explore the university's urban roots and Jesuit mission. Thanks to the unwavering support of President Michael J. Garanzini, S.J., and his staff, my research took off midyear 2005.

But how to tell Loyola's story from the scanty relevant sources available? By the time Brother Michael J. Grace, S.J., established the archives in the early 1980s, chunks of the university's past had been lost. For example, the naming of Loyola University in 1909 appears as only a single line in a Jesuit ledger! While the extant records in the archives under the supervision of Kathryn Young helped me construct broad outlines, I found myself making pilgrimages to other archives and libraries in search of crucial documents and photographs. Invaluable were David Miros, PhD, archivist at the Midwest Jesuit Archives in St. Louis; James F. X. Pratt, S.J., who sent me 1850s and 1860s letters from the Jesuit archives in Rome; and from St. Ignatius College Prep, Donald Hoffman, archivist, and Raymond J. Heisler, who provided Latin translations. More generous assistance came from the archives of the Sisters of Charity of the Blessed Virgin Mary in Dubuque, Iowa; the Society of the Sacred Heart in St. Louis, Missouri; and Loyola's own Women and Leadership Archives under the direction of archivist Elizabeth Myers, PhD, and archivist emeritus Sister Ann Ida Gannon, B.V.M.; the dedicated staffs of the Chicago History Museum Research Center; University of Chicago's Special Collections; Chicago Public Library; DePaul University Archives; Georgetown University; Marquette University; St. Louis University; Garrett Theological Seminary; and the Concordia Historical Institute.

Martin J. Lane (BA, 1965), assistant director of Alumni Relations, shared his voluminous knowledge as I chased down documents in proverbial attics and basement. This first published history of Loyola University benefited from the enormous skill of editor Sylvia B. Bace. Its visual appeal is due to the talents of designer Beth Adler, the staff at Herman Adler, and photographer Mark Beane.

It is my hope that *Born in Chicago* will serve as the beginning of a new exploration of the impact of Loyola University Chicago upon the city, nation, and world.

Ellen Skerrett

Chapter 1

"Why we go to Chicago"

1856–1895 |

As Chicagoans flocked to a church downtown in August 1856 to hear a dynamic young Jesuit missionary from St. Louis, they unknowingly set into motion a new era in Chicago history. Night after night, for three straight weeks, more than 12,000 Catholics—and Protestants—came to hear the message of Arnold Damen, S.J. The crowds were so great that the congregation had to be moved from St. Mary's Cathedral at Madison and Wabash to a new church across the river. Eventually, Father Damen's mission would evolve into an engagement between a university and urban life that has extended over the decades. The mission would progress from a simple frame church, Holy Family, near Twelfth Street to a comprehensive educational establishment—Loyola University Chicago—which spread to several sites, including an impressive lakefront campus.

John Comiskey window, Holy Family Church

The history of Loyola University of Chicago cannot be separated from the history of the city itself.

Loyola's Founder Arrives in Chicago

Father Damen's three-week mission gave Chicagoans their first glimpse of the priest who would soon be identified with the city's first Jesuit parish and college. Although Damen had to compete with such popular amusements as Matilde Heron in *Camille*, Thorne's national theater and vaudeville review, and Dan Emmit's variety and minstrel show, he didn't disappoint. The *Chicago Times* characterized him as "one of the most zealous and forcible preachers" ever heard in the city, and prominent residents agreed that the

Jesuits ought to make a permanent foundation in Chicago. The decision in 1856 to build a Jesuit church and a college was an investment that paid dividends for the Society of Jesus and Loyola, as well as for the larger city. The history of Loyola University of Chicago cannot be separated from the history of the city itself. Since its earliest days, the school drew its student body from the very heart of the city's immigrant population, and its graduates, in turn, contributed to the growth and development of Chicago.[1]

The city that greeted Damen and his colleagues was vastly different from the one James Oliver Van de Velde, S.J.,

encountered seven years earlier when he became bishop of the Chicago diocese in 1849, succeeding Bishop William J. Quarter. The city had grown up around the river, but by the time of Damen's arrival, the railroads had begun to transform Chicago's economy and its landscape. In 1850, several thousand miles of track had been laid, connecting the city to the country beyond and to new markets—corn, cattle, lumber, and agricultural machinery. The modern city emerging on the shores of Lake Michigan boasted new landmarks, such as the great passenger depot of the Illinois Central Railroad at the foot of Water Street, described by the

Chicago in 1857: The Palmatary Map

The first bird's-eye view of Chicago looking west from Lake Michigan depicted the city that Loyola's founder, Father Arnold Damen, encountered in 1856. In painstaking detail, artist James T. Palmatary rendered the city's distinctive grid of streets, and he captured Chicago as it was becoming the railroad capital of the world. Palmatary's map also featured St. Mary's and Holy Name churches, where Damen preached, as well as the future site of Holy Family parish and St. Ignatius College.

1 St. Mary's Cathedral, Madison Street and Wabash Avenue

2 Holy Name Church and the University of St. Mary of the Lake, Chicago Avenue and State Street

3 Illinois Central Railroad, east of Michigan Avenue

4 Chicago Courthouse, Clark Street between Washington and Randolph streets

5 Haymarket, Randolph and Desplaines streets

6 Future site of Holy Family parish and St. Ignatius College, Twelfth Street (now Roosevelt Road) west of Blue Island Avenue

By the time Chicago was incorporated in 1837, Fort Dearborn had already become a quaint reminder of the city's beginnings as a military outpost in 1803. Located at what is now Michigan Avenue and Wacker Drive, the fort was rebuilt after it was burned by Native Americans in 1812. This lithograph of Fort Dearborn also portrays the Lake House, a former hotel (shown at right) that became a hospital and remained under the direction of the Sisters of Mercy from 1851 to 1853.

Chicago Tribune as a stupendous building of white stone with four brick towers, and the nearby Sturges and Buckingham grain elevator. Chicago's Catholics contributed to this architectural boom with buildings such as the Church of the Holy Name and the four-story "Bishop's Palace" at Madison Street and Michigan Avenue, designed by the architectural firm of Van Osdel and Bauman for Van de Velde's successor, Bishop Anthony O'Regan.[2]

It was obvious that by the time Damen arrived, Chicago's pioneer past was fast receding. Only months earlier, the city had taken bids for the removal of Fort Dearborn, which had been rebuilt after its destruction by Native Americans during the War of 1812. The last of its troops had left the garrison in 1836, and there was little sentiment in favor of preserving the old wooden soldiers' barracks, carpenter house, log-hewn blockhouse, or even the officers' substantial brick quarters.

Of great interest to Chicagoans in the summer of 1856 was the panoramic view of their city captured by artist James T. Palmatary. Measuring 83 inches in length and 48 inches in width, his colored engraving illustrated the metropolis that had developed since the arrival of the Illinois Central Railroad. The *Chicago Times* praised Palmatary for portraying

View of Chicago looking east toward Lake Michigan, 1858, from the courthouse at Washington and Clark streets. Built in the Greek Revival style in 1844, the spire and cross of St. Mary's (shown with arrow) were visible to travelers approaching the Chicago harbor "from the lakes, or far away upon the prairie."

Chicago's First Jesuit Bishop

Instead of viewing his appointment as Chicago's first Jesuit bishop as an honor, James Oliver Van de Velde (1795–1855) was profoundly disappointed and immediately began a vigorous campaign to resign.

Unlike St. Louis, where he had been a professor and president of the Jesuit university, Chicago had little in the way of refinement or culture. After consulting with several American bishops, however, Van de Velde "constrained to bend my neck to the yoke" and accepted his new position in February 1849.[3]

The diocese of Chicago at that time embraced the entire state of Illinois. Van de Velde calculated that he traveled some 6,000 miles during his four years as bishop, often over "abominable roads" in rough wagons lacking springs, only to arrive at remote Catholic settlements completely drenched and covered in mud. In his first pastoral address, he outlined the need for houses of worship and recalled how "astonished and grieved" he had been at the "miserable condition" of country churches in which he celebrated mass and administered the sacrament of confirmation. Van de Velde's experience on the Illinois frontier contrasted sharply with his travels out east. After attending the second public session of the Baltimore Council in May 1849, for example, he stopped at Georgetown, his alma mater, and then visited President Zachary Taylor in the White House.[4]

One thing Van de Velde did appreciate about his new location was the University of St. Mary of the Lake. Chicago's first institution of higher learning had been founded by Bishop William

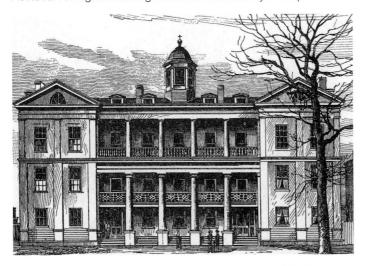

The University of St. Mary of the Lake, designed by architect Daniel Sullivan and dedicated on July 4, 1846, was Chicago's first institution of higher learning.

Quarter, and its stately frame building, dedicated on July 4, 1846, was a landmark on the North Side. Its extensive grounds, bounded by Chicago Avenue, Superior Street, State Street, and Cass (later Wabash) Avenue, were located in close proximity to Lake Michigan but "sufficiently removed from the business portions of the city." Its eighty students enjoyed spectacular views of Chicago from the third-floor balcony and cupola. The cosmopolitan nature of the university—and the city—was reflected in the 1850 commencement with addresses in Greek, Latin, French, Dutch, Spanish, Gaelic, and English. The main oration was "This, Our Country," delivered by James A. Mulligan (1830–64), who later became Chicago's first Catholic Civil War hero.[5]

Unfortunately, Van de Velde was unable to persuade the Jesuits to take over the university. Moreover, he found himself in conflict with the Sisters of Mercy when he claimed their hospital as diocesan property. Adding to his troubles, in 1852, the president of the University of St. Mary of the Lake and three faculty members filed charges against Van de Velde with the Congregation of the Propaganda Fide in Rome. They questioned his management of the diocese and called for his removal.[6]

Van de Velde kept the city at arm's length, and his private correspondence revealed his deep unhappiness with Chicago. He wrote his old friend Archbishop Anthony Blanc of New Orleans that even at mass in St. Mary's Cathedral "the draughts pierce right through me," and he despaired that winter would ever end. Although the bishop could see Lake Michigan from his residence, he considered it a liability rather than an attraction. In May, he was still complaining that while "everything was green and blooming around St. Louis; along the lake here just now there is neither leaf nor blossom and we cannot do without a fire." For him, the city's impressive record of growth could not dispel negative impressions of Chicago's climate "and the land about here, swampy and full of stagnant green water . . . fit only for rats and frogs.[7]"

When Van de Velde finally received his transfer to the diocese of Natchez, Mississippi, in 1853, his friends expressed regret. However unwilling, Chicago's first Jesuit bishop left his mark on the city and the diocese: of the 119 Catholic churches in Illinois, 70 had been constructed during his tenure.[8]

the "hurry and bustle" of the city, with its omnibuses and carriages and "all the bridges together with each and every new house and improvement." This bird's-eye view of Chicago, claimed the newspaper, could be used as a map because it showed "every street and alley as far as the Bull's [H]ead to the west" and as far south as Bridgeport.[9]

Damen's mission impressed not only Chicagoans; news of its success spread to St. Louis as well. In an August 1856 article in the *St. Louis Leader*, Father Mathew Dillon, pastor of Chicago's Holy Name church, described the Jesuit missionaries' grueling schedule—"from four in the morning till after midnight"—and praised their efforts at reaching out to Catholics and Protestants alike. In Dillon's view, the mission revealed "fresh evidence of the vitality of the Catholic spirit," and he was not alone in believing that in Chicago "a new harvest is found already mature." Privately, he reminded Father Damen that the Jesuits had missed a great opportunity when, early in 1856, they turned down an invitation to establish a foundation in Chicago and take over the University of St. Mary of the Lake. "This very day, Sir," Dillon wrote, the bishop "would have both places in a flourishing condition."[10]

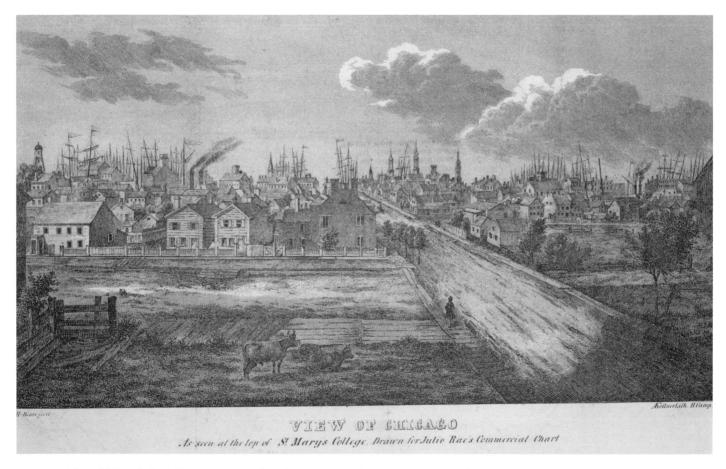

VIEW OF CHICAGO

As seen at the top of St. Marys College. Drawn for Julie Rae's Commercial Chart

This unusual view of Chicago's North Side in 1848 shows State Street (on the right) as an unpaved thoroughfare extending south from Chicago Avenue (in the foreground) to downtown. Visible in the distance are the masts of ships docked along the Chicago River. German-born artist August Hermann Bosse climbed to the cupola of the University of St. Mary of the Lake to make his sketch. Although Father Damen rejected the opportunity to take over St. Mary's College in 1856, ninety years later the Jesuits reclaimed this part of Chicago for their Water Tower Campus.

Philip Conley, United States Collector of Customs (d. November 22, 1900)

Chicagoans Plead for a Jesuit Foundation

When Damen returned to St. Louis after completing his mission, pressure continued to build for the Jesuits to establish a foothold in Chicago. Among the ardent boosters was Philip Conley, a Catholic and one of the city's most respected citizens. Conley wasted no time in urging Father Damen to come back to Chicago. Since his arrival from New Orleans in 1840, Conley had developed a valuable perspective on the city's growth, first as a hotelkeeper and alderman and then as Collector of Customs, an appointment he received from the United States Senate on August 8, 1856. In letters to Damen, he renewed his promises to accompany the priest "all over town and beg enouf [sic] money to build a church." Conley emphasized the good that had already been accomplished through the recent mission.[11]

O'Regan, bishop of the Chicago diocese, was not a member of the Society of Jesus, but no one was more anxious than he to have the Jesuits put down roots in the city. O'Regan's early years in Chicago had had some difficult moments, chief among which was his dismissal of four faculty members of the University of St. Mary of the Lake. One of those removed was Father Jeremiah Kinsella, the popular pastor of Holy Name. The bishop's order ignited a firestorm of controversy. Catholics gathered for a mass meeting at North Market Hall on January 17, 1855, to register their disapproval, but it was to no avail. O'Regan would not change his mind. In fact, he followed his decision by making an offer to Edward Sorin, C.S.C., founder of Notre Dame University: the use of the former university building for a day school for boys and for a still-to-be-established

industrial school. In August 1856, Sorin accepted the bishop's offer. O'Regan's official announcement expressed hope that "as at Notre Dame, so likewise in Chicago, religion and education will advance under the holy and successful exertions of the Congregation of the Holy Cross."[12]

Before coming to Chicago, O'Regan had been head of the Theological Seminary in Carondelet, Missouri, near St. Louis. There he had become familiar with Damen's reputation as an eloquent preacher and an effective pastor. The Jesuit mission in Chicago only confirmed O'Regan's belief that Damen "would be a most efficient instrument to build up religion in this city & diocese." O'Regan decided to move ahead with his plans. He asked permission from the Jesuit superiors in Rome to establish a permanent Jesuit presence in Chicago, and he promptly sent Damen suggestions on possible sites for a parish and a college. He warned Damen "not to correspond *on this matter with anyone whatever in Chicago* . . . Already Catholics . . . are actually speculating on the subject and if they knew you or I had a preference for a particular place they would soon have it bought up."[13]

While O'Regan continued to encourage Damen, he expressed regret that he could offer only $1,000. After acknowledging that he "[couldn't] do a better work for religion, for the diocese, or for my own soul than by establishing here a House of your Society," the bishop pleaded indebtedness and cited a litany of prior obligations: "to erect a Hospital, two Asylums, a House of Refuge, and a House of Mercy— We must build School Houses, Priests' Houses . . . churches . . . [and] provide a cemetery which will cost about $32,000, without any prospect of much revenue in my lifetime." Despite the lack of financial support from the Chicago diocese, Damen was heartened to learn that Father General Peter Beckx, S.J., took O'Regan's request seriously as "an enterprise worthy of our zeal and [compatible] with our Institute." The official letter of approval, written in Latin, was sent from Rome on January 7, 1857. It expressed confidence that the Jesuits "can be of great service in promoting the Catholic faith in that central city which seems to be ever on the increase." Shortly thereafter, John Druyts, S.J., superior of the Missouri Province, gave Damen his marching orders among which was "Remember why we go to Chicago viz. A.M.D.G. (*Ad Majorem Dei Gloriam*, "to the greater glory of God") the good of Religion—the good of Souls."[14]

Becoming an American

Damen breathed new life and meaning into the old Jesuit proverb *Amat magnas Ignatius urbes* ("Ignatius loves great cities"). Over the next thirty years, he would devote his enormous energies to creating a church, a college, and a system of education that would become a model for American urban life. Chicago's astonishing growth from 4,000 people in 1837 to 109,000 in 1860 "made it the youngest city in the United States with more than 100,000," and in terms of Midwestern rivalry, it soon overtook St. Louis and Cincinnati. During the 1850s, thousands of Germans, Irish, Bohemians, Scandinavians, and French Canadians poured into the city, along with prosperous New

Arnold Damen, S.J. (1815–90), c. 1862

England Yankees who quickly rose to positions of prominence in civic and business circles.[15]

Damen, like half of Chicago's population, was foreign-born, so he understood what it was like to land in this new country and have to learn to speak and read English. Born in Leur, Holland, in 1815, he spent his early years in Brabant. He later enrolled in the college at Turnhout in Belgium, and there, at the age of 22, he met the charismatic Peter De Smet, a Belgian Jesuit well known for his work with Native Americans. After hearing De Smet's tales of the Western frontier, Damen asked to join other Jesuit recruits headed for the seminary near St. Louis. The small group

The Jesuits "can be of great service in promoting the Catholic faith in that central city which seems to be ever on the increase."

Father Damen as a newly ordained priest, c. 1844

arrived in New York after a twelve-day voyage from France and began their trek west, reaching Florissant, Missouri, on November 22, 1837.

The speed with which Damen became acclimated to life in America is reflected in a letter he sent to his parents and siblings in 1839. He apologized for not writing more often but acknowledged that "I have almost completely forgotten my mother tongue . . . so don't be surprised if you find an English or French word." His proficiency in French and Latin notwithstanding, Damen concentrated on his English skills so that he might be able to preach more effectively. His progress was slow but steady, and three years after his ordination in 1844, he was appointed pastor of the college church of St. Francis Xavier in St. Louis. There he drew large crowds of "all classes of persons." According to one Jesuit observer in 1853, the parish's comprehensive activities, from devotions to sodalities and soup kitchen, "electrifies the most indifferent [and] Father Damen, a Hollander, is the soul of it all."[16]

Damen's spirited exchanges with O'Regan and his own Jesuit provincial reveal a man willing to take risks and to challenge authority. He rejected O'Regan's offer to make Holy Name a Jesuit parish and also dismissed the bishop's persistent suggestions to purchase six acres of land for the new church and college near Bull's Head on Madison Street near Ogden Avenue. Bull's Head was one of Chicago's early landmarks, a 100-room tavern and hotel built by Matthew Laflin and William

Loomis, that became a favorite gathering spot for cattle dealers and farmers who conducted business at the nearby stockyards. Military groups often concluded their parades through the city with grand dinners at Bull's Head, and crowds numbering in the thousands gathered to watch executions on the prairie southwest of the tavern. What influenced Damen's decisions more than anything else, however, was what he observed when he visited the neighborhood of the tavern. In a letter to a fellow Jesuit, dated March 10, 1857, he said he "could not find a dozen [Catholic] families around the place." Another equally serious drawback was the opinion that the Jesuits would have "to put up $10,000 improvements the first year."[17]

In 1839, Damen wrote to his parents and siblings in Holland in Dutch but apologized to them because after a few years in the United States he had "almost completely forgotten my mother tongue." Although English was not his first language, by the late 1840s, Damen had become one of the most powerful Catholic preachers in America.

Chicago's First Jesuit Parish

The location for Chicago's first Jesuit parish and college was an extremely significant matter. Damen's preference for three acres of property on Twelfth Street near the intersection of Blue Island Avenue was based on his conviction that "here we will have a large Catholic population at once, sufficient to fill a large church." And he was right. Already hundreds of working-class immigrants, predominantly Irish and German, had begun to settle within walking distance of the shipyards and lumber district located along the south branch of the Chicago River and within proximity of the new railroad lines east of Canal Street. As in other Catholic parishes formed throughout the city, Damen resolved to build a church that would become the center of neighborhood life.

Unlike wealthy Protestant congregations in Chicago that were able to finance churches in brick or stone, however, Damen's new Catholic parish would invest in a temporary frame house of worship that could later be used as a school. These modest beginnings in no way precluded his outsized plans for the future. As Damen's correspondence makes clear, he was already dreaming of a permanent church that would rival the grand edifices elsewhere in the city. He understood that wise investments in real estate "will help us to build the college and the new church," but first he had to get the frame church of Holy Family up and running. Only then could he move ahead with this greater plan, a massive church *and* a school system.[18]

The new project took on extreme urgency, fueled by the sense that there was not a minute to lose. On March 21, 1857, O'Regan wrote to Damen, expressing congratulations about the Twelfth Street site and advising him to move quickly. O'Regan told Damen to "define your Parish, announce it" and begin work "as soon as possible [or] some one else might be walking over your ground unless you come in good time." Damen took to heart the instructions he had received from Druyts about conducting business in Chicago and the necessity of reporting "weekly your good & bad success," but he also left nothing to chance. On May 4, 1857, just days after arriving in Chicago, he fired off a letter to Joseph A. Miller, the St. Louis architect who had drawn plans for the church, putting him on notice. "I can have very good architects in Chicago for one half of what you charge," he wrote, adding that "your living so far away from us will expose us to constant delays and annoyance." Moreover, Damen continued to pursue a discount from real estate dealer N. P. Iglehart. He reminded his provincial that Iglehart "is a sharp Yankee. I am trying to get a subscription from him in land."[19]

News of Damen's bold plan to build a church and a college on Twelfth Street spread rapidly. On May 19, 1857, the *Chicago Daily Democratic Press* announced that the Jesuits "have resolved to establish a Church, College and Free School in this city, on a scale of magnitude equal to any of the same character in the United States . . . The church will be one of the handsomest in the West and will cost about $100,000." Among the first in Chicago to pledge support was Philip Conley with a generous subscription of $1,000.

The reaction of the *Chicago Tribune* was swift and harsh. In a long editorial on May 25, the city's leading abolitionist newspaper begged Protestants "to think twice before they aid in any way the founding of Jesuit institutions in this city."

DAILY TRIBUNE.

No. 53 CLARK STREET.

CITY OF CHICAGO.

Monday Morning .... May 25, 1857.

Proposals for a Jesuit College.

We see that one of our city cotemporaries manifests no little anxiety for the erection of a Jesuit Church and University at the corner of Twelfth street and Rock Island Avenue, and that it calls loudly upon Protestants who own real estate in that vicinity to be liberal in their contributions for the furtherance of the enterprise. As it is clearly within the province of a public journal to urge its readers to give to any project toward which it may be favorably inclined, so it is within editorial line of duty to urge the withholding of benefactions, when asked for a dangerous or unworthy purpose. The *Times* chooses to assist in the spread of Jesuitism; and, hence it pleads that it may have the contributions of the liberal. The TRIBUNE, regards Jesuitism as eminently anti-Republican and anti-American; it begs Protestants to think twice before they aid in any way the founding of Jesuit institutions in this city. We do this not in a spirit of intolerance, but upon the warrant of facts which show that the Society of Jesus is the most virulent and relentless enemy of the Protestant faith and Democratic government. Jesuitism is the embodiment of despotism in religion and politics—so dangerous in its aims and ambition that it is scarcely allowed in countries where Catholicism is the belief of nine-tenths of the people. Jesuitism is the same now as when it was suppressed in Catholic France and Spain. It has not abated an iota of its lofty pretensions, nor has it been dispossessed of the least of its propensity for mischief. That Protestants who hold to a purer and better faith, should be influenced to aid in establishing it here, where it has already proved its anti-democratic tendencies, is preposterous, be the plea upon which that aid is asked, ten times more specious than it is. It is sufficient that they give it the protection of our institutions and laws. We trust that no Protestant will be caught with the bait though it is artfully gilded. Jesuitism can take care of itself,

The *Chicago Tribune* editorial, May 25, 1857, warned Protestants against donating money to the proposed Jesuit parish and college founded by Father Damen.

Georgetown University, c. 1863

We do this not in a spirit of intolerance," claimed the *Tribune*, but because "the Society of Jesus is the most virulent and relentless enemy of the Protestant faith and Democratic government." Throughout the 1850s, the newspaper railed against "the influence which the Catholic priesthood exercises over the majority of the Irish in our country," claiming that instead of helping themselves, "servant girls and laboring men, now in want of food, shelter, and fire" had spent hard-earned money on Catholic churches and parochial schools. Far from welcoming Damen and his Jesuit brothers to Chicago as men of education and culture, the *Tribune* characterized their plans to build a college and a church as dangerous and unworthy.[20]

The *Tribune* was not alone in its belief that Catholic immigrants, especially the Irish, threatened the moral fabric of the nation by "continually infringing law and good order." In June 1857, the *Northwestern Christian Advocate*, the prestigious Methodist weekly published in Chicago, warned readers of the challenges posed by the "Irish population in our midst . . . It burrowes amid the filth of our cities, kennels where none else can live. It is ready for fun, frolic, or fight . . . They are unfit for the duties of citizenship when

they come among us, grossly and shamefully so." Little wonder that Damen and his parishioners regarded the building of a Gothic church and schools as a sign of faith in their own future—as well as a stinging rebuke to the conventional wisdom that Catholic institutions imperiled urban life.[21]

Building a Great Edifice

The laying of the cornerstone for Holy Family Church on August 23, 1857, was the first of hundreds of parish events that began to reshape the public image of working-class Catholic immigrants. The *Chicago Times* reported, favorably, that the new house of worship "will surpass in size any other in Chicago" and informed its readers that the Jesuits intended to establish "a collegiate institution . . . [which] will eventually rival that of Georgetown, District of Columbia." Georgetown, established in 1789 as the first institution of Catholic higher education in the United States, had set the standard for all Jesuit colleges founded during the nineteenth century. Its beautiful campus overlooking the Potomac River included several massive brick buildings among which was an observatory, started in 1843 and funded in

The Gothic church and the college were designed to "give glory to God and to beautify our young city."

The five-day Ladies' Fair that began on December 28, 1857, to raise money for completing Holy Family Church drew Chicagoans from all parts of the city. In addition to offering chances for valuable prizes and jewelry, the fair featured "the most gifted vocalists in the Northwest."

part by revenues from a sixty-three acre farm that produced oats, potatoes, tobacco, cattle, and sheep.[22]

Although the Society of Jesus was one of many religious orders in America, by the middle of the nineteenth century, it had established an enviable record for building churches that dominated urban landscapes. St. Ignatius Church (1856) at Calvert and Madison streets in Baltimore, adjoining Loyola College, for example, included such distinctive features as enameled glass windows, a massive marble altar, and a fine oil painting in the center of the altarpiece. But unlike Baltimore's Jesuits who had been "intimately connected with the ecclesiastical history of Maryland," Father Damen and his colleagues were breaking new ground, literally and figuratively, on Chicago's West Side. They were dealing with a rising tide of anti-immigration and nativist sentiment as they worked to create an urban parish that would meet the spiritual, educational, and social needs of Catholic laborers and middle-class residents who were settling on the prairie west of the south branch of the river.[23]

From the start, the Jesuits reached out to the larger city for financial support through a Ladies Fair, held downtown in Metropolitan Hall between Christmas and New Year's 1857. The fair was organized with the explicit intention of surpassing any other church festival in the city, Catholic or Protestant. It featured vocal and instrumental music, and Chicagoans found "rich fruits and abundant sweetmeats," as well as tables filled with artwork and material culture. Proceeds of the fair were earmarked for building "one of the finest church edifices in the North-west," which promised to become "an ornament to our city, and a triumph in architectural art."[24]

Keeping Faith During the 1857 Panic

Although the surrounding neighborhood was decidedly working-class, Damen made sure that the Gothic church and the college were designed to "give glory to God and to beautify our young city." His letters to St. Louis and Rome provide a behind-the-scenes look at the challenge of creating sacred space on the prairie, a difficult business under the best of circumstances but especially so after the financial panic of 1857. Just a few weeks after the cornerstone laying, Damen reported that although there were fewer bank failures in Chicago than in St. Louis, Philadelphia, Boston, and New York, times had changed. He continued, "We find it next to impossible to collect money at present." Yet he rejected as "out of the question" his provincial's suggestion "to reduce the stone work at present." Damen informed him, "About 150 men are at work at the church," and he pointed out that any changes now "will bring in bills for extras afterwards." In spite of the bad news, there was some good news. He reported, "We have just opened our free schools, we have already 300 children . . . and the boys' free-school costs us nothing, except the board of Mr. Seaman, (the converted Episcopalian minister)."[25]

As construction of the new Holy Family Church got underway, Damen was gratified by what was occurring in the neighborhood. He told Beckx that Holy Family parish had begun to create a community on Chicago's West Side. Calling it "alltogether a new establishment commenced principally at my suggestion," he reported that about 8,000 men, women, and children crowded into the four masses each Sunday, and even though the frame church

continued on page 18 ▶

Holy Family Church: "an ornament to our city"

From the day of its dedication, August 26, 1860, the Gothic church of the Holy Family has been considered one of Chicago's architectural wonders. Holy Family had been erected in three years' time. By contrast, St. Patrick's Cathedral in New York City, begun in 1858, would not open its doors for another twenty years. And, as the Chicago Tribune *predicted, the brick church on Twelfth Street would become "an ornament to our city."[26]*

◀ *1893*

This rare photo, taken by the St. Ignatius College Camera Club, depicts the 1865 main altar as it was originally illuminated by gas jets.

▲ *2007*

As part of Holy Family's restoration, the authentic color scheme of the Victorian stenciling from the 1890s has been carefully replicated.

Although Holy Family is the second oldest church in Chicago after St. Patrick's on Adams and Desplaines streets, its interior has remained virtually intact for more than a century. Built with the nickels and dimes of predominantly immigrant families, the Gothic edifice on Twelfth Street (now Roosevelt Road) continued to be a work in progress for nearly forty years. According to Chicago newspaper editor James W. Sheahan, in 1866, Holy Family's sanctuary was "larger and more convenient than that of any other church in this city, [able to accommodate] grand festivals."[27]

The main altar with its gas jets was a marvel of technology in 1865, and after 1899, when incandescent lights were installed, it "glowed with a new brilliancy."[28] Among the church's cherished features are many beautiful statues: of Faith, Hope, and Charity, which nearly reach the ceiling; of St. Patrick, St. Frances Cabrini, and St. Martin de Porres; and of golden angels and saints, all playing musical instruments and decorating the organ case. Also enriching the interior are the handsome organ case itself, the portrait of the Holy Family, the communion railing, the clerestory windows—the oldest stained glass in all Chicago—the side altar painting that depicts St. Joseph wearing a derby hat on the flight into Egypt, and the seven vigil lights that have burned continuously since 1871, fulfilling Father Damen's promise if the church escaped destruction in the Great Fire.

An Architectural Wonder

Built on a grand scale, Holy Family Church continued to be an object of intense public fascination throughout the nineteenth century.

Contributing to the splendor of the Gothic church were immigrant craftsmen such as Anton Buscher from Baden, Germany. According to local lore, Damen had found Buscher carving cigar store Indians and persuaded him to devote his talents to the church. *Chicago Republican* editor Sheahan claimed that Buscher's main altar "has no equal in the west" and praised it as a "striking and elaborate piece of work . . . abounding with religious imagery and ornamentation. The niches are occupied by statuettes of apostles, evangelists, or saints, and the intermediate spaces are filled with beautiful carved work." In 1899, modern illumination was provided through the installation of 1,500 incandescent lights that shown on the main altar and in the sanctuary.[29]

Young Sebastian Buscher had come from Baden, Germany, to help in his uncle Anton's work at Holy Family. Sebastian created the Last Supper scene on the main altar, statuettes for the elaborate confessionals, and carvings for the side altars.

The blessing of the main altar in 1865 drew thousands of Chicagoans, Protestants as well as Catholics, to Holy Family. James Sheahan, a Chicago editor, described the dedication of the main altar as a "scene which one is not likely soon to forget."

Since the early 1860s, Anton Buscher's statue of St. Patrick has occupied a place of honor. In 1889, a Jesuit priest moved the statue of St. Ignatius into St. Patrick's spot. Parishioners vehemently protested, and Ireland's patron saint was returned to his original location facing the congregation.

Whether Sebastian Buscher was poking fun at the pretensions of Irish laborers or injecting a bit of whimsy is not clear, but St. Joseph is clearly wearing a derby as he flees to Egypt. This side altar has been restored to its original beauty through the generosity of Loyola benefactor Joseph Gentile.

One of the seventeen communion-railing panels carved by Louis Wisner (shown above at the top) depicts a pelican feeding her young, an ancient symbol of the Eucharist. The second panel carving is that of the face of the crucified Christ.

Another great artisan was Louis Wisner, a German Lutheran and Freemason, who in 1866 carved the communion railing from a solid block of walnut. Father Damen used to visit him daily in his home workshop at Fourteenth and Halsted streets, offering advice about themes for the seventeen panels.[30]

Louis Mitchell of Montreal, Canada, built the organ, and its case was embellished with life-sized statues designed by the well-known French Canadian sculptor Charles-Olivier Dauphin. When installed, it was the largest organ in the United States. Chicago's most famous organists, A. J. Creswold and Dudley Buck, inaugurated the great instrument in a concert on October 20, 1870. The *Tribune* noted, approvingly, that although "the church is 'a long way out of town' [and] the night an uninviting one . . . the vast edifice was well filled at an early hour. A considerable number of those present were, of course, regular worshippers in the church, but the majority were from the outer world—men and women who love music . . . [along with] a large number of professional musicians."[31]

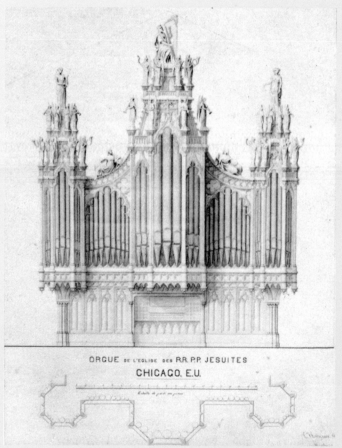

ORGUE DE L'EGLISE DES R.R. P.P. JESUITES
CHICAGO, E.U.

Holy Family's organ, with 64 stops and 3,944 pipes, was installed in 1870. Father Damen had paid $3,690 ("gold duties") when the organ arrived in Chicago on August 11, 1870.

▶ continued from page 13

had been enlarged twice, more space was needed. The figures for school attendance were equally impressive: in addition to "two day-schools for the poor," nearly 500 children attended Sunday school every week. Damen took pains to describe to Beckx the makeup of Holy Family parish: "The people . . . are almost all very poor, yet are willing to assist us as far as they are able to build the new church." He also reminded the Father General that the Jesuit order "has certainly nothing like it in the United States. It will be two hundred and twenty feet long, seventy feet wide, and in the transept (for it is cruciform) one hundred and twenty seven feet wide."

Damen reported that he had "made no debts" and had paid out over $25,000 and still had "a little trifle of money in the bank, perhaps one or two hundred dollars." But after the panic of 1857, he was not optimistic that he could redeem $30,000 in pledges to the new church because "America has never seen as difficult and severe a time as the present." Damen reflected that "when I signed the contracts for the completion of [the] church, I had no idea that the times would turn out as they have done . . . We foresee nothing but misery and poverty." Still, he remained confident of "the good accomplished in this city, in our church" and expected that Holy Family would serve thousands of parishioners in the coming winter. He emphasized to the Father General that the future of Holy Family parish was intimately connected to completion of the church, where construction "is now about twenty-five feet above the ground." Damen begged for a $7,000 loan "to put the roof on the church, to preserve the walls from being injured by the weather."[32]

The help he needed came from the St. Louis Jesuit community—75,000 francs ($15,000)—and by May 1859, the new slate roof was in place. But Damen's thanks were framed in a way that the provincial probably did not expect. Damen conceded that Jane Brent Graham's St. Louis property at 14th and O'Fallon had been sacrificed for $7,000. However, he stood his ground, insisting to his provincial that "we Chicago people" regard the sale as "a great favor" to the Missouri Province! Damen reminded Druyts that by completing Holy Family Church, the Jesuits in Chicago would be able to "do more good, and secure a larger revenue" than if the church were left unfinished. Ever the pragmatist, he had already purchased 22,000 feet of lumber, which was then "rising in price," and he was about to sign a contract for plastering the church. But more construction help was needed. Where, Damen continued to ask the provincial, was the carpenter Brother Hutten with his tool bag? Jesuit Brother Francis A. Heilers had been supervising much of the construction of Holy Family, and he needed assistance. Damen reminded his superior that "every week we look for Brother Hutten . . . and I have been speaking about it so long . . . [that] our folks here have turned unbelievers."[33]

As Damen's correspondence confirms, he was making ambitious plans for a brick church that would compete with Protestant edifices. He stood fast in his belief that creating a place of great beauty for a predominantly poor congregation at the edge of the city was a necessary first step if the Jesuit mission in Chicago was to succeed. This radical notion contrasted sharply with the experience of the city's mainline denominations whose elegant houses of worship clustered around the public square bounded by Randolph, Washington, Clark, and La

John M. Van Osdel

Salle streets. By locating near Chicago's courthouse, the city's "first" Baptists, Presbyterians, Methodists, Universalists, Unitarians, and Episcopalians formed a "religious precinct," and their steeples provided definitive proof that Protestants had put their imprint on the urban landscape. But class mattered: although building monumental churches was regarded as a respectable activity for the wealthy, similar investment by poor congregations was criticized as scandalous. Indeed, the *Tribune* suggested, Bishop O'Regan's house should be "surrendered to the widows

and orphans of his flock" and Holy Name Cathedral ought to be converted "into a workshop for the unemployed."[34]

As the new Gothic church continued to rise on Twelfth Street, there were clear signs that it would soon take its place among Chicago's finest houses of worship. Damen had chosen an impressive architect to complete the interior of Holy Family. Not only was John Van Osdel (1811–95) Chicago's first registered architect, but over the preceding two decades, he had designed "some of the finest buildings in the city [and] in the State," including the courthouse, the First Presbyterian Church, the convent and academy of the Sisters of Mercy on Wabash Avenue, and Bishop O'Regan's house in St. Mary's parish downtown. Robert Carse, the noted stained-glass expert who had recently moved to Chicago from New York, was also hired. Damen spelled it out: "The style and finish" of Carse's windows in Holy Family "shall be equal to the stained glass work in the St. James [Episcopal] church in

MASON'S SPECIFICATIONS
FOR

Lathing & Plastering
and Ornamental Stucco & Plaster
work
for The Church of the Holy Family

JOHN M. VAN OSDEL,
ARCHITECT,
NO. 8 MASONIC TEMPLE,
CHICAGO.

Specifications for the ornamental stucco and plaster work in the Holy Family Church interior.

Mother Margaret
Gallwey, R.S.C.J.
(1805–73)

of German immigrant craftsmen. Working alongside Van Osdel was Brother Heilers (1826–91), a native of Westphalia, whose skill as a carpenter "sometimes surprised even professional architects." And Louis Wisner, who lived in the neighborhood, worked onsite to carve the confessionals and communion rail described by Damen as "a gem of beauty . . . in keeping with the grandeur and style of the church."[36]

The Religious of the Sacred Heart Put Down Roots

While Damen never wavered from his original plan to establish both a church and a college, he knew that in a working-class city like Chicago, elementary and secondary schools took precedence. In August 1858, he welcomed the Religious of the Sacred Heart on their first day in Chicago and celebrated mass for them in their rented quarters on Wabash Avenue. Like their Jesuit counterparts, they were an international order with a remarkable track record in education. Members of their congregation, which was based in Paris, France, had been pioneers on the frontier in St. Louis, where they opened schools well in advance of the public school system. Although the boarding and day school on Rush Street attracted the daughters of Chicago's elite, its proximity to the river was far from ideal. In January 1860, Mother Margaret Gallwey, a native of County Cork, Ireland, welcomed the opportunity to build a new convent academy in Holy Family parish, and she hired Van Osdel to draw up plans for a four-story brick structure on Taylor Street near Vernon Park, with enclosed grounds that were described as an attractive adornment to the city. On moving day, August 22, 1860, an "imposing procession of forty

the North division of the city of Chicago." Unlike Chicago's Protestant churches, however, the windows in Holy Family would honor the rich tradition of Catholicism, with images of "the Sacred Heart of Jesus and of Mary, the Ecce Homo and Mater Dolorosa, St. Joseph and St. Patrick," as well as cherished figures in the Society of Jesus. To provide the stained-glass painters with models, Damen asked his provincial to send pictures of Jesuit saints, preferably in color, among them "St. Ignatius in chasuble with constitution in hand; St. Francis Xavier . . . [Blessed] Peter Claver . . . Martyrs of Japan."[35]

In addition to well-known architects and artists, the Jesuits also drew on the talent

In 1866, Holy Family Church was one of fifty-two Chicago landmarks included in Otto Jevne and Peter Almini's illustrated guide to the city. Chicagoans were encouraged to visit the Gothic church and see its fine interior because "no mere words will convey a true idea of its splendor."

drays and thirty five express wagons" made the trip from the North Side with the Sisters' "ordinary household goods, chattels and fixtures."[37]

Dedicating the "Cathedral on the Prairie"

The culmination of Damen's bold plans to build a Gothic church on Twelfth Street was celebrated on August 26, 1860, when more than 6,000 Chicagoans attended the solemn ceremony of dedication. Completion of the building in three years' time had been nothing short of phenomenal, and even the *Chicago Tribune* weighed in, calling it a "splendid structure . . . [whose] interior is one of the most elegant we ever remember to have seen and will challenge comparison certainly with any in the Northwest." In a city unused to religious spectacle, the singing of Mozart's Twelfth Mass, accompanied by a full orchestra and several choirs, provided a rare glimpse of high culture, and the sight of

so many bishops—from as far away as Boston, Buffalo, Detroit, and Nashville— only added to the "the imposing ceremonies of the Roman ritual." Not surprisingly, Chicago's Jesuit church received national attention, and newspapers such as the New York *Freeman's Journal* emphasized the sheer size of the structure and the orderliness of the celebration. Like so many other Catholic parishes in urban America, however, pressing needs for schools and charitable work meant that Holy Family Church remained a work-in-progress for the next forty years. But the public fascination with the "mother church" of the Jesuits in Chicago never dimmed, and each improvement was hailed as another sign of the growth and development of Catholicism in the city.[38]

If Damen thought the completion of Holy Family Church in such a short time—in the midst of a financial panic— would make it easier to build a college, he was dead wrong. The Civil War broke out just eight months after the dedication of

Holy Family, and raising money became increasingly difficult. In addition, the Missouri Province did not have enough priests to send to Chicago to aid in any expansion. Indeed, Bishop James Duggan, who had succeeded O'Regan as bishop of Chicago in 1859, urged the Jesuits to take over nearby St. Francis of Assisi Church and make it a model parish for the city, but none of the German-speaking priests could be spared.

Meanwhile, the demands on Damen's time and energy increased dramatically, not only as a pastor in Chicago but also as a missionary. His fame as a preacher had spread, and between 1861 and 1863 he adhered to an incredible schedule, traveling beyond the Midwest to Philadelphia, Canada, and finally New York City, where he made a dramatic—and lasting—impression. For three weeks, "people from every corner of the city and from nearby towns" came to the Jesuit church and college of St. Francis Xavier on West 16th Street to take part in the mission of Damen and Cornelius Smarius, S.J. American Catholic historian John Gilmary Shea (1824–92) recalled the mission as "the most notable ever preached in this city," and, according to one account, "the street in front of [St. Xavier's] was so blocked with the crowds that it was impossible to make one's way through. 'Why haven't the Fathers a bigger church?' was the question heard on all sides."[39]

Damen's preaching was adding not only to the national reputation of Holy Family but also to its coffers. The twenty-five or fifty cents paid for each ticket to his lecture after the mission services in church was used "to build up our establishment in Chicago." However, raising the kind of money necessary for a college would take much more than nickels and dimes.

On November 18, 1862, the consultors, or official advisers to the provincial in St. Louis, acknowledged that "the time seems highly opportune for buying property on which a school-building may some day be erected" but lamented that "we cannot just now supply the teachers."[40]

News that the University of St. Mary of the Lake was being reorganized under the direction of Rev. John McMullen added to the pressure felt on Twelfth Street. The Congregation of Holy Cross had failed to maintain university courses at the seminary, but there was every reason to believe that McMullen, the new thirty-one-year-old president, would succeed. As one of the early graduates of St. Mary's, McMullen knew the central role the institution had played in the life of Chicago, and five years of study at the Urban College in Rome had only strengthened his resolve to return his alma mater to its former glory. With Duggan's support, McMullen hired architect George Randall to draw up plans for a new brick building, and the cornerstone was laid on May 24, 1863, amid great fanfare. More than 8,000 Chicagoans attended—including Damen's old friend Phil Conley, who served as grand marshal. According to the *Tribune*, "Every available space from which a view could be obtained, was occupied. Not only all the doors and windows, but the roofs of several buildings, and the trees in and around the grounds were alive with spectators." In his sermon marking the event, Bishop Thomas Rosecrans of Cincinnati predicted that the university's "benign influences" would again be felt "by men in all the higher walks of life."[41]

Despite this competition, Damen did not give up hope for a Jesuit college in Holy Family parish. As things turned out, he was right to keep the faith. When

McMullen was unable to raise sufficient funds to pay a $6,000 debt, the university program ended in 1866. However, the seminary department, under the direction of James J. McGovern, continued for two more years. Its abrupt closing by Bishop Duggan became a major source of dissension in the Chicago diocese and ultimately resulted in the bishop's transfer to a sanitarium in St. Louis.

Establishing an Educational System

Throughout the 1860s, the schools of Holy Family parish set the pace for all Chicago Catholic parishes. Even when faced with the disaster of an early morning fire at the original Holy Family Church on May 10, 1864, Damen refused to relinquish that lead. The frame church had been put to good use as a school, but "owing to the strong wind which was prevailing," firefighters were "unable to prevent its destruction." Undaunted, the pastor hired noted architect Augustus Bauer to design "a first class" modern brick school, to be located on Morgan Street. The building would have cut-stone trim and a gable roof, and it would accommodate more than 1,000 students, making it comparable in size to local public schools.[42]

Educational facilities were expanding elsewhere in the parish as well. An addition to the convent academy on Taylor Street, another Bauer design, had been commissioned by the Religious of the Sacred Heart. In earlier reports to Rome, Damen had acknowledged that the sisters "render immense service to our church" in teaching the poor girls of the parish "which would cost us $1,000 a year."[43]

Damen also kept moving on his plans for a college. On June 8, 1865, he took the first step by signing a warranty deed for property on Twelfth Street, an agreement with an unlikely group, the trustees of the Immanuel German Evangelical Lutheran Church. Since the arrival of Holy Family, tensions between the two congregations had intensified, and it was with a great sense of relief—on both sides—when, in 1864, the Lutherans relocated to Taylor and Brown (Sangamon) streets. But it would be five long years before the dream of the college materialized.

Two years after acquiring this property, Damen expanded the educational opportunities in the parish in yet another direction when he invited the Sisters of Charity of the Blessed Virgin Mary (B.V.M.s) to open a school for girls. Sister Mary Agatha (Ellen Hurley), a native of Cloyne, County Cork, Ireland, and a small group of sisters left their motherhouse in Dubuque, Iowa, to establish a foundation in Chicago. For the next thirty years, Sister Agatha would be as closely identified with St. Aloysius School as Father Damen was with Holy Family parish. The B.V.M. Sisters not only lived in proximity to the children they taught, but they shared similar conditions.

In 1865, Father Damen secured the deed for land on Twelfth Street from trustees of the German Lutheran congregation of Immanuel Church. Nearly three more years would elapse before construction could begin on St. Ignatius College.

The Jesuit–B.V.M. Connection

Although Mundelein College for women did not formally affiliate with Loyola University until 1991, the B.V.M–Jesuit partnership began 124 years earlier on Chicago's West Side.

Sister Mary Agatha Hurley, B.V.M. (1826–1902)

Father Damen's dream of a men's college was still in the making when he invited the Sisters of Charity of the Blessed Virgin Mary from Dubuque, Iowa, to establish a foundation in Holy Family parish. The need was critical. "We now have 1,000 boys in our school, and we should have as many girls," Damen told the B.V.M. spiritual advisor Terence Donaghoe. But he had confidence that this "evil" situation could be remedied, he said, if only the sisters would agree to come to Chicago. Because he felt that appearances mattered, Damen insisted upon getting "good teachers, so as to make a good impression, for the first impression is generally the lasting one."[44]

Sister Mary Agatha Hurley and several sisters arrived on August 6, 1867. Among the young girls waiting for their first glimpse of the Sisters was ten-year-old Mary Kane. Born in Carrighaholt, County Clare, Ireland, she had come to Holy Family parish in 1865 with her widowed mother. This first meeting was destined to shape the future of the B.V.M.s in Chicago.[45]

In 1870, Kane joined the order, the first of hundreds of girls from Holy Family parish to do so. She rose steadily through the ranks and in 1919 was elected head of the order. As Mother Isabella, she was involved in opening thirty-three schools in the Midwest and in California. In Chicago, she hired the noted Prairie School architect Barry Byrne to design Immaculata High School (1922), at Irving Park Boulevard near Lake Michigan. The school was one of Chicago's most prominent Catholic secondary institutions; it had earned an outstanding reputation for preparing young women for college and for careers as public schoolteachers.

Mother Isabella's crowning achievement came in 1929 when she played a key role in the construction of the "temple of classic beauty" known as Mundelein College. She not only arranged financing for the multi-million-dollar liberal arts college during the depths of the Depression but also oversaw the interior design and furnishings. Loyola acknowledged her great vision in 1933 with an honorary doctor of laws degree, proclaiming her an "eminent builder."[46]

Charles Coppens, S.J., remembered the little frame house on Halsted Street where twelve Sisters first lived in "three rooms, namely, a parlor and a community room on the ground floor, with a diminutive appendage for a kitchen and a common dormitory above. On the landing at the head of the stair-case was placed an altar, at which I daily said Mass, the Sisters kneeling between their beds in the dormitory, whence they came singly to the door to receive Holy Communion." Within just a few months of their arrival in Chicago, the B.V.M. Sisters were teaching 850 students "with 150 more striving for entrance."[47]

In fewer than ten years, Damen had successfully established the largest parochial schools in the entire city, so it must have been a great disappointment that his own consultors disagreed about the wisdom of building a college. Nevertheless, he forged ahead and took advantage of the fact that his provincial, Ferdinand Coosemans, S.J., was on an extended trip to Rome, well beyond reach. Damen enlisted the support of Cooseman's assistant, Joseph E. Keller, S.J., who had recently convinced his colleagues in St. Louis to purchase property on Grand and Lindell avenues as the future site for St. Louis University. For Keller, seeing *was* believing: after a visit to Chicago in the summer of 1867, he "marvelled at the achievements" of the Jesuit mission "in that great city." Writing

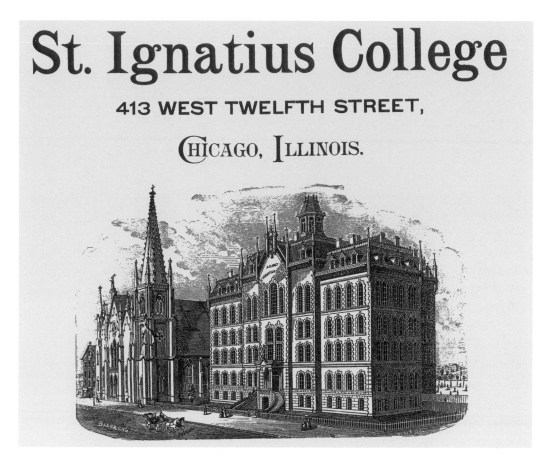

St. Ignatius College

413 WEST TWELFTH STREET,

Chicago, Illinois.

William Baker's engraving for St. Ignatius College bore the date 1867. This bit of artistic license underscored Damen's long struggle to build the college, against the advice of his Jesuit consultors.

in Latin to Father General Beckx in Rome, he expressed surprise and delight at the "noteworthy and splendid house of worship, such as one would scarcely expect in America; a parochial school for boys with 1600 in attendance; schools for girls, one registering 400, another, nearly the same number, a third, 300, this last group taught gratuitously by [the Religious of the Sacred Heart]." Keller did not mince his words when he continued: "The college is the only thing lacking and . . . then will the Society truly flourish in Chicago."[48]

Going First Class

In keeping with his ambitious plans for a first-class institution, Damen hired William D. Baker, Chicago's most prominent engraver, to create a visual image that featured the new building directly east of Holy Family Church. In a bit of artistic—and historic license—the date "A.D. 1867" appeared above the name St. Ignatius College. Although work had barely begun,

the "photographic plan" spoke volumes about the aspirations of the Chicago Jesuits to build "a most noble structure." The Baker engraving became an icon used for many years in local advertisements, college brochures, and parish calendars, as well as in national publications. Writing from St. Louis, Keller assured Beckx that initially only the central section of the building would be constructed and

THE LARGEST AND OLDEST

Wood Engraving Establishment

IN THE WEST.

(*ESTABLISHED IN 1857.*)

SEVEN PREMIUMS · FOR SUPERIOR WORK.

DESIGNING, DRAWING AND WOOD ENGRAVING

IN ALL ITS BRANCHES.

10,000 MISCELLANEOUS WOOD CUTS ON HAND — COPIES FOR SALE.

Ad for Baker's firm, which designed the engraving of St. Ignatius College shown above

'Le bâtiment a été commencé sur un plan un peu grandiose afin de pouvoir rivaliser avec les Collèges Protestants et les Écoles publiques qui sont comme des palais. Ceci était nécessaire pour emmener les parents à nous donner la préférence, car l'extérieur fait beaucoup d'impression sur l'esprit américain.

This 1868 letter, in French, compares the St. Ignatius building to "the Protestant colleges and public schools that are like palaces."

that the two wings would be added later, as finances permitted, "until the entire façade as you see it in the photograph is completed, giving a frontage [along Twelfth Street] of 160 feet."[49]

When Coosemans returned from Rome, he learned that the foundations of St. Ignatius College had already been laid and that its walls had begun to rise. Far from criticizing Damen for circumventing his authority, however, the provincial interceded on his behalf to secure a loan when progress on the building stalled due to a lack of funds. Instead of borrowing money in Chicago at 10 percent, Damen sought permission to travel to Holland where his Holy Family colleague, James Van Groch, S.J., could arrange a better deal through

Architect Toussaint Menard's children honored him with a window in Holy Family Church. The clerestory windows, created in 1860 by Robert Carse, are the oldest stained glass windows in Chicago.

his brother: 50,000 florins (about $20,000) at 4 percent.

The argument Keller and Coosemans used in their appeals to Rome sheds light on the role they expected the new St. Ignatius College to play in the life of Chicago. On February 16, 1868, Keller wrote to Beckx, recounting the history of the college and expressing his opinion that "I see nothing of greater utility . . . The hope of our Province almost depends on it for this college will be a nursery for Jesuit vocations." Coosemans agreed, pointing out to the Father General that since the University of St. Mary of the Lake no longer existed, the Jesuit college would be the only Catholic institution of higher learning in Chicago, educating future priests as well as laymen. The St. Louis provincial concluded his plea by making a strong case for Damen's ambitious plans: "The building was begun on a somewhat grandiose scale so as to compete with the Protestant colleges and public schools that are like palaces." Coosemans explained that "this was necessary in order for the parents to give us preference, because the exterior makes a big impression on the American mindset." The letters had the desired effect: Damen and Van Groch received approval from Rome and traveled to Holland in the summer of 1868 to secure the necessary funding.[50]

Did the bricks and mortar of the college matter? Absolutely. Even before the basement was completed, Chicago newspapers gave the project their imprimatur and hailed it as a welcome addition to the city. In October 1868, the *Chicago Times* asserted that the new school was one of the most significant "educational enterprises projected in this city" and predicted that it would become "one of the largest and best appointed educational institutions in the country."

There was no doubt that the Jesuits were building for the future: Toussaint Menard's architectural plans called for a basement "of Athens stone, laid in the most substantial manner, the outer walls being three feet thick, and the inner walls from one and a half to two and a half feet. The foundation is seven feet wide, laid on two feet thickness of concrete." One of the most respected contractors in Chicago, Menard had built the new brick addition to the University of St. Mary of the Lake in 1863, and his shop was located near Holy Family Church, where his children had honored him with a stained-glass window. Menard promised to finish the basement and window casements in "red cedar, the most durable wood known . . . the first story with butternut, and the remainder with [grained] pine."[51]

Plans for the $300,000 building featured a mansard French roof and, according to the *Times*, a dome rising "40 feet high, surmounted by a spire." The entrance of the new college, designed to reflect the Jesuits' engagement with urban life, would face directly onto Twelfth Street "through a portico matched by a spiral staircase, thirty feet high, and costing $30,000." From its "niche at an elevation of one hundred and twenty feet" a marble statue of St. Ignatius would proclaim the school's identity. By July 1869, the prestigious *Chicago Land Owner* included the "large and handsome Catholic college" among the most notable buildings in the city, along with the new Palmer House on State Street, and reported that its walls were nearly completed.[52]

All the favorable press notwithstanding, the local Jesuit community remained divided about investing scarce resources in the college building. A few months after Damen bought another piece of property on Twelfth Street for the school, the consultors went on record as unanimously opposed to opening the college because of the financial expense. On December 23, 1869, they were still debating whether the whole interior should be plastered, or only part of the interior.

Racing to the Finish

Meanwhile, rumors flourished that Damen was to be appointed bishop of the Chicago diocese. Alerted to the strong possibility, Coosemans pleaded with Beckx to intervene in Rome to allow Damen to complete the college project. Writing in French, he recounted the many twists and turns the process had taken since 1866 but assured Beckx that "I have no doubt with the help of heaven both interest and capital will be paid off in due season provided Father Damen be not taken away."[53]

For the Chicago Jesuits, the selection of Baltimore-born and -educated Thomas Foley to succeed Duggan early in 1870 was both a reprieve and a blessing. Coosemans expressed to Beckx his confidence that Foley would be "favorable to the Company" (meaning the Society of Jesus), but never could he have imagined how accurate that assurance would be. Within months after his arrival, the new bishop held the first clergy conference in "the new and splendid college of the Jesuits" where eighty-four priests "were entertained in a liberal style by Very Reverend Father Damen, S.J."[54]

Throughout 1870, events continued at a fever pitch as the focus remained

From Prairie to City Neighborhood

When Father Damen began organizing Holy Family parish in 1857, the area was sparsely settled, but over the next thirty years, the surrounding prairie was transformed into a densely populated urban neighborhood. The colorful map at the right, made for fire insurance purposes, reveals the "footprint" of Holy Family Church, St. Ignatius College, and the nearby Convent of the Holy Heart of Mary. Brick structures were identified in pink and frame buildings in yellow. Also clearly visible is Aberdeen Street, vacated by the city council in 1870, thanks to the political clout of Alderman "Honest John" Comiskey. With the closing of Aberdeen Street, St. Ignatius College was able to create a campus in the heart of the city. Below is a larger version of the 1886 fire insurance map. Its perspective is looking west from Morgan Street to Centre (now Racine) Avenue between Harrison Street and Twelfth Street (now Roosevelt Road).

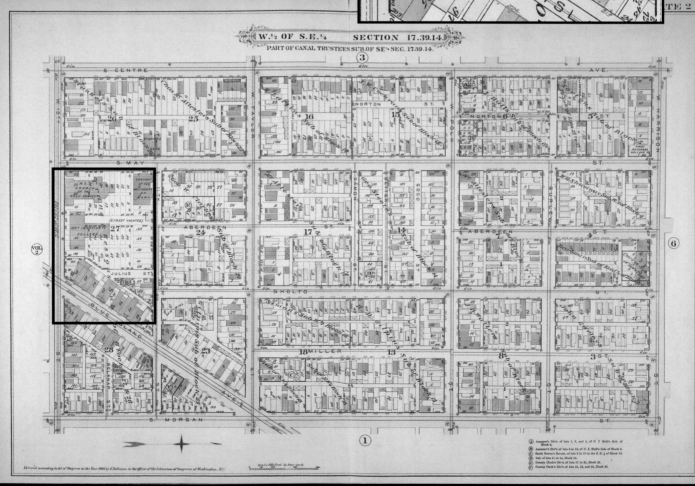

on a fall opening date. On June 13, the Illinois legislature granted a charter for St. Ignatius College. Work progressed rapidly on the building's interior as Heilers supervised the installation of three sets of stairs, fifteen flights in all, and maple and pine flooring. Then Damen discovered that, in addition to all the obstacles he had overcome over the years, he still had one more hurdle before the institution could open. He confided to his provincial on June 15, "We are in difficult circumstances at present, trying to finish the College, and paying enormous prices for adjoining lots to close the street." Fortunately, John Comiskey was president of the Chicago City Council when it met that summer to discuss vacating Aberdeen Street between Eleventh and Twelfth streets. As one of Holy Family's earliest members, Comiskey had gone door to door in 1859, collecting for stained-glass windows, and he was able to use his considerable influence to ensure that the church and college would not "be separated forever by Aberdeen Street."[55]

Damen's missions throughout the country had helped to build the new college on Twelfth Street, but keeping it afloat, along with the parish schools that annually enrolled 4,000 children, remained a delicate balancing act. Thanks to the donated services of Jesuit priests, faculty salaries were not an issue, but the lack of an endowment—or even the hope of one—was an issue. Unlike St. Louis University, which had realized nearly $70,000 in the 1860s from a generous donor, John Doyle, Chicago had no long tradition of Catholic philanthropy. Seeking financial contributions beyond the immediate neighborhood was essential. The college began to help in this respect even before its doors opened for classes. As part of its efforts, "a new feature [in

fundraising] was introduced" during a fair at the college in August 1870—a "popular voting" contest between two of Chicago's most prominent insurance executives, William E. Rollo, founder of the Merchants' Insurance Company, and J. R. Payson of the Republic Company. According to the *Chicago Tribune*, "Each has an army of friends who will not fail to demonstrate their zeal in this friendly contest" and the "lively campaign" for votes filled the new college hall every evening for nearly two straight weeks. Each vote represented not only an endorsement for a contender but also a paid admission.[56]

Exactly ten years after Holy Family Church was dedicated, the original dream of a college finally became a reality. The *Chicago Tribune* of August 26, 1870, praised the building's "lofty and magnificent front," its main entrance "reached by two flights of circular stairs," and its "small, but neat cupola, from which the entire city, and a large area of the surrounding prairie and lake, can be seen."

This colored postcard of St. Ignatius College, produced around 1906, continued a long tradition of publicizing the school as one of Chicago's notable buildings.

COMISKEY - 1ST BASE ST. LOUIS.

Future White Sox owner Charles Comiskey (1859–1931), one of the first students at St. Ignatius College, signed with the St. Louis Browns in 1882 and is credited with changing the way first base was played.

The entire project, costing more than $200,000, included a thirty-classroom building on Twelfth Street and a field at the rear of the college measuring 300-by-200 feet "where the boys can play base ball or anything else." The field was an attraction that endured for decades. One of the recurring themes in the school vice president's diary is the students' preoccupation with baseball, then the fastest growing sport in urban America. Among those who threw himself into the sport was Charles Comiskey, the alderman's son and one of the first students to enter St. Ignatius in 1870. The young man had grown up playing baseball on the prairies around Maxwell Street, a pastime his father derisively referred to as "a sport for town boys and loafers."[57]

Opening Day

The first page of the *Diarium of St. Ignatius College* for September 5, 1870, provides a poignant reminder of the challenge involved in creating a place of beauty in a working-class city. "Though the College is far from complete within, there are rooms enough prepared for all college purposes. Desks were ordered and placed in the rooms, but upon close examination they were considered too common, consequently Father Damen procured the present desks which are the latest improvement. These desks are up just in time but not an hour too soon." Finally, on October 28, 1870, workers installed a beautiful pane of etched glass above the front door with the street number "413" and "St. Ignatius College" and returned the next day to set in place "stained glass windows in the parsonage door near the parlor." Thanks in part to Damen's years of preaching on the East Coast and his ensuing popularity, news of the college's opening was reported by the *New York Tablet*—verbatim—from the Chicago papers.[58]

From its very first day, the college aimed at providing a classical education consistent with the *Ratio Studiorum*, the Plan of Studies used in Jesuit colleges since 1599. The original *Ratio* plan provided for starting boys at an early age and educating them along a given track right through the college years. The first catalog for St. Ignatius College emphasized that its six-year curriculum would "impart a thorough knowledge of the English, Greek, and Latin languages; of Mental and Moral Philosophy; of pure and mixed Mathematics; and of Physical Sciences." The college, however, also offered a four-year commercial course that "embraces all the branches of a good English Education." Whether business and scientific courses were compatible with the *Ratio* was a subject that Jesuit colleges across the country debated. It appeared that the colleges of the Missouri Province had broken ranks with East Coast institutions such as Georgetown, Holy Cross, and Boston College, which favored only the classical course. The issue was featured at the very first annual exhibition of St. Ignatius College through a spirited debate, "Which is the more advantageous, a Classical or a Commercial Education?"[59]

As the only Catholic institution of higher learning in Chicago, St. Ignatius College cast a wide net, but the $60 cost of tuition for ten months represented a sizeable investment, well beyond the means of most city dwellers. While its modern building on Twelfth Street compared favorably with Northwestern University in suburban Evanston and the first University of Chicago on 35th Street, it remained a relatively small school for its first twenty-five years.

Original University of Chicago, 1866

University Hall, Northwestern University, 1870

The Hidden Strength of Chicago's Commuter College

Still, there were distinct advantages in its being a commuter day-school. Because they lived at home and walked or traveled on public transportation, students at St. Ignatius College were not insulated from urban life. As historian James O'Toole notes, this had not been the case in the 1860s and 1870s at Georgetown University, which "kept its distance from the rest of the capital . . . Professors were rarely seen in local society . . . [and] students were discouraged from venturing downtown too frequently, lest they succumb to temptations that could be more closely regulated on the campus." Quite the opposite was true at St. Ignatius College, which opened its doors wide to the public for exhibitions that reflected the burning issues of the day. The very first event, on June 29, 1871, included an elaborate program with "music and songs and speeches" that appealed to immigrants as well as their American-born children. Ambrose Goulet presented "Chicago the Coming City"; William H. Hughes rendered an impassioned declamation, "The Wrongs of Ireland and the Genius of Her Sons"; and Simon Blackmore read his essay on Daniel O'Connell, the

founder of modern Irish nationalism and a folk hero to thousands of Chicago men and women who continued to advocate Ireland's emancipation from British rule.[60]

A breakdown of the 1870–71 student body, the school's first, reveals the challenges facing St. Ignatius College: although 57 of the 99 students enrolled were registered in the classical program, none were ready for college work. But there was no talk of changing the original educational plan since it was only a matter of time until the college would be "fully equal, in all respects" to the Jesuit colleges "which flourish in other parts of the country." Although Damen was elected president of the college in 1870, he did not teach, but continued his retreat and missionary work. This took him away from the parish for considerable periods of time, and the day-to-day operations of the school fell to John Verdin, S.J., vice president; John De Blieck, S.J., secretary; and Maurice Oakley, S.J., treasurer.[61]

That a Jesuit community had put down deep roots on the West Side of Chicago was confirmed by the 1870 federal census. Filling twenty lines on the census form were the names of priests and brothers, only one of whom had been born in

At the time of the Great Fire of 1871, Father Damen was preaching a mission at St. Patrick Church in Brooklyn, New York.

The January 1, 1872, pulpit announcement reminded Holy Family parishioners that a collection would be taken after all the masses "to keep lights constantly burning before the Statue of Our Lady of Perpetual Help." The seven lights honor the promise Damen made after the Jesuit church and college escaped destruction in the Great Fire of 1871.

the United States. The picture was much the same for the Religious of the Sacred Heart and the B.V.M.s, whose convents and schools had become a familiar part of the urban landscape they shared with Irish and German immigrants.

Chicago Ablaze

The dreams, hard work, and financial investment in Holy Family parish all seemed doomed when on October 8, 1871, a fire started on nearby DeKoven Street. It rapidly developed into the Great Chicago Fire, which "destroyed three and a half square miles in the heart of the city, leveling more than 18,000 structures." The myth of a cow starting the fire by kicking over a lantern in the barn of Catherine and Patrick O'Leary quickly became popular. News reporters, many of whom dug up old stereotypes, descended on the O'Learys. Catherine O'Leary, a respected member of Holy Family parish who owned five cows and operated her own milk business, was transformed into an old Irish hag and nicknamed Our Lady of the Lamp.[62]

Soon, a different legend emerged. It involved Father Damen, who learned that Chicago was in flames as he was giving a mission in St. Patrick Church in Brooklyn, New York. As the story goes, he prayed on his knees all night, making a solemn vow that if the Jesuit church and college on Twelfth Street were spared, he would keep seven lights burning in Holy Family Church. The wind did shift and the fire spread east across the river, burning the business district and the North Side all the way to Lincoln Park. Whether the story was true no one knows for sure, but after all the masses on January 1, 1872, a collection was taken "to keep lights constantly burning before the Statue of Our Lady of Perpetual Help."

Although these urban legends quickly became ingrained in the public psyche, a more fascinating, true story was unfolding. Catholic nuns, priests, and brothers were playing a major role in helping to restore order and stability through the donation of food, clothing, and money, much of it sent them from distant cities where their religious communities lived and worked. So beloved was Sister Mary Agatha Hurley, for example, that the Committee for Chicago Orphan Relief in Dubuque donated $130 to the Sisters of Charity at St. Aloysius School, along with barrels of flour and clothing. Writing in French to the motherhouse in Paris, a Religious of the Sacred Heart reported that at the convent academy on Taylor Street "one heard continually the sound of the doorbell announcing that one of the victims of the fire had come to us seeking aid." Sacred

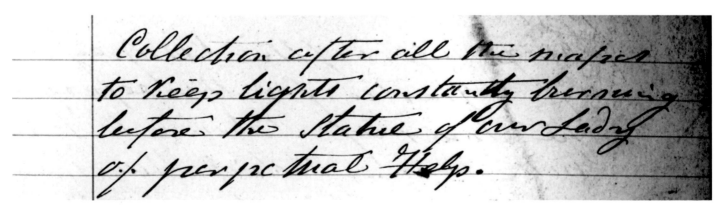

32

The Great Chicago Fire

The Great Fire of October 8 and 9, 1871, was a defining moment in the history of Chicago. Ironically, the scale of destruction contributed to the city's rebirth and laid the groundwork for its leadership in architectural design.

This haunting illustration of victims of the Great Fire in Chicago appeared in the Berlin journal *Illustrirte Zeitung* on November 18, 1871.

Nearly 300 hundred men, women, and children perished in the blaze that destroyed Chicago's business district and large sections of the North Side all the way to Lincoln Park. Many people claimed the inferno reflected God's displeasure at the evils of city life. Closer to home, an urban legend developed that Catherine O'Leary's cow had kicked over the lantern in her barn on DeKoven Street and burned Chicago down.[63] Elements of both stories surfaced in news coverage throughout Europe, where the Chicago disaster was compared with the burning of Rome, Moscow, London, and Hamburg. In describing the extent of the devastated region, the London *Graphic* urged its readers to think of an area comparable to that "from the Tower [of London] to Buckingham Palace, extending a mile back from the river." The French journal *L'Illustration* depicted the spread of the fire with a map showing its origins in the O'Leary barn. The publication predicted, however, that the grace and incomparable energy of Chicagoans would soon erase any sinister traces of the fire.[64]

The first to invoke the image of the phoenix, the mythical bird that is consumed by fire but emerges intact, was the nationally known preacher Henry Ward Beecher of the Plymouth Church in Brooklyn, New York. Five days after the fire began, Beecher confessed his inability to comprehend the disaster but said he was comforted by the thought that Chicago "like another Phoenix" would rise "from her ashes, fairer and more beautiful than ever before."[65]

Having struggled against great odds to create churches, schools, hospitals, orphanages, and asylums, Chicago's Catholics had to begin all over again. Although Holy Family and St. Ignatius College survived the fire, St. Mary's and Holy Name, where Father Damen had preached in 1856, were destroyed. Also lost in the fire were the German parishes of St. Peter, St. Joseph, and St. Michael; the French parish of St. Louis; and the Irish parish of Immaculate Conception. Help to rebuild came from Catholic dioceses across the nation. Bishops and priests exhorted parishioners to remember the "poor [and] homeless, shivering with cold, and starving," and the outpouring of money and supplies was immediate. New Yorkers were especially generous, due in large measure to the fame of Damen's missions.[66]

For many years, the anniversary of the Great Fire was an occasion for noting the extent of Chicago's rebirth. Daily papers printed long articles about the modern city that had emerged like a phoenix. But Catherine O'Leary shunned any semblance of fame or notoriety, refusing all offers to be interviewed or to have her photograph taken. Year after year, she dreaded the anniversary and chased reporters from her home at 5133 South Halsted Street. When she died in 1895, newspapers across the country took notice, retelling the story of the cow and its role in the Great Chicago Fire. The *Washington News* joked that "the cow departed this life some years ago and did not repent before its demise." In an interesting twist, the *American Architect and Building News* thanked Mrs. O'Leary's cow for "her great act by which Chicago was freed of more second-rate buildings in a shorter space of time than had any other similarly burdened city." The fire, the magazine pointed out, was a "blessing in disguise," one that cleared the way for "the brightest flowers of architecture." Although Catherine O'Leary's title as the patron saint of Chicago architecture remains disputed, she did receive absolution finally when the city council in 1997 declared that neither she— nor her cow— was responsible for starting the Great Fire of 1871.[67]

House and barn of Catherine and Patrick O'Leary on DeKoven Street

Heart communities in St. Louis and St. Charles, Missouri, sent food and money, "making it possible for us to help those who needed it." She lamented that "those in authority were almost all protestants" who refused to give money to her poor neighbors on the West Side, telling them to "go to your priests, go to your Church." Many did. She estimated that "the Jesuits had cared for seven or eight thousand people for several weeks." In a letter to the Catholics of Baltimore, Bishop Foley acknowledged that "the Jesuits have taken all the orphans in their college."[68]

Recounting what it was like to live "surrounded for miles in every direction, by a vast tinder-box of wooden houses," a St. Ignatius professor wondered whether the neighborhood would burn "like all the rest." He reported that the priests and brothers "gathered together fourteen men and kept them patrolling the block till morning." As soon as the college opened its doors as a relief station, supplies "poured in at once from all parts of the country," so quickly that "a stranger passing by would have thought that the building had been suddenly turned into a vast Commission Warehouse."

What is astounding is the speed with which life returned to normal. The pulpit announcement at Holy Family on October 22, 1871, two weeks after the fire started, simply stated, "Tomorrow the College will open its usual classes." Back in the classroom, Jesuit professors discovered that many of their students who lived on the North Side "had lost everything but their lives. Yet they were anxious to get back to their books, and with three or four exceptions, all of them returned almost without delay."[69]

Along with an appeal to his old friend Archbishop Martin Spalding of Baltimore, Bishop Foley gave a report on the devastation: "Our cathedral, six churches, asylum, three convents, Good Shepherd House, hospital, and various schools . . . reduced to ashes. Six square miles in the heart of the city . . . " Although Foley lamented the loss of his personal library, he admitted that it could not compare with the sad experience of removing "the remains of poor Bishop Quarter [who had been securely entombed beneath the sanctuary] from the rubbish of St. Mary's."[70]

Reinvesting in the College

Foley took shelter with the Jesuits and in gratitude donated $1,000 to the college, which promptly used the money to create a natural history museum. A powerful sign of reinvestment in the city, the museum quickly became a public attraction. It featured ornate cases, crafted by the J. M. Brunswick Billiard Table Company, and "splendid specimens," thanks to

Natural History Museum, St. Ignatius College

34

Advertisement from 1873 for St. Ignatius College in *The Land Owner*

missionary Francis X. Schulak, S.J., who collected them during trips out west. Born in Moravia in 1825 and assigned to St. Ignatius College in 1869, Schulak was instrumental in organizing St. Stanislaus Kostka, the mother parish of Chicago Polonia. He also celebrated mass and heard confessions of Bohemians in nearby St. Wenceslaus Church at DeKoven and Desplaines streets.

The Jesuits' living quarters in the college building may have been austere, but community life had its pleasures. After the semiannual exhibition in February 1873, professors, scholastics, and clergy celebrated "with a little refreshment and smoke." Across the hall, reporters and policemen "were treated to beer, cakes & segars."

The size and scale of the college continued to amaze visitors, especially after the completion of the west wing. Father Coppens, who had spent time in Chicago in 1869, could hardly believe his eyes when he returned four years later. Not only did the new college dwarf Holy Family Church, he declared, but "the photographed pictures of the College are far

from doing justice to the magnificence of its front." Little wonder that in order to boost enrollment, Father Coosemans, now the college president, paid $50 (about $800 in 2006 dollars) for a feature story that ran in April 1873 in the city's most prestigious real estate journal, *The Land Owner*. Four months later, he authorized $75.44 for ads in nine Chicago newspapers, including the German-language *Staats-Zeitung*. The results were dramatic: "157, of whom 54 are new scholars," enrolled in the fall of 1873. Although nine young men left due to the effects of bank failures, 178 were still attending in December, "25 more than at the same date last year."[71]

Professors and students celebrated the third anniversary of the Great Chicago Fire in a unique way: watching the installation of new fire pipes in the college, a project dear to the heart of Aloysius A. Lambert, S.J. The popular science teacher supervised the installation of a "large 3 inch iron pipe running from the ground to the roof of each wing, to be connected with the [fire]plug at the sidewalk; the water to be forced up by steam-fire engine in case of fire." Although the city had tightened its

The nationally known Brunswick Billiard Company crafted the ornate cases for the Natural History Museum in St. Ignatius College.

Aloysius A. Lambert, S.J. (1842–1909)

building codes, the threat of fire was still a reality because the college was located near the lumber district along the south branch of the river, where many immigrants had settled. On October 21, a great crowd gathered as firemen tried out the new system and watched with fascination as "a stream [of water] was thrown up at least 10 ft. above the cross of the college." The demonstration concluded quietly and successfully with Father Lambert and John Van Agt, S.J., treating the firemen "to a splendid lunch in the Engine-house" across the street.[72]

Awarding the First Baccalaureate Degrees

In a city where the Catholic population remained predominantly working-class, the awarding of academic degrees to seven students in 1876 was cause for celebration. The college's "competent professors and a wide and useful range of studies" attracted eighty students to the classical department, eighty to the commercial, and forty-two younger boys to the preparatory program. Without an endowment and wealthy benefactors, however, there was little chance that St. Ignatius would catch up anytime soon to Northwestern University, which also offered programs in medicine and law. By contrast, the Jesuit commitment to education from elementary through college was paying dividends in an environment very different from that of suburban Evanston. Emphasizing this difference, Northwestern University president Charles Fowler regarded the progress of that Methodist university as inextricably linked to its location "just outside of the great city, and so out of its dust, and din, and saloons, and great temptations." Account after account of the Jesuit mission in Chicago emphasized that the

parochial schools compared favorably with the public schools in terms of buildings and curricula and that the church was a place of great beauty beloved by ordinary working people. Even critics grudgingly agreed that the construction of Catholic churches and schools such as Holy Family and St. Ignatius College "improves and helps to fill up the surrounding neighborhood and swells and enhances the value of property."[73]

Carter H. Harrison, Jr. (1860–1953), the Protestant son of Chicago's popular mayor, regarded his years at St. Ignatius College as excellent preparation for a political career in a city of immigrants. As a six-year-old boy growing up in a mansion at Ashland Boulevard and Jackson Street, he was familiar with Holy Family parish and its legendary founder. The family's Irish servants frequently took him to mass, and on the way he listened to them talk about Father "Diamond." By the time Harrison enrolled at St. Ignatius College in 1876, he had already traveled extensively in Europe, and as a result of his two-year stay in Heidelberg, he said, his German was "much better than my English."

Although Harrison passed his entrance exam for Yale in 1877, he decided to remain at St. Ignatius, where he played a prominent role on the debate team. In fact, while he was serving as its vice president, the Chrysostomian Debating Society underwent a dramatic change. Founded in 1875 as the first student organization, the debate club took as its patron the eloquent Greek prelate, St. John Chrysostom, a name that translated to "golden mouthed." But as of September 24, 1880, it was rechristened the Loyola Debating Society, the first time the founder of the Jesuit order was so honored at the school that eventually would carry his name.

Despite the constant distraction of baseball games during the fall and spring, debaters argued the great issues of the day: women's suffrage, Chinese-immigration restriction, voter literacy qualifications, Sunday theater closings, secret societies, and, of course, whether "the Irish Race is justified in demanding Repeal of Land Laws." Harrison, who was already showing well-honed political skills, in 1879 donated two sets (13 volumes) of the *Congressional Record* from his father's office to the debating library, which also held 543 volumes of history, biography, essays, and fiction, as well as Catholic periodicals and the college journals from Georgetown and Notre Dame. In a trademark flourish, the future five-term Chicago mayor thanked his fellow debaters for "electing him [recording secretary] . . . for two consecutive terms for the first time in the history of the society."[74]

The college became a pioneer among Jesuit schools in the Midwest when it adopted a four-year college curriculum in 1880–81, but the rigors of the classical course with its emphasis on Latin and Greek still meant that very few students graduated. Harrison and Thomas B. Finn were the only two students awarded bachelor of arts degrees on June 27, 1881. Finn was one of seven children born to Catherine and Patrick Finn. Although his Wexford-born father was not as famous as Mayor Harrison, he did enjoy a reputation as one of Chicago's legendary "lake captains." Thomas joined the Jesuit order after graduation and later served as chair of rhetoric at Creighton University in Omaha. Religious life also appealed to two of Finn's siblings, Mother Esperance, superior of St. Theresa Convent in Hastings, Minnesota, and James, a Jesuit on the faculty of Woodstock College in Maryland.[75]

continued on page 40 ▶

Carter H. Harrison II, 1881. When he was elected mayor for the first time in 1897, his alma mater sent a floral arrangement of red and white roses depicting the school's coat of arms.

𝔗𝔥𝔢 𝔏𝔬𝔶𝔬𝔩𝔞 𝔇𝔢𝔟𝔞𝔱𝔦𝔫𝔤 𝔖𝔬𝔠𝔦𝔢𝔱𝔶

Was organized on the 10th of November, 1875. Its object is to promote the cultivation of eloquence, the acquisition of sound knowledge, and a taste for literary studies. The exercises, at the weekly meetings, consist chiefly in the reading of original essays and the discussion of subjects approved by the President. A select library of 600 volumes is at the service of the members. None but students of the more advanced classes are eligible to membership. The President is appointed by the Faculty; the other officers are elected by the members.

OFFICERS.

Mr. M. A. McGINNIS, S. J., - - President.
Mr. CARTER H. HARRISON, Jr., Vice-President.

The earliest use of the name Loyola appeared in 1880 when the Chrysostomian Debating Society of St. Ignatius College honored the patron saint of the Jesuit order. In 1909, St. Ignatius College would be renamed Loyola University.

Thomas Finn (1860–1920), as a Jesuit missionary in British Honduras, c.1900

The Terror of Haymarket

Did anarchists provoke a riot on May 4, 1886, by exploding a bomb during a workers' rally at Haymarket Square, as prominent businessmen and civic leaders believed? Or was this yet another deadly confrontation between predominantly German workers and Chicago's largely Irish Catholic police force?

After nearly 125 years, historians continue to debate the meaning of Haymarket. There is little or no disagreement, however, about the events leading up to the tragedy. On May 1, 1886, thousands of workers advocating the eight-hour day had walked off their jobs and formed processions throughout the city. Sympathetic strikes took place over the next two days. The killing of two strikers by police at the McCormick Reaper Works on Blue Island Avenue near Western Avenue on May 3 sparked another protest. The *Arbeiter Zeitung* printed circulars urging workers to meet the following night at Haymarket Square at Randolph and Desplaines streets.

About a thousand people turned out to hear August Spies, Albert Parsons, and Samuel Fielden speak from atop a wagon that served as a makeshift platform. Observing the reaction of German and Bohemian workers, Mayor Carter Harrison I decided there was no reason to disperse the crowd because there had been no call "for the immediate use of force or violence." He headed for home and, while getting ready for bed in his nearby mansion on Ashland Boulevard, heard the blast at Haymarket.[76]

A short time earlier, as the crowd had dwindled, Police Captain William Ward raised his hand and "commanded this meeting, in the name of the People of Illinois, to peaceably disperse." Then an unknown person threw a bomb into the ranks of the police, instantly killing Officer Mathias Degan. The police returned fire. In all, eight policemen died from wounds suffered at Haymarket, and more than sixty officers and unidentified civilians were injured by shrapnel and bullets.[77]

Mayor Harrison's proclamation on May 5 reflected the popular belief that this had been a terrorist event. He deplored the "use of weapons never resorted to in CIVILIZED LANDS, EXCEPT IN TIMES OF WAR or for REVOLUTIONARY PURPOSES, [CAUS-ING] GREAT BLOODSHED AMONG CITIZENS AND AMONG OFFICERS OF THE MUNICIPALITY who were simply in the performance of their duties." Police arrested hundreds of suspected anarchists and enforced the mayor's order to "break up and disperse all crowds."[78]

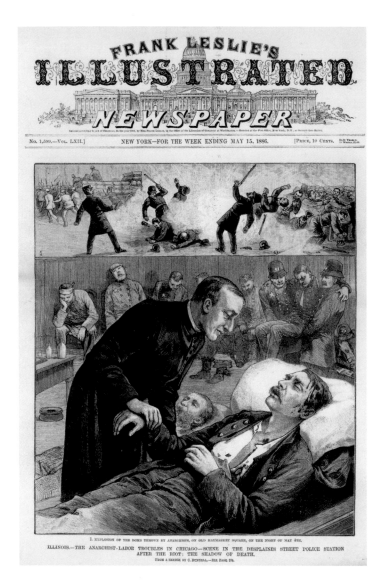

The most sympathetic rendering of the Haymarket tragedy appeared on the cover of *Frank Leslie's Illustrated Newspaper*, May 15, 1886. A Catholic priest gives absolution to a dying police officer in the Desplaines Street station.

For students at St. Ignatius College, the tragedy of Haymarket was inescapable. Not only were they aware of the labor battles fought along Blue Island Avenue but, on May 12, the funeral procession for Officer Michael Sheehan made its mournful march through the neighborhood. Sheehan was a twenty-nine-year-old Irish immigrant who had come to America from County Kerry, Ireland, about 1879. After working in the freight department of the Fort Wayne railroad, he joined the police department in 1885, where he was regarded as a "sober, faithful officer." The coroner's jury ruled that he died "from shock and hemorrhage caused by bullit wound received in the riot of May 4th, 1886." Sheehan had left behind his parents in Ireland, and only a brother, Daniel,

For students at St. Ignatius College, the tragedy of Haymarket was inescapable.

represented the family at the solemn requiem mass at Holy Family, celebrated by Florentine Boudreaux, S.J. (1821–94). Afterwards, the funeral cortege passed the Desplaines Street police station where Sheehan's fellow officers paid their last respects. His body was taken by carriage to the Milwaukee and St. Paul depot for the funeral train to Calvary Cemetery.[79]

The death of the eight officers at Haymarket barely registered in the public mind. Of far more interest were stories about suspected anarchists, and the daily papers provided extensive coverage day after day, week after week. During the summer of 1886, Spies, Parsons, Fielden, and five other defendants were tried on a single count, the murder of Officer Degan. Although prosecutors failed to provide evidence linking the defendants to the bomb, the jury agreed that they were all guilty of conspiracy. The *Chicago Tribune*, along with other newspapers, covered the trial in great detail and with sensational headlines such as "Nooses for the Reds." Appeals to the Supreme Court failed, and on November 11, 1887, Spies, Parsons, George Engel, and Adolph Fischer were hanged in Cook County Jail. Louis Lingg had ended his life with a dynamite cap the day before he was to be executed.[80]

On June 26, 1893, Governor John P. Altgeld granted an absolute pardon to the three surviving defendants, Samuel Fielden, Oscar Neebe, and Michael Schwab, and they were immediately released from Joliet Penitentiary. Altgeld's unpopular decision ended his political career, but he agreed with supporters of the "Haymarket Martyrs" that the defendants had been tried illegally, that the jurors were prejudiced, and that the judge had conducted the trial with "malicious ferocity."[81]

Over the years, the Haymarket tragedy has been commemorated with memorials that reflect different interpretations of the tragic events. Johannes Gelert's sculpture, unveiled on May 30, 1889, portrays a policeman raising his right hand in a "Command Peace" gesture. It honors the memory of Mathias Degan, John Barrett, George Miller, Timothy Flavin, Michael Sheehan, Thomas Redden, Nels Hansen, and Timothy Sullivan. Even before the monument was completed, it provoked controversy. Critics maintained that the statue looked too Irish, despite the fact that six of the officers killed were of Irish birth or descent. The statue has been bombed several times, the first time in 1890, and although it was moved to other sites, it remained a target for protestors. It is now located at the headquarters of the Chicago Police Department at 35th Street and Michigan Avenue.[82]

The anarchist monument in Waldheim Cemetery in suburban Forest Park memorializes the five Haymarket defendants who died in Cook County Jail. Albert Weiner's monument depicts the Lady of Justice crowning a workingman with laurels and holding a sword in her right hand to avenge his death. It was dedicated on June 25, 1893, the day before Governor Altgeld's pardon.[83]

After years without a permanent memorial to Haymarket near its original site, the City of Chicago commissioned Mary Brogger to create a sculpture, which was formally dedicated on September 14, 2004. The bronze figures symbolize free speech and assembly, and the cart evokes the simple wagon on which Spies, Parsons, and Fielden delivered their speeches on the fateful night of May 4, 1886.[84]

Haymarket riot or massacre? While the debate continues in earnest, the 1886 bombing in Chicago and the subsequent trial of suspected anarchists are remembered "throughout the world in speeches, murals, and monuments."[85]

THE FRIEND OF MAD DOGS.
Governor Altgeld of Illinois is freeing the Anarchists bitterly denounced Judge Gary and the jury that convicted them.

Governor John P. Altgeld's pardon of three Haymarket defendants in 1893 ended his political career. The cartoon depicts him unleashing the "mad dogs" of socialism, anarchy, and murder.

▶ *continued from page 37*

The College and Urban Life

The faculty and the students of St. Ignatius College were not isolated from the great labor battles of the 1880s, in which workers fought for the eight-hour day. After all, the school was located near Blue Island Avenue, the diagonal street that led directly to the McCormick reaper plant, the site of bitter strikes.

On May 4, 1886, a bomb exploded at a workers' rally at Haymarket Square, and, as the annals of the college make clear, "a state of alarm [pervaded] the city." While professors understood that Chicagoans would react with anger and confusion, they were faced with a practical matter. What should they do about the school's big science exhibition, planned for the evening of May 5? After considerable debate, they

agreed that "notwithstanding the excitement of the day," the student lectures should go on as planned. Ironically, the topic of the evening was combustion! A full house waited patiently in College Hall for the strains of the "Saengerfest March" and the "Bridal Rose" to fade so that John D. Baggot could begin his analysis of fire. The student orchestra played the Strauss "Fire Galop" as a prelude to Patrick Grogan's discussion of forms of combustion, and the program ended with William P. Whelan's scholarly lecture on explosions caused by gunpowder, dynamite, hydrogen, and oxygen.[86]

During 1886 and 1887, professors from St. Ignatius and Marquette College in Milwaukee, which several years earlier had become part of the network of Jesuit schools in the Midwest, joined

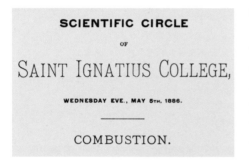

SCIENTIFIC CIRCLE

OF

SAINT IGNATIUS COLLEGE,

WEDNESDAY EVE., MAY 5TH. 1886.

———

COMBUSTION.

On the evening after the Haymarket tragedy, a science program at St. Ignatius featured lectures on fire, combustion, and explosion.

St. Ignatius College Hall

Holy Family's 300-foot tower and steeple, designed by architect J. P. Huber in 1874, made the Gothic church the highest structure in the city. Still visible in this 1893 photo are the statues of Jesus, Mary, and Joseph created by Anton Buscher in 1867.

The annual Confirmation Day procession in Holy Family parish drew thousands of Chicagoans. In 1895, Archbishop Patrick A. Feehan reviewed the parade from the portico of St. Ignatius College.

vigorous debates on curriculum. It became abundantly clear that what worked in one city did not necessarily work in another. As part of the ongoing debate about the form Jesuit education ought to take, St. Ignatius discontinued its commercial course for three years, starting in 1888. Statistics published in *The Woodstock Letters*, indicate St. Ignatius enrolled only 237 students in 1887–88, which put it ahead of Georgetown and Marquette but behind Jesuit colleges in New York, Cincinnati, Buffalo, Boston, St. Louis, and Detroit. *The Woodstock Letters* was a Jesuit journal that provided information unavailable elsewhere on the progress being made in colleges, universities, and missions. But it was becoming increasingly difficult to attract young men who lived in new residential areas, especially near fashionable Lincoln Park.

Dealing with the problem head-on, in 1888, the Chicago Jesuits launched a new initiative: a branch college on LaSalle Street, just a few blocks west of Archbishop Patrick A. Feehan's mansion at North Avenue. According to the prospectus, "repeated entreaties of the Catholic laity in that division of the city" had forced the

issue and the decision had received "the cordial approval and sanction of the Archbishop." Significantly, the branch school would be "strictly Classical," and enrollment the first year would not surpass eighty students. Boys who had made their First Communion or reached the age of twelve were eligible to attend, and non-Catholics were also welcomed with the expectation that they would "conform in a respectful manner to the ordinary exercises of public prayer." Heading up the branch school was Thomas Fitzgerald, S.J., former vice president of Marquette College, who was well known in Chicago. Born in Tipperary, Ireland, during the Famine, he had grown up in Holy Family parish and attended the Brothers' school on Morgan Street before joining the Jesuit order.[87]

For a very brief moment in its history, St. Ignatius College was listed in Jesuit publications of 1890 as being "Exclusively Classical." But the experiment failed. In a city like Chicago, with its large working-class population, a classical curriculum such as that at St. Ignatius and some of the city's public high schools had limited appeal. It didn't help that the branch college on the North Side was abruptly closed after John P. Frieden, S.J., the provincial in St. Louis, issued an ultimatum. He insisted that the Chicago Jesuits seek permission to build "a new academy or College and a Church, but without a parish." Archbishop Feehan knew that local Catholic pastors would regard a Jesuit church as unfair competition, and so he rejected Frieden's request. The only recourse left for the Jesuits in Chicago was to close their branch school and return to the Twelfth Street location.[88]

Looking to the Future

Reinvesting in the original 1870 building appeared to be a pragmatic move, especially in light of Holy Family's parish population of 20,000 and its well-organized system of "feeder" schools. There certainly could be no doubt about the commitment of religious orders to building up this part of Chicago. When Father Damen observed his fiftieth year as a member of the Society of Jesus in 1887, for example, the celebration received intense coverage in both the secular press and Jesuit journals. Characteristically, Damen used the occasion of his jubilee to highlight the continuing educational work of the parish, this time a school for the deaf, which had been organized in 1884. A similar outpouring of affection and appreciation greeted Sister Mary Agatha on December 13, 1894, when she celebrated her fiftieth jubilee as a member of the Sisters of Charity of the Blessed Virgin Mary. Thirteen hundred people crowded the chapel where Archbishop Feehan celebrated mass and read the telegram from Pope Leo XIII. Festivities continued into the evening with a banquet and musical event.[89]

By the 1890s, Chicagoans had become familiar with the Jesuit mission in

Chicago, especially the annual Confirmation Day parades. Daily newspapers routinely devoted extensive column space to descriptions of young girls in white dresses and veils and young boys wearing suits, all marching in orderly procession on unpaved streets to the great Gothic church next to St. Ignatius College.

Early in 1893, the Jesuits were already planning for their future with a modern addition to St. Ignatius. The consultors "all favored facing it on 11th Street. It should provide for a hall—playroom—reading (library) room—additional class rooms—complete scientific department—minor society (debating hall)." As had happened in the past, there was spirited discussion about costly features such as iron stairs, but by April 29, 1895, workmen got the green light: "plaster ceilings were determined on . . . [and] iron stairs are to be put at both ends." Moreover, the Jesuits

In 1894, Pope Leo XIII sent congratulations to Sister Agatha Hurley on her fiftieth anniversary as a Sister of Charity of the Blessed Virgin Mary.

How Damen Avenue Got Its Name

Nearly forty years after his death in 1890, the legacy of Father Damen was clearly visible in Chicago. The college he founded in 1870 had blossomed into Loyola University with a beautiful campus bordering Lake Michigan in Rogers Park, a university college downtown, and a medical school on the West Side. Holy Family Church, in its seventieth year of service, was still a Chicago landmark, along with St. Ignatius High School next door. This was certainly reason enough, then, to honor Damen in typical Chicago fashion—with a street name.

But when the city council unanimously passed an ordinance on June 15, 1927, renaming Robey Street as Damen Avenue, war broke out. Merchants protested that Robey Street, one of Chicago's longest north-south streets (at 2000 west), was familiar to Chicagoans and that they would incur great expense if forced to change signage, stationery, and catalogues. The Damen Avenue Committee responded, pointing out that shopkeepers would benefit by "the talismanic character of the name of Damen . . . [since he] had the reputation of being the best business man that came to Chicago within his generation."[90]

The showdown came at a July 12 meeting of the city council's committee on streets and alleys. Patrick H. O'Donnell, a Loyola law school founder and prominent criminal defense attorney, and Assistant Corporation Counsel Joseph J. Thompson represented the Damen group. They squared off against Emmanuel Goldenberger, secretary of the Greater Robey Street Improvement Association, and Joseph R. Noel, representative of the Wicker Park Chamber of Commerce. The businessmen argued that they would lose significant trade "if the well-known name of Robey were dropped for the little-known name of Damen." O'Donnell was loudly applauded when he asserted that "we are building roads and avenues as never before and what could be more fitting as a memorial to our great spiritual men than giving their names to thoroughfares."[91]

Finally, after months of delay, aldermen voted 28 to 7 on December 14 to honor Loyola's founder. The businessmen nevertheless vowed to continue their fight, buoyed by three editorials in the *Chicago Tribune*. Ironically, decades earlier, in 1857, the *Tribune* had also railed against Father Damen's plans to build a church and a college! Now the paper claimed that the council's action was "inconsiderate and unnecessary" and recommended that the merchants "can retain the name on their letterheads and they can even paint it alongside their street numbers on their signs." Contrary to the dire prediction by Alderman Max Adamowski that "the name of Damen avenue will never receive popular usage," the new name quickly became part of Chicago life. It has endured as a fitting tribute to the Jesuit Hercules whose labors at Holy Family laid broad and deep foundations for Catholic higher education in Chicago.[92]

ST. IGNATIUS COLLEGE
West Twelfth Street
CHICAGO

View of Holy Family Church, St. Ignatius College, and related parish buildings, c. 1892

Had Father Damen "placed (the college) in an aristocratic district many young men would have been unable to enter its classrooms."

decided that in order "to have good drinking water it was agreed to put a Pasteur filter on the second floor of the College building."[93]

For graduates of St. Ignatius College, the construction of the new wing may have been the inspiration for the formal organization of an alumni group in 1895. They wasted little time in organizing a three-day celebration of the college's twenty-fifth anniversary, beginning with a special mass in Holy Family on June 23, 1895. In a front-page story, the *Chicago Inter Ocean* commented on the dense crowds that gathered to watch the "picturesque procession" of acolytes wearing red soutanes and lace surplices and the Jesuit priests who had devoted their lives to the education of young Chicago men. In a stirring homily, Father Edmund M. Dunne recounted the history of the college. He pointed out that had Father Damen "placed it in an aristocratic district many young men would have been unable to enter its classrooms," and he praised the modern-day followers of Ignatius Loyola for their commitment to educating "the rising generation."

On June 24, every seat in the fashionable Auditorium Theater on Michigan Avenue was filled for the silver jubilee commencement. Included in the ceremony was the presentation of twelve honorary doctor of laws degrees, nineteen master of arts degrees, and twelve bachelor of arts degrees as well as thirteen certificates to graduates who had completed the scientific course. In a lavish banquet the next evening in their beloved College Hall, St. Ignatius alumni proclaimed their faith in their alma mater, toasting "Our Future" with glasses of malvoisie, charboneau, cabernet, muscatel, and mumm.[94]

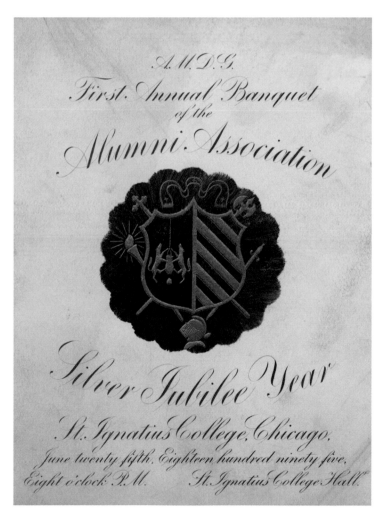

The silver jubilee program for St. Ignatius College featured two wolves feasting at the kettle. In 1909, the university's seal incorporated this traditional image of the hospitality of the House of Loyola.

Chapter 2

Landlocked on Twelfth Street

1896–1908

When students returned for classes in the fall of 1895, they found modern science laboratories on the fifth floor of the new addition. But only time would tell if these new quarters would enable St. Ignatius College to increase its enrollment and continue the Jesuit mission in Chicago. During the 1860s, Irish and German immigrants had built up the prairies around Holy Family Church with modest frame cottages. Within the following thirty years, the neighborhood had been transformed into one of the most densely populated areas of Chicago, home to thousands of new immigrants: Italians, Eastern European Jews, and Greeks. From the top floors of the college building on Twelfth Street, students could appreciate the dramatic view of the neighborhood changes that had taken place, and they also encountered it up close on their daily commutes.

Original St. Ignatius College building

By 1906, when this color postcard was printed, Holy Family Church and St. Ignatius College had become landlocked on Twelfth Street (later Roosevelt Road).

growing public perception was that this neighborhood on the West Side was in a serious state of decline.[4]

Understandably, when James Hoeffer, S.J., former president of Creighton University in Omaha, was installed as the ninth president of St. Ignatius College on December 8, 1894, he faced enormous challenges. Holy Family parish still claimed a membership of 20,000 men, women, and children, but many of its financially secure families had moved out of the neighborhood to newer parishes in outlying districts, such as St. Agatha in Lawndale. How to attract and stabilize enrollment was a major concern, along with paying the remaining cost of the recent addition and the $15,000 indebtedness to the Jesuit Province.

One strategy Hoeffer advocated involved cultivating enthusiasm among prominent Chicagoans in the fields of law, medicine, and business, and acknowledging the achievements of alumni. From 1878 through 1894, the college had awarded only two doctor of law degrees. All that changed in 1895, however, when twenty-two civic leaders accepted honors, among them pioneer surgeon John B. Murphy; Chicago Board of Education member and lawyer Thomas Brenan; and General George W. Smith (the latter two having championed the rights of the Sisters of the Good Shepherd and their industrial school in 1888); former Chicago City Collector William J. Onahan, a recipient of Notre Dame's prestigious Laetare medal; and newspaper editor Martin J. Russell. Also singled out were men whose influence would soon be felt throughout Chicago, especially Richard S. Tuthill, first judge of the Cook County Juvenile Court; Father Edmund M. Dunne, founding pastor of the Italian parish of Holy Guardian Angel; Edward F. Dunne, future Chicago mayor and Illinois governor; and William Dillon, first dean of Loyola's law school.[5]

When it came to influential alums, few rivaled Richard Prendergast, who had received one of the first bachelor of arts degrees granted by St. Ignatius College. His inclusion among Chicago movers and shakers was well deserved. A loyal supporter, he helped the college continue

Richard J. Prendergast (1854–99)

DEATH REMOVES PRENDERGAST

Noted Lawyer Dies After Long Suffering from Anæmia

BRILLIANT CAREER

Ex-Judge Richard Prendergast is dead. The well-known lawyer, who had been hovering between life and death at the Chicago

Richard Prendergast, Former County Judge, Who Died Today

Despite receiving blood transfusion, Prendergast died in 1899 at the age of forty-five.

its long tradition of public speaking by contributing money for a gold medal, won in 1895 by Francis O'Rourke for his speech "Religious Intolerance, an Enemy to American Liberty."

Prendergast was born in Claremorris, County Mayo, Ireland, in 1854 and, when ten years old, left Ireland with his widowed father. He attended school for two years in LaSalle, Illinois, and then started working in a store in Chicago, "reading in his spare moments everything that came his way." In 1872, Prendergast enrolled in college in Laurents, Montreal, but transferred to St. Ignatius; upon graduation in 1876, he ranked second in his class of seven. Prendergast's rise in Chicago public life was speedy. While clerking in the office of Judge Thomas Moran, he enrolled in the Union College of Law, where he was awarded the Horton Prize for his essay "The Law of the Land." Prendergast began practicing law in 1878, after scoring 100 on an examination administered by the appellate court, the only one in the class of that year, or in the State of Illinois up to that time. Four years later, he was elected

circuit court judge and in 1889 led an independent campaign and was elected a trustee of the sanitary district. When he died in 1899 at the age of forty-five, the entrance to the Cook County building was draped in black and white bunting and the U. S. flag was flown at half mast.[6]

Although support from some alumni contributed to the high profile of St. Ignatius College, there was still a desperate need for wealthy Catholic donors. Jesuit records make no direct reference to the University of Chicago on the South Side, but John D. Rockefeller's $3.6 million contribution in 1892 was front-page news and a poignant reminder that colleges needed money in order to grow and prosper. U. of C. president William Rainey Harper praised the Baptist philanthropist's generous gift establishing a perpetual endowment. Harper noted that although Rockefeller had never seen the new institution on the Midway, "he evidently believes that Chicago is the location for developing the university of the future, and he shows his faith by his work." The new university also benefited

Architect Henry Ives Cobb's Gothic design for the new University of Chicago, financed by philanthropist John D. Rockefeller, created the illusion of centuries-old buildings.

Herman Meiners, S.J. (1854–1919)

from the donation of ten acres of land by Marshall Field. The Gothic-style campus on Chicago's Midway, designed by noted architect Henry Ives Cobb, quickly gained national attention. In a review of collegiate architecture in the United States in 1894, *Harper's Weekly* recognized the University of Chicago for "having a homogeneity which the ordinary college campus distinctly lacks."[7]

Science and Business Education Take Hold

The Jesuits may have credited the 40 percent increase in enrollment between 1891 and 1897 to the school's "reputation for thoroughness and general scholarship," but the new emphasis on applied science also appears to have played a key role. Herman Meiners, S.J., was featured in a *Tribune* story of February 1896 devoted to a public lecture and demonstration he gave on the new form of radiation known as X-rays, which had been discovered just months earlier by German physicist Wilhelm Roentgen. The scientific community in Europe and America took great interest in Roentgen's theory of a new kind of ray and his photographic plates made just four months earlier, showing the bones of his wife Bertha's hand, complete with wedding ring. In the new lab at St. Ignatius College, Meiners and his assistants, Henry Dumbach, S.J., and Professor William N. Brown, an 1886 graduate, entertained visitors with "shadowgraphs of various articles—pencils, knives, coins, and different metallic substances" and demonstrations of how Roentgen rays were produced. The college's collection of thirty Crookes tubes, purchased from the Columbian Exposition for experimentation, was considered "the most extensive in the United States," and the student catalog devoted significant space to describing—and picturing—the X-ray work done by the science department.[8]

In spite of the general interest in scientific advances, debate continued among

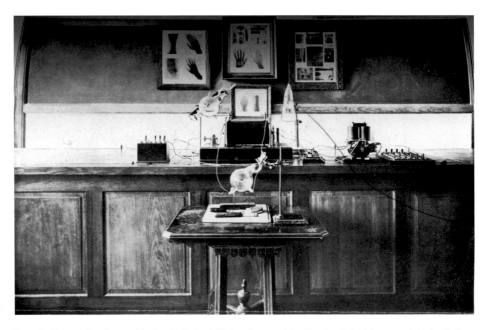

To make X-rays of ordinary objects, students at St. Ignatius used the Crookes tube (shown on table) with its "bulb as large as an ostrich egg, [and] four wires sealed in the glass."

The mineralogy department at St. Ignatius College featured rare specimens collected by missionary Father Francis Schulak from his travels out West.

Jesuit Colleges in the Midwest concerning the place of science and business courses in the curriculum. From the day St. Ignatius College opened its doors in 1870, it had attempted to remain faithful to the *Ratio Studiorum* by offering a classical curriculum that emphasized Greek, Latin, and English literature, but it also recognized the concerns of many parents and businessmen that young men be prepared "for the learned professions, for scientific pursuits or for commercial life." How was the college to achieve this balance? An important step had occurred in 1878 when the collegiate department expanded its program to four years. Although the courses kept their distinctive titles—Philosophy, Rhetoric, Poetry, and Humanities—these names would now correspond "to the Senior, Junior, Sophomore and Freshman Classes of other colleges."

Also significant was the introduction of a four-year course "designed to qualify young men for scientific pursuits, such as Civil and Mechanical Engineering, Mining, Assaying, etc." The expectation was that upon completion of the course, students would earn a bachelor of science degree and would be eligible for a master of science degree after two years of practical life. At some point, the scientific courses were folded into the commercial course, but the curriculum continued to emphasize mathematics and various sciences, notably physics and chemistry, as solid preparation for careers in business and commercial pursuits. In fact, the description of the commercial course in the 1878–79 student catalog would leave no doubt in parents' minds that its two-year program was "intended to be an *immediate* preparation for business life."[9]

While St. Ignatius College continued to provide a classical education, the layout of the fifth floor of the new addition made clear the school's commitment to the sciences. The physical department on the west side of the floor featured a lecture

During the bitter 1894 Pullman strike, *Harper's Weekly* depicted American railway union president Eugene Debs as a king who brought the nation's railroad traffic to a halt.

hall with seating for 200, along with "a laboratory, an apparatus-room, a science library and a dynamo room." The chemistry department on the east side included another lecture hall and a laboratory with eight large slate-topped tables for qualitative analysis, arranged to accommodate seventy students, as well as a "balance room, a science library . . . and a photographic studio and a dark-room." The Camera Club, under Father Dumbach's direction, claimed more than thirty members during the 1890s and wasted little time in making good use of "the splendid dark-room" at its disposal. The group recorded scenes of college life and the exterior and interior of St. Ignatius College and Holy Family Church, producing images that were used repeatedly in student catalogs.[10]

An innovation endorsed by the faculty in 1896 centered on a "plan of historical readings and discussions . . . to alternate with the regular debates" ranging from such topics in American history as the adoption of the US Constitution to President Andrew Johnson's impeachment trial in 1868. Moreover, living as they did in Chicago, many students were passionately interested in the contemporary issues of the day, and their debates continued a long tradition of engagement with the city. On October 20, 1897, for example, the hotly contested issue was whether "the agitation among the laboring classes as conducted by Eugene Debs is for the best interests of the working man." Two members of the class of 1900 found themselves in opposite corners of the debate: Arnold D. McMahon, a future secretary of Loyola's law school, for the affirmative view (the winning side), and Louis J. Mercier, a future French professor at Harvard and Georgetown, for the negative view.[11]

Competing for Catholic Students

What the reaction of Jesuit professors was to the news that the Vincentian Fathers were going to open a college in St. Vincent de Paul parish on the North Side is hard to judge, but it may not be a coincidence that St. Ignatius College suddenly began emphasizing its location. Stressing the school's proximity to commuter rail lines, the 1897–98 catalog noted that St. Ignatius students "daily make the pilgrimage" from Hyde Park, Austin, Evanston, River Forest, Joliet, Waukegan, Englewood, Grand Crossing, LaGrange, Oak Park, Edgewater, and Lawndale. Young men who lived in small towns in Illinois, Indiana, Wisconsin, and Iowa and who wanted an urban Catholic education were encouraged to "take lodgings in the vicinity of the College." The officers of the college took no responsibility for "faults committed outside the premises," and they warned students that "should any serious charge be fairly substantiated, the guilty shall be punished according to the gravity of the offense."[12]

At the turn of the twentieth century, only 63,618 young men attended college nationwide, and in a predominantly working-class city such as Chicago, many Catholics were fortunate if their children graduated from grade school, much less high school. Moreover, relatively few of Chicago's industrial leaders had attended college or studied Greek and Latin, which were still regarded as defining characteristics of a Jesuit education. Attracting enough students who could afford to pay $40 tuition was difficult enough, but now for the first time, St. Ignatius College faced Catholic competition. In September 1898, seventy young men began attending classes in the original church of St.

Vincent de Paul at Webster and Osgood (Kenmore Avenue), a modest structure that had none of the beauty or collegial feel of the school on Twelfth Street. While the Jesuit college was enjoying a momentary edge in terms of faculty and facilities, still another rival appeared on the scene. In September 1900, the Carmelite fathers opened St. Cyril College and made plans for a brick structure at 6413 South Dante Avenue in the Woodlawn neighborhood, directly south of the University of Chicago. The Carmelites continued to operate their collegiate department until 1918, and six years later, the institution was renamed Mount Carmel High School.[13]

In relation to higher education, gender also mattered, as the Sisters of Charity knew so well from teaching young women who wanted to pursue careers, primarily as teachers in Chicago's public schools. Catholic families were willing to invest in their daughters' education because it prepared them for salaried positions as teachers, nurses, and secretaries. On September 5, 1899, the B.V.M. Sisters opened St. Mary's, the first central high school for girls in Chicago, with seventy-two students. St. Mary's, located about a mile and a half west of St. Ignatius College, quickly became "the largest Catholic high school for girls in the United States." Its modern building at Grenshaw and Cypress streets (Hoyne Avenue) was enlarged three times between 1900 and 1924.

Although the B.V.M. Sisters took great satisfaction in the number of their graduates who won admission to the

St. Mary's High School, founded in 1899 by the Sisters of Charity of the Blessed Virgin Mary at 1031 South Hoyne Avenue, became the largest Catholic high school for young women in the United States.

Photo. by the College Camera Club.

ST. IGNATIUS COLLEGE—VIEW FROM ELEVENTH STREET.

The 1895 addition (at right) with its modern laboratories overlooked the field where students had played baseball since 1870.

Chicago Normal College, the specter of so many Catholic teachers in the public school system became a matter of grave concern to some Chicagoans. In 1915, School Superintendent Ella Flagg Young tried to impose a quota system for students entering the teachers' college from private institutions. Since St. Mary's drew 600 young women from forty-seven parishes in Chicago, the proposed policy would dramatically restrict their opportunity to pursue teacher training. The effort was defeated, however, and St. Mary's continued to flourish. Not only did the school play a critical role in upward social mobility for the daughters of working-class Catholics but it also helped to lay the foundations for Mundelein College, established in 1930.[14]

Beyond Baseball

Although the science curriculum at St. Ignatius College captured a great deal of interest, so too did sports. Baseball had been the most popular pastime since the school opened in 1870. Official records confirm the intensity with which games were played—and how distracting they proved to be for members of the debate society as they argued the great issues

of the day. Dr. Edward Garraghan, who began his education at St. Ignatius in the late 1880s, recalled that before the 1895 addition was built "a high fly between second and third [base] often fell into . . . the beautiful flower garden laid out around a small pool and fountain." In fact, so many windows were broken over time that in 1897, Father Hoeffer decided to place screens "on all the windows of the east corner of the old college building; & on all the windows northeast of the [Jesuit] residence."

During the 1890s, a new, more physically demanding sport, rugby football, began to claim the time and attention of St. Ignatius students. Garraghan remembered that he and his friends preferred football to soccer and that "'Jim' (Big Hoss) Quinlan went into the new game with so much enthusiasm that his leg was broken in a scrimmage. We didn't have the 'revised rules' then."[15]

The organization of a football team in 1892 was regarded as yet another sign that students were looking for competition beyond the school's familiar grounds. Records are fragmentary, but they suggest that the St. Ignatius eleven accepted invitations from local public high school teams in addition to their legendary Jesuit rivals, Marquette and Detroit universities. Although daily press coverage continued to feature mainly East Coast teams such as Harvard, Yale, Princeton, and Cornell as well as Midwestern powerhouses such as the University of Chicago, Northwestern, and the universities of Illinois, Wisconsin, and Michigan, St. Ignatius students had reason to be hopeful. Their coach, Victor Sincere, had been a pupil of the famous University of Chicago coach Amos Alonzo Stagg and provided much-needed expertise for his players. In 1902, J. F. Byrnes, a former halfback from the University of Wisconsin, coached the St. Ignatius team to several victories, including a 6–0 win over Rush Medical College on October 28, 1902, and a 6–6 tie against Marquette a month later. Playing in that game were two sons of the late Judge Prendergast: John, the center, and Richard, who scored a touchdown before "time was called at the end of two desperately fought halves." A large number of St. Ignatius rooters improvised a college cheer based on the popular ditty "Mr. Dooley," and, according to the *Tribune*, the stands at the American League Park "reverberated with the song."

The St. Ignatius football team in 1900 included future Loyola president Samuel Knox Wilson (highlighted), who headed the university from 1933 to 1942.

The stands at the American League Park "reverberated with the song."

Catholic Colleges Under Fire

While collegiate spirit remained strong, provided in large part by activities such as football, behind the scenes, Jesuit professors expressed deep concerns about the school's future on Twelfth Street. John F. G. Pahls, S.J., who had succeeded Father Hoeffer as president in November 1898, believed that better publicity would help attract students. In June 1899, St. Ignatius College printed 3,000 catalogs and prospectuses and ran ads in a variety of publications ranging from the Catholic weekly *The New World* to the *Polish Daily News* and the Benedictine *Bohemian Daily*.

But enrollment was only part of the problem. How could Catholic schools such as St. Ignatius compete with state and private institutions? The reforms adopted by the Missouri Province in 1886–87 may have brought greater uniformity in terms of textbooks, but the course of study was still not comparable to that of secular colleges. Gilbert J. Garraghan, S.J., who received his BA from St. Ignatius College in 1889, and later became a noted Jesuit historian, summed up the curriculum of his youth as "one of marked rigidity, practically no elbow room at all for electives being allowed."[16]

The news that graduates of Boston and Holy Cross colleges would no longer be admitted as regular students to Harvard University Law School starting in 1898 sparked deep debate among Jesuit colleges on the East Coast, but its effects were also felt in the Midwest. If a diploma from a Catholic college was unacceptable at a university's professional school, few parents would invest in tuition money, no matter how reasonable that cost. Although Georgetown had been given a reprieve

by Harvard, its president, J. Havens Richards, S.J., wondered whether the Harvard ruling represented "a systematic and deliberate intention . . . to discredit Catholic education, and to drive us from the field." Despite repeated requests for clarification, including a letter from the rector of Catholic University in Washington, DC, President Charles Eliot of Harvard remained insistent that "the Jesuit colleges of the United States do not stand, and have never stood" on the same level as "Dartmouth, Amherst, Williams, Haverford, Lafayette, Oberlin, Rutgers [and Connecticut's] Trinity, and Wesleyan." The solution, in Eliot's view, was for Jesuit colleges to "amplify their courses of instruction and raise their standards of admission."[17]

An equally serious challenge to the existence of Catholic colleges in Illinois occurred in January 1899 when the state legislature introduced the Curtis bill, which would have prevented colleges from granting diplomas unless each had an endowment of more than $100,000. President Henry Wade Rogers of Northwestern University took the lead in calling for a state commission that would regulate and proscribe standards for degrees and literary honors as the most effective way of shutting down "diploma mills" such as the Illinois Health University headquartered in Chicago. In a speech before the Illinois State Teachers' Association in Springfield, Rogers had lambasted the institution, which existed only on paper, claiming that it had "discredited American degrees in Europe and Asia, and been publicly denounced in the British Parliament." Despite such obvious abuses, St. Ignatius alumni, at their smoker and banquet on February 7, 1899, protested that the Curtis bill would limit the ability of

View of Boston College and Immaculate Conception Church on Harrison Street in the Sound End in the 1870s

U.S. Jesuit Colleges Across the Centuries

Currently there are twenty-eight Jesuit colleges and universities in the United States plus two Jesuit schools of theology. Listed below are the colleges and the years in which they were founded.

Marquette College, dedicated in 1881, at Tenth and State streets in Milwaukee

1789   Georgetown University, Washington, DC

1818   St. Louis University, St. Louis, Missouri

1830   Spring Hill College, Mobile, Alabama

1831   Xavier University, Cincinnati, Ohio

1841   Fordham University, New York, New York

1843   College of the Holy Cross, Worcester, Massachusetts

1851   St. Joseph's University, Philadelphia, Pennsylvania

1851   Santa Clara University, Santa Clara, California

1852   Loyola College in Maryland, Baltimore, Maryland

1855   University of San Francisco, San Francisco, California

1863   Boston College, Boston, Massachusetts

1870   Canisius College, Buffalo, New York

1870   Loyola University Chicago, Chicago, Illinois

1872   St. Peter's College, Jersey City, New Jersey

1877   University of Detroit-Mercy, Detroit, Michigan

1877   Regis University, Denver, Colorado

1878   Creighton University, Omaha, Nebraska

1881   Marquette University, Milwaukee, Wisconsin

1886   John Carroll University, Cleveland, Ohio

1887   Gonzaga University, Spokane, Washington

1888   University of Scranton, Scranton, Pennsylvania

1891   Seattle University, Seattle, Washington

1910   Rockhurst University, Kansas City, Missouri

1912   Loyola University New Orleans, New Orleans, Louisiana

1914   Loyola Marymount University, Los Angeles, California

1922   Weston Jesuit School of Theology, Cambridge, Massachusetts

1934   Jesuit School of Theology at Berkeley, Berkeley, California

1942   Fairfield University, Fairfield, Connecticut

1946   LeMoyne College, Syracuse, New York

1954   Wheeling Jesuit University, Wheeling, West Virginia

Over time, several Jesuit establishments, such as Campion College in Prairie du Chien, Wisconsin, ceased to function as colleges but continued as preparatory schools.

Postcard showing St. Louis University, c. 1915

John P. McGoorty (1866–1953)

Carter Harrison II (1860–1953) reminded voters that "Chicago is fortunate in having a mayor who keeps his hands in his own pockets."

their alma mater to grant degrees. John P. McGoorty, leader of the Democratic minority in the Illinois house, wasted no time in organizing opposition to the bill. He informed Mayor Carter Harrison, the school's most famous graduate, that the proposed legislation could sound the death knell for "every small denominational institution in the State . . . many of which are doing good work." Although the Curtis bill was defeated, the position of Catholic colleges remained tenuous.[18]

In April 1899, Jesuit college presidents and professors from the East (Massachusetts, New York, Maryland, and Washington, DC) and the Midwest (Ohio, Missouri, and Nebraska) joined diocesan priests and representatives from eleven other religious orders at a historic meeting in Chicago, the first conference of Catholic educators ever held in the United States. In the opening address, Catholic University president Monsignor Thomas J. Conaty acknowledged the challenges facing Catholic colleges "in this day of trust and syndicate" but reminded his colleagues that they had a duty to "question the methods of improvement . . . to shape and mold our instruction so as to produce the best results for those committed to our care." Concern was mounting, based not only on President Eliot's criticism, still fresh in the delegates' minds, but also on the survey of Catholic higher education in the United States completed by Notre Dame professor Austin O'Malley. Confirming that there were more Catholic students enrolled in state and secular institutions than in Catholic colleges, O'Malley lamented the fact that aside from Catholic University in the nation's capital, America's ten million Catholics "have [only] a handful of institutions . . . worthy of the name college."

Still, there were reasons to hope, as the conference's newly elected secretary Francis Cassilly, S.J., prefect of studies at St. Ignatius College since 1897, could attest. Even before the conference, Chicago's Jesuit college had begun implementing changes by separating its preparatory department from the collegiate division and devoting more attention to the sciences and athletics. In addition to providing more uniformity in the college curriculum, Catholic educators agreed on the need for strengthening courses "with particular regard to history, history of philosophy, philosophy of history, political economy and the addition of advanced courses in English and the modern languages."[19]

The Conference of Catholic Educators also unanimously voted "to condemn all unwarranted state interference with private rights and privileges." In their view, recent legislation aimed at restricting the liberties at private institutions was a move by large universities to crush small colleges. They emphasized that their institutions "without any help or subsidy from the state, have contributed so much to the intellectual and material progress of our Nation."

The closing ceremonies in Steinway Hall at 64 East Van Buren Street on April 14, 1899, left no doubt about the commitment of Catholic colleges to American life and provided the Jesuits with an opportunity to showcase their students' mastery of oratory and their love for history and appreciation of science. Facing nearly a thousand men and women from a stage decorated with American and college flags, one St. Ignatius student, future Penn State history professor and translator Francis J. Tschan, opened the event with a speech on Abraham Lincoln, and a second student,

THE ATHLETIC AND GAME-ROOM ASSOCIATION,

Supported by the voluntary contributions of its members, possesses a well-furnished Gymnasium, and a large collection of interesting and instructive games. Its end is to afford indoor amusements during severe or inclement weather ; to promote the physical development of its members by manly games and healthful exercise, and also to create and foster a *College Spirit* among the students.

OFFICERS:

MR. HUGH B. MacMAHON, S. J.................PRESIDENT.
JAMES J. CLANCY....................VICE-PRESIDENT.
VINCENT J. WALSH...........CORRESPONDING SECRETARY.
JOHN L. BABICKY................RECORDING SECRETARY.
DOLAMORE D. HENRY......................TREASURER.
WILLIAM J. FARRELL, ⎫
JOHN A. McCABE, ⎬ ....CENSORS.
HENRY G. NOLAN, ⎭

MEMBERS, 267.

St. Ignatius students regarded athletics as the key to creating and sustaining college spirit.

Henry Dumbach, S.J. (1862–1909)

Louis J. A. Mercier, was awarded the gold for his presentation on Louis Pasteur.[20]

Clearly aware of its competition in Chicago, St. Ignatius College took the unusual step in 1898–99 of appealing to generous donors to provide "liberal patronage and endowment" so that the school might "broaden its scope and raise to a still higher plane its standard of scholarship." Though they realized they were unlikely to attract million-dollar endowments like those bestowed upon the University of Chicago and Northwestern University, Jesuit professors believed that the larger Catholic population in Chicago ought to contribute financially to the "many deserving and ambitious boys" who wanted to continue their education beyond high school. Any donor who might be unable to endow a perpetual scholarship was encouraged to pay the tuition of a student for one session. Also significant was the school's appeal for $8,000 to $10,000 to build a gymnasium "worthy of the college." By 1900, the Athletic and Game-Room Association had emerged as one of the college's most important organizations, and its thirteen officers coordinated the annual field day exercises that kicked off commencement week. Although no names of benefactors survive, the impressive fourth-floor gym was dedicated on March 20, 1902, and became one of the most popular spaces in the school.

In 1900, when Dumbach, the former science professor, was appointed school president, the student body of 443 included 109 students in the collegiate

THE PRINCE AND
❧❧❧ PAUPER ❧❧❧

Dramatized from Mark Twain ❧❧❧ First Production in Chicago

PRESENTED BY

The Students of St. Ignatius College

AT THE

COLUMBIA THEATRE

Thursday, December 28, 1899, at 2 o'clock

CAST

King Henry	EDWARD HAYES
Edward, Prince of Wales	GEORGE CARROLL
Earl of Hertford	EDWARD GUEROULT
Prince Godfrey	RAYMOND FOX
Page to Prince	CHARLES CLANCY
Court Physician	JOHN MOORE
Archbishop of Canterbury	JOSEPH CORRIGAN
Humphrey Marlow, Whipping Boy	WILLIAM MAGEE
Miles Hendon, a Soldier	CLARENCE MERCER
Tom Canty, the Pauper	THOMAS McDONALD
John Canty, his Father	JUSTIN McCARTHY
Dan Canty, Tom's Brother	HORACE MacROBERT
Sykes, Tom's Uncle	CHARLES CAMP
Yokel, a Vagabond	PAUL MUEHLMANN
Mad Sam	THEODORE ADAMS
Anthony Gorse ⎱ Men-at-Arms	MICHAEL DOLAN
Hugh Gallord ⎰	WILLIAM GAYNOR
Servant to Hendon	PAUL MUEHLMANN
Herald	WILLIAM J. RUSSELL
	ANDREW HELLGETH
Vagabonds	THOMAS McNALLY
	LEO KONKELL

Royal Choristers, Courtiers, Rabble, etc.

STAFF

PLAYWRIGHT	JOHN F. SYNNOTT, S. J.
WORDS AND MUSIC OF JESTERS' SONG BY	A. F. FRUMVELLER, S. J.
DRAMATIC INSTRUCTOR	JOHN LANE O'CONNOR
MUSICAL DIRECTOR	M. A. ROY
COSTUMERS	FRITZ SCHOULTZ & CO.

ROYAL COURT JESTERS

SIDNEY BLANC, LEADER

HERBERT KENDRICK   WILLIAM EPSTEIN   THEODORE REINERT
JOHN SNOWHOOK   FRANK MEHREN   EDWARD O'GRADY
JOSEPH WARZYNSKI   MICHAEL KLEIN   ALOYSIUS SCHMITZ

ROYAL DANCING PAGES

LOUIS BEAUVAIS   HERBERT KENDRICK   WILLIAM MAGEE
CLARENCE WILLIAMS   FRANK CAVANAUGH   CHAS. FOWLER
GEORGE BERNATZ   EDWARD O'GRADY

Program for *The Prince and the Pauper*, performed at the Columbia Theater, Monroe and Dearborn streets.

division and 103 in the commercial department. The academic department, which corresponded to a secondary high school, enrolled 199 students with an additional 32 young boys in the preparatory department. Although relatively few young men completed all four years of the collegiate program, those who did so enjoyed a remarkable range of activities. Football player Andrew W. Hellgeth, for example, also was a member of the debating society and took part in theatrical productions such as *The Prince and the Pauper*. In 1900, competing against students from St. Louis University, Creighton, Xavier, Detroit, Marquette, and St. Mary's Kansas, he became the school's first recipient of the prestigious Inter-Collegiate Latin award. During December of that year, the school celebrated the debut of its first orchestra at the Studebaker Theater downtown in connection with the ambitious student staging of *The Black Arrow*, based on the novel by Robert Louis Stevenson. Financial support for the play was provided by more than

Andrew W. Hellgeth (1877–1944)

The first St. Ignatius College orchestra, organized in 1900

St. Ignatius College 1900 graduates: front row, seated, Charles B. Collins, Louis J. Mercier, M. C. Edward Gueroult, Theodore T. Adams, Charles P. O'Connor; second row, Charles J. Scott, Stanley S. Walkowiak, Joseph T. O'Donnell, Bernard E. Naughton, Austin E. Torney, James P. Whelan; third row, Leo F. Zuchola, Nicholas N. Britz, Charles A. Meehan, Francis A. Crowe, Stanislaus A. Warzynski; not pictured, Arnold D. McMahon and Michael J. Morrissey

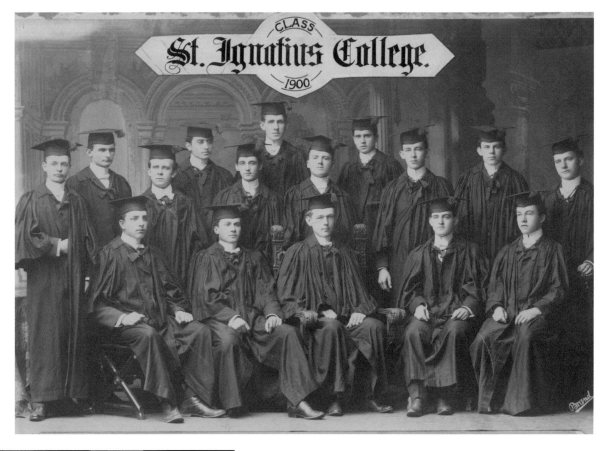

1900 commercial class

addresses explored the students' relationships to twentieth-century politics. Significantly, the school awarded 1881 alumnus Mayor Carter Harrison a doctor of law degree and conferred similar honors on Chicago grocery magnate Franklin Mac Veagh; Chicago Law School Dean George W. Warvelle; and Patrick H. O'Donnell, one of the city's most colorful criminal defense lawyers.[22]

fifty women, among them Sacred Heart alumnae Agnes Ward Amberg, Katherine Michie Bremner, and Genevieve Amberg, who had recently led the drive to organize the Italian mission of Holy Guardian Angel on Forquer Street.[21]

Students at St. Ignatius College were not immune from the dramatic changes taking place outside their classrooms, and their struggle for understanding was reflected in the 1900 commencement speeches. Titled "The Problem of Want" and "The Problem of the Citizen," the

The Future of St. Ignatius College

By far some of the most poignant correspondence found in the Jesuit archives in St. Louis and at Loyola University focuses on the great debate over the future of St. Ignatius College and the schools of Holy Family parish. Once regarded as the "banner schools of America," enrollment had declined as a result of rapid ethnic change in the surrounding neighborhood. As early as 1896, the Jesuits expressed concern that the B.V.M. schools had become "less

continued on page 66 ▶

▶ *continued from page 63*

St. Aloysius School, 631 West Maxwell Street

& less self supporting" and voted in favor of closing St. Aloysius School at 631 West Maxwell Street. Their hope was to make the schools of Holy Family parish free as soon as possible, so that they would be on a par with the public schools, but decreasing parish revenues rendered this impossible. In 1899, the Jesuit consultors agreed to sell St. Aloysius School to the city of Chicago "for the education of the Maxwell Street Hebrew [children]," and it subsequently was reopened as the Oliver Goldsmith School.[30]

By the turn of the twentieth century, there was widespread agreement among the Chicago Jesuits that the location of its college on Twelfth Street had become a liability. In 1899, the front of Holy Family Church was painted, its doors and vestibule refurbished, and the old plank sidewalk in front of the college "torn up and filled in [with] granitoid pavement." These improvements contrasted sharply with the deteriorating condition of many of the neighborhood's streets and alleys, and therefore the Jesuit consultors were dismayed to discover that property owners opposed the paving of nearby May Street. Despite believing that their "own interests would be best served by a new pavement," the Jesuit community reluctantly went along with their neighbors. Throughout the 1890s, Jane Addams had battled the local alderman, John Powers, over garbage collection in the Nineteenth Ward, and although she and her Hull-House colleagues were unable to defeat him, they did succeed in calling attention to the unsanitary condition of the streets and the overcrowding of frame cottages that had become "alley tenements." In a study of the Jewish and Italian districts on the Near West Side in 1901, for example, the City Homes Association claimed that "one house in every five was considered dangerous" and pointed out the health risks to children whose only playgrounds were alleys. While not as densely populated as the Polish neighborhood on the Near Northwest Side, the area still harbored an overabundance of basement dwellings and a lack of sanitary facilities that contributed to high rates of infant mortality and tuberculosis.[31]

Beginning in September 1901 and continuing for the next several years, Dumbach and his Jesuit colleagues explored many strategies to ensure the Jesuit mission in Chicago. First and foremost would be the establishment of a new parish, perhaps in suburban Oak Park, seven miles west of St. Ignatius College. The consultors unanimously agreed that "while we may not be able to locate in the most fashionable district of town . . . further delay in the matter will only lessen our chances." Obtaining permission from Archbishop Patrick A. Feehan for the parish, however, was no sure thing. After all, a decade earlier the Jesuits had spurned his offer of establishing a parish and a college north of Lincoln Park when they wanted to expand their North Side branch. Edward A. Higgins, S.J., remembered that Feehan had been surprised when the Jesuits abruptly closed the college department on North Avenue. Higgins afterward

Tuberculosis Threat

In 1904, Dr. Theodore Sachs challenged the widespread assumption that Jewish immigrants enjoyed immunity from tuberculosis. He documented the number of tuberculosis cases in the neighborhood directly east of St. Ignatius College (the college's location indicated by the arrow), where "the largest percentage of the Jewish poor of Chicago" lived. Sachs described deplorable living conditions in the area bounded by Taylor Street on the north, 14th Place on the south, Blue Island Avenue on the west, and Canal Street on the east, and he called for city authorities to improve conditions in the area.

CHART I.– Showing distribution of cases of Tuberculosis in the Jewish district of Chicago. (May 1, 1902 to November 1, 1903.) By Dr. THEODORE B. SACHS.

Francis B. Cassilly, S.J. (1860–1938)

regarded Feehan as "a good friend to have overlooked such a fiasco and to treat us as if we had not caused the people and himself such a disappointment."[32]

Cassilly provided a behind-the-scenes look at the deliberations of his Jesuit colleagues as they tussled with the decision to establish an annex or academic department in an outlying neighborhood. Recording the minutes of the consultors' meeting on March 7, 1902, Cassilly lamented that "one by one magnificent opportunities have slipped through our hands. The North and South Sides are now practically closed to us. . . . If any religious body enters the territory west of us, our field of work in the city will be reduced to a vanishing point." The Jesuits were aware that they had no time to lose since "there is rumor that the Notre Dame people are striving to get a foothold on the west side."

The neighborhood under consideration was Garfield Park, named for the spacious city park west of Central Park Avenue between Madison and Lake streets, originally designed by William LeBaron Jenney in 1871. With its modern homes and apartments, the surrounding area was experiencing rapid development and attracting former members of Holy Family parish. Not only had two of Chicago's most prominent Catholic realtors, John F. Cremin and Thomas Brenan, "subdivided and improved hundreds of acres on the west side between Garfield Park and Oak Park" but Feehan had relied on them to purchase property for the Catholic Church in Chicago. After Cremin's death in 1899, his son, Joseph, took over the firm, and it is likely that he advised the Jesuits on possible West Side locations.[33]

While St. Ignatius College had no intentions of abandoning its long-standing

tradition as an urban day-school, Cassilly acknowledged that many parents were "loathe to send their younger boys a long distance to school . . . particularly where the street cars and streets are always overcrowded." Yet Cassilly believed that if Feehan did not grant the Jesuits permission to establish a parish, "half a loaf is better than no bread" and that his colleagues ought to be "content with an academy." He reminded them that "as circumstances change, we must adapt ourselves on non-essential points, or else drop out of the race."[34]

The New Century's First Question: Location?

Throughout 1902, the Chicago Jesuit community discussed with great passion the issue of a new location. Letters sent to Joseph Grimmelsman, S.J., the provincial in St. Louis, revealed a keen appreciation of real estate issues and changing residential patterns in the city. John F. X. Tehan, S.J., enthusiastically reported that Chicago was experiencing "a building boom, second only to that after the great fire" of 1871 and that "now is the most propitious time to select a location here" for the expansion of the Jesuit mission in Chicago. Edward Gleeson, S.J., argued that Chicago should have three large Catholic colleges, one in each division of the city, and he reminded the provincial that "the North and South Sides are at present occupied [by DePaul University and St. Cyril College]." Gleeson asserted that St. Ignatius no longer commanded the field because the area around the school was a deteriorating neighborhood, and he predicted that it "may some day have to be abandoned like old St. Louis University."

Gleeson had attended St. Louis University in the late 1860s when it was located at Washington Avenue and 9th Street, before the business area of downtown Saint Louis engulfed the campus. Many Jesuits in the Missouri Province clearly remembered the controversy involving the relocation of the campus to Grand and Lindell in 1888. St. Louis University officials had argued for the new location in the city's fashionable West End as early as 1874, and, according to historian Barnaby Faherty, S.J., "The delay in moving had set the school back immeasurably." No doubt reflecting on the experience of his alma mater, Gleeson asserted that steps should have been taken twenty years earlier to assure the future of St. Ignatius College, and he expressed doubt that an academy building in the Austin–Oak Park area, then under consideration, would "secure the field for ourselves without special agreement with the Archbishop."[35]

Cassilly, however, remained optimistic that "there is a wide field in Chicago and plenty of room for another Jesuit establishment" and was heartened by the practical unanimity among his colleagues. He favored the opening of two or three branch academies in the choicest locations obtainable to serve as feeder schools for St. Ignatius College. He expressed reservations, however, about the wisdom of having a parish church and college together since the resulting physical plants are "badly cramped in America." Cassilly strenuously argued for "choos[ing] our own building sites for colleges" and pointed out to Grimmelsman that "this problem does not occur in European countries, where [our Jesuit colleagues] do not have to wrestle with the parish problem." In his view, the only territory left to the Jesuits was the west side and the extreme north side, but he believed that the west side with its "extension of ten or twelve miles each way" was the better choice.[36]

Tensions over the urban mission of St. Ignatius College were clearly evident in the letter consultor A. K. Meyer, S.J.,

View of the Austin neighborhood looking southwest from Lake Street and Central Avenue in 1888

"Going out of the city to a place where [there] are no inhabitants is most unwise."

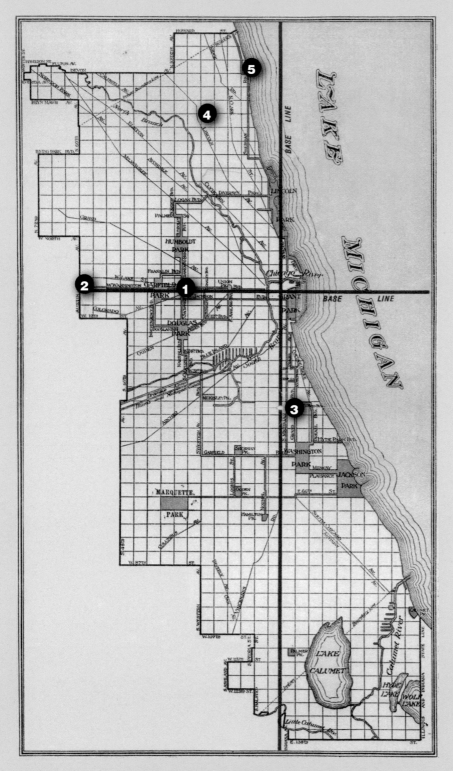

Beginning in 1901, Jesuit consultors debated the merits of several new sites for their Chicago college, including (1) Garfield Park (2) Austin, (3) Grand Boulevard, and (4) Ravenswood before deciding on lakefront property (5) between Devon and Hayes avenues.

wrote to Grimmelsman on April 5, 1902. "Going out of the city to a place where [there] are no inhabitants is most unwise," he maintained, claiming that "the college people don't seem to realize that it would take from fifteen to twenty years before we would have a decent College & parish." Although he questioned whether it was advisable "to run away from the people or from town," Meyer acknowledged that differences in economic backgrounds could not be overlooked. If the "poorer class were to follow us and build their homes around the Church and College," asked Meyer, "what assistance could they give us and how soon?" J. F. Neenan, S.J., regarded the recent robbery of a St. Ignatius College student on Taylor Street as a bad omen and insisted that "there are dozens of young men going to Cornell, Yale, and Harvard, and to the Public Schools who would come to us if we were in another locality." He encouraged the provincial to establish parishes in Morgan Park and Oak Park that might prove suitable in time for a college, warning him that "year after year good locations are being taken up by others, and we who were first in the field are worse off now than we were ten years ago, and unless we do something we will be in much worse conditions ten years hence."[37]

West Side or South Side?

On April 16, 1902, Bishop Peter Muldoon, pastor of nearby St. Charles Borromeo parish on Twelfth Street, called on Dumbach at St. Ignatius to discuss the Jesuit plans for a site in suburban Oak Park. When he learned that the "matter was hanging fire," Muldoon confidentially informed Dumbach of two potentially ominous developments: "The Christian

GRAND BOULEVARD, CHICAGO, ILL.

This colored postcard shows that after the 1893 Columbian Exposition in Jackson Park, Grand Boulevard (now King Drive) became a fashionable residential district.

Brothers were looking out for a new college on the West Side, also that the Paulists were casting longing glances toward the West Side for a Church establishment." Due to Feehan's declining health, Muldoon had been appointed coadjutor bishop to manage the diocese, which then served more than half a million Catholics living in Chicago as well as 300,000 outside the city limits. He expressed his opinion that Oak Park was too far out for a college and recommended that the Jesuits buy property "between Douglas and Garfield Park, about four or five miles west of here and about a mile north."

Clearly, immediate action was necessary, but what was the best strategy? Dumbach advised his provincial, "We must simply drop the idea of a Parish and look to a College, to save ourselves." He suggested, "If we did nothing more than choose a site, take an option on property and announce the fact that we are in the field for another College or Academy on the West Side we would thereby shut out other [religious] orders and retain control at least of this territory."[38]

A few weeks later, Dumbach had another unexpected visitor, Marshall Boarman, S.J., who arrived at the Jesuit college residence on May 26, 1902, "in red hot haste." He wasted no time in telling Dumbach that a former St. Ignatius student, Father Francis S. Henneberry, had made an unusual offer: to exchange the diocesan parish of Corpus Christi for the Jesuit parish of the Sacred Heart at 19th and Peoria streets. Boarman described Corpus Christi at 49th and Grand Boulevard on the Side South as "the finest spot in Chicago . . . located within a block of the L road and two miles from the Christian Brothers [of De La Salle Institute]." He argued that because of the Muldoon-Henneberry friendship, "we have a better chance now than ever before to get what we want from [Archbishop Feehan]." Since the Columbian Exposition of 1893, this part of Chicago had experienced tremendous growth, and land adjoining Grand Boulevard [now King Drive] had dramatically increased in value. Dumbach suggested to Grimmelsman that "perhaps Fr. Boarman could do something as he has influence and push and lots of nerve," but

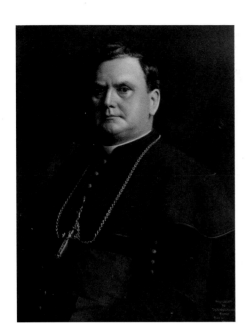

Archbishop James E. Quigley (1854–1915) who headed the Chicago diocese from 1903 to 1915

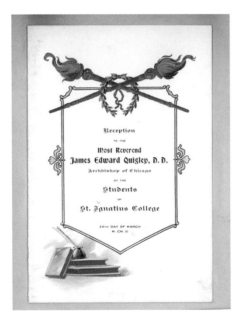

March 24, 1903, reception for Archbishop Quigley

added that the real question was "will the authorities agree to the exchange of parishes & allow us to put a College there."[39]

Although the Chicago Jesuits had favored establishing an academy on the Far West Side of the city, "the decision became known prematurely," effectively halting the property sale. Feehan's death on July 12, 1902, further delayed any action on plans for expansion, and the future of St. Ignatius College now lay with his successor, Archbishop James E. Quigley. Continuing a long tradition, the Jesuits welcomed Quigley to the college, where he paid his first visit on March 24, 1903, just two weeks after his installation. According to the *Chicago Tribune*, the new archbishop had long been associated with Jesuit schools in Buffalo and on the East Coast but "in none of them had he ever found a more promising class of students than in St. Ignatius college." Although heartened by Quigley's remarks and the fact that enrollment in 1903 was the highest in its history, the Jesuit consultors nevertheless agreed that Dumbach ought to pursue "permission for a new parish." Meanwhile, they made plans to further improve the building on Twelfth Street since "the probability is that we shall remain indefinitely. . . . It is our duty then, to develop our plant, so as to enable us to do all the good we can."[40]

But the issue of a new site did not die out. On the contrary, in March 1904, after much spirited discussion, Dumbach and his consultors drafted a letter to Quigley outlining the bleak prospects for St. Ignatius College if it remained at its original location. Stating that "most of the substantial Catholic families have moved away" and that the neighborhood "is becoming thickly settled by Russian Jews and other foreigners," they observed that when parents visited

the school and saw the surroundings, they "go away and place their sons elsewhere." Although the consultors acknowledged that "good work is being done at the college," they conceded that "still we realize that a neighborhood more accessible and more agreeable to the better class of Catholics, would give far better results from an educational point of view."[41]

In the final version of the letter to Quigley, Dumbach stressed, "We do not desire to give up our present location; but to start another college [on the North or the South side of the city]," and he offered in return "the well-established Sacred Heart parish, which is fully equipped with church, parochial residence, school, hall and sisters' residence." He also made it clear that the Jesuits preferred a site "on the lake front north of Lincoln Park, as we consider the far north side to be the growing part of the city, where many of the Catholics who are likely to patronize higher education will probably take up their residence." He concluded his plea with a reminder that "as a matter of history . . . the Jesuits were amongst the pioneer workers of Chicago, and we think the records of the archdiocese will show that we have done our fair share of labor in building up the magnificent diocese as it exists today."[42]

Like other religiously affiliated universities such as Northwestern (Methodist) and the University of Chicago (Baptist), St. Ignatius College had a long track record of preparing students for the seminary. In a meeting with the archbishop in August 1904, Dumbach informed him that since 1870 "some 125 Priests of the Diocese made their College studies at St. Ignatius & that the majority of his present Seminary students are the graduates of our Institution." He took no small satisfaction in pointing out that the one-year course in philosophy at St. Ignatius "is fully equivalent" to the two-year course offered at Kenrick Seminary in St. Louis.

One evening, after smoking cigars on the veranda of the archbishop's residence on North State Parkway, the two men began to discuss the future of St. Ignatius College. In summarizing that conversation for his provinicial, Dumbach emphasized that Quigley had studied the conditions on the North Side and that he had concluded "we must have a College there & Parish." Further, Dumbach reported, Quigley believed that Ravenswood "was best located in regard to [railroad] and streetcar facilities & that property could be had for our purpose." The archbishop confided to Dumbach that the local parish in Ravenswood, Our Lady of Lourdes at Ashland and Leland avenues, was "in deep water financially" but lamented that because Chicago pastors "live long . . .

one cannot figure on vacancies which would solve certain difficulties." Still, the archbishop remained hopeful that the Jesuits would ultimately open a college on the North Side as well as an academy on the South Side because he believed "the Carmelites & Christian Brothers were not filling the need."[43]

There was no doubt that Catholics had put their imprint on Chicago by 1904 with 148 parishes in the city alone, most with parochial schools. As a result of massive immigration from southern and eastern Europe, Chicago's population grew dramatically—from one million in 1890 to 2.2 million in 1910—and so did its Catholic population. Quigley's policy of dividing older parishes to form new ones in outlying neighborhoods had long-term positive consequences for the growth of the diocese, but from the Jesuit perspective, the announcement could not come soon

Our Lady of Lourdes parish at Ashland and Leland avenues in the Ravenswood neighborhood on the North Side in 1900

The Catholic archbishop's mansion at 1555 North State Parkway, with its fifteen chimneys, quickly became a North Side landmark after its construction in 1885. The conservatory at the right no longer exists.

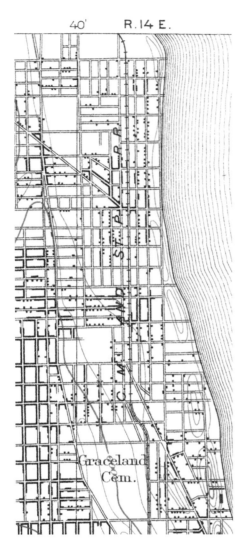

enough. On June 29, 1905, nearly a year after his conversation with Quigley about plans for expansion, Dumbach wrote the archbishop, imploring him to act quickly. Dumbach reminded him that "our sphere of usefulness in the city is considerably narrowed by the character of the neighborhood in which our College is at present situated. If we do not soon provide for the future, we fear that the time is not far distant when we shall be able to do very little for higher education in Chicago."

What emerges from Dumbach's letter is the degree to which Catholic parishes had become a familiar part of the urban landscape. On the far North Side, he informed the archbishop, "the proposal to extend the elevated road to Evanston has set the real estate business booming in Edgewater and Rogers Park." He added that before long "it will be necessary to form another parish between St. Jerome's and St. Ita's." Dumbach proposed a solution

to the thorny question of parish boundaries, encouraging Quigley to assign the Jesuits "a territory north and south of Devon Avenue and adjacent to the lake [because] we would deprive the existing parishes of practically no families as this territory is not yet built up." There was another, equally important reason for the new site in Rogers Park: it would be more than five miles from DePaul University in Lincoln Park so that the Vincentians' college "will suffer no detriment." In fact, Dumbach pointed out, "the location suggested is further from St. Vincent's than St. Vincent's is from St. Ignatius College."[44]

The Vincentians (the Congregation of the Mission) and their friends, however, did not share the Jesuits' viewpoint and "protested so vigorously against the establishment of another college on the North Side anywhere" that Quigley refused to grant permission "until the objections are removed." In July 1905, Dumbach organized a massive campaign aimed at persuading the archbishop to change his mind. He reported to his provincial that his supporters "have gone to work . . . to obtain the signatures of 1000 Catholic men on the Northside for a petition to the Archbishop in our favor." A map showing parishes and distances was prepared, and he remained confident that "there is only one obstacle to be overcome & I believe this is quite possible [and] we shall very soon be successful." Time was of the essence: Dumbach informed his supporters that "they must move and . . . rapidly."[45]

On September 19, 1905, the idea of relocating to Corpus Christi parish resurfaced when Father Henneberry died. Once again the Jesuit consultors indicated their eagerness to take over the parish property in "the very choicest neighborhood of the South Side" and all "were

Shown in the colored postcard is property at 51st Street and Grand Boulevard (now King Drive) in Corpus Christi parish, an area in which the Jesuits expressed a renewed interest in 1905.

strongly in favor of [Dumbach's] seeing the Archbishop at once." But this time they agreed "that perfect secrecy on our part should be observed." The archbishop, however, still refused their request to assume the Corpus Christi property, promising instead "a parish along the lakefront "in the neighborhood of Devon Ave."[46]

In the last months of his appointment as Midwest Jesuit provincial, Grimmelsman traveled to Chicago to see the proposed site and was delighted with it. Although the Jesuits often argued about the cost of improvements on the original St. Ignatius College building, when it came to the land owned by the Chicago, Milwaukee & St. Paul Railroad, there was surprising unanimity. They understood that the city was growing so fast that it would be difficult to secure another piece of property suitable for their purposes, and they believed that "twenty acres ought not to be considered an excessive amount of property for our purposes, as there is no telling what the future growth of our work in Chicago may be."[47]

Going North to Rogers Park

On the evening of November 1, 1905, a special delivery package arrived on Twelfth Street from Quigley's residence. Inside was a short letter granting permission to establish a new English-speaking parish, subject to the approval of the Sacred Congregation in Rome. As Dumbach had hoped, the new Jesuit parish would be formed from territory taken from St. Jerome's and St. Ita's, "north and south of Devon Avenue & the west without limits." The rector of St. Ignatius College fired off a letter to Grimmelsman with the good news, adding that Quigley's approval arrived at 9:00 p.m. "while we were in the

Church saying the Office of the Dead; so we owe our success to the Poor Souls."[48]

On November 23, 1905, the front page of the *Chicago Record-Herald* announced that after fifteen years of planning, the Jesuits were seeking permission for a new parish and university at Devon and Evanston [Sheridan Road] "which will be perhaps the largest Roman Catholic institution of learning in the United States." When Dumbach informed his colleagues the next night that the Chicago, Milwaukee & St. Paul Railroad had refused the Jesuits' bid of $7,500 per acre, all "unanimously agreed to . . . offer $8,500." They reasoned that the college "had the greater part of the amount necessary for the purchase on hand" and expressed confidence that "in case we found the burden of debt too expensive, we could always . . . [sell] a portion of the property." But Dumbach hesitated and asked his colleagues to reconsider the asking price. According to Cassilly's handwritten notes, the meeting began on November 26, 1905, at 1:30 p.m., and "the consultors unanimously agreed at once, and without discussion, on closing the deal as soon as possible at the price stated."[49]

While no records exist to verify that realtor Joseph W. Cremin and lawyer Morris St. Palais Thomas influenced the

Joseph W. Cremin (1879–1969)

The Cremin & O'Connor real estate firm advised archbishops Feehan and Quigley.

My dear Mr. Cremin:

Thank you very much for forwarding to me Father Henry J. Dumbach's characteristic letter regarding our Lake Shore Campus. I take it that I may keep the letter which may be of use when the history of Loyola University is written. It may interest you to know that we have called the first building on the campus "Dumbach Hall." From all accounts, Fathers Dumbach and Cassilly were chiefly responsible for giving us a start on this campus.

Excerpt of a letter from Father Kelley acknowledging Joseph Cremin's advice regarding the purchase of more Devon Avenue frontage for the Lake Shore Campus

Hauman G. Haugan

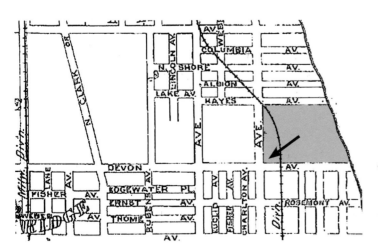

Haugan's reassuring letter to Dumbach, January 5, 1906, regarding the new Lake Shore Campus

Chicago, Milwaukee & St. Paul Railroad to reduce the asking price to $8,250 an acre, it is clear that these two Catholic laymen offered the Jesuits excellent advice about the transaction. Cremin and Thomas were concerned at the lack of a formal contract and the Jesuits' desire to pay in cash, and they insisted on having a survey of the land made by "some competent person." After a meeting in the Chicago office of Hauman G. Haugan, comptroller for the railroad, they reported to Dumbach on the spirit of cooperation that surrounded the sale. According to Dumbach, Haugan had reassured them that his correspondence with the president of St. Ignatius College "amounted to a contract; that he regarded the property as sold to you and had refused an offer of a larger price." Born in Christina, Norway, in 1840, Haugan spent considerable time in Wisconsin before moving to Chicago, where he was a member of several prestigious clubs. In a follow-up letter to Dumbach, Haugan's Midwestern sensibility shone through when he counseled that it might take several more weeks but reminded him that "large bodies move slowly!"

By late January 1906, Dumbach had agreed to take out a mortgage for the property and informed Haugan that "whatever arrangement you may see fit to make will be for the good of St. Ignatius College." In reporting the $161,254 sale on March 9, 1906, the *Chicago Tribune* informed its readers that the new site for the college "consists of twenty acres lying along the lake shore two miles south of Calvary [Cemetery], and bounded on the west by Sheridan road. The land is 253 feet north of Devon avenue and 135 feet south of Hayes ave."[50]

Considering the tight money market in 1906 resulting from the failure of several Chicago banks, the Jesuit purchase of property in Rogers Park was cause for celebration. But try as they might, Thomas and Cremin could not convince Dumbach to purchase more land on Devon Avenue. Thomas had been awarded a doctor of law degree in 1895, and he took to heart his status as an honorary alum and worried about the future of the campus adjacent to Lake Michigan. On December 11, 1905, he wrote Dumbach that "the more I think of it the more important it seems to me that you should obtain some frontage on Devon

> *"...twenty acres lying along the lake shore ... 253 feet north of Devon avenue and 135 feet south of Hayes ave."*

The future site of Loyola University's Lake Shore Campus (highlighted) included a triangular plot of land (arrow) that was eventually sold and developed as the Granada Theater.

DePaul University's new building on Webster Avenue, 1907, shown in this colored postcard, was built next to St. Vincent de Paul Church (1895–97).

Avenue to give you an entrance to the grounds. As they are now there is really no suitable entrance." Cremin's plea also was rejected. The president thanked him for his advice but responded, "We are not in a position even to think of buying more land . . . I am looking for the generous man to buy us an entrance into our property & can't find him."[51]

News of the Jesuits' ambitious plans to create a university on the new lake shore property ignited a firestorm of controversy among the Vincentian priests who staffed St. Vincent de Paul parish and college in Lincoln Park. And who could blame them? Like other religious orders in the United States, the Congregation of the Mission had incurred heavy debt in building its parish complex on Webster Avenue. In spite of the economic depression that followed the World's Fair, they had forged ahead with the construction of a magnificent Romanesque church designed by James J. Egan that finally was dedicated in 1897. In 1905, a spacious residence for the priests was completed, and plans were underway for a theater, a six-story college building, and a lyceum that would include a gymnasium, billiard hall, reading rooms, and meeting halls. Little wonder that William Barnswell, C.M., the Vincentian provincial in Perryville, Missouri, protested

to Quigley about the impact the new Jesuit college in Rogers Park would have on their Lincoln Park foundation. The archbishop's response was blunt. On January 24, 1906, he informed Barnswell that he was "perfectly free to give the Jesuit Fathers or any other Fathers permission to establish a college on the North Side of Chicago" and that he had not seen plans for the new building on Webster Avenue. Moreover, Quigley took the opportunity to point out that the Vincentians did not enjoy "the privilege of a perpetual or even long time exemption from competition on the North Side." He further suggested that it was "part of wisdom" to revise their plans in light of the likelihood of "competing colleges on the North Side."[52]

The Turf Battle: S.J. versus C.M.

But the archbishop's letter was not the only piece of bad news the Vincentians received in 1906. A handsome brochure prepared by Dumbach and Cassilly pointedly asked the public, "Would you like to see a Catholic university established in

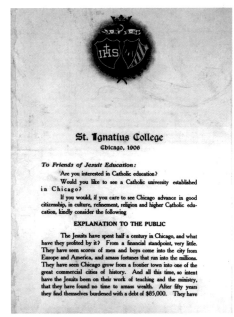

The Jesuit plea for a new Catholic university in Chicago

Loyola University makes an effort to raise $135,000 to cover existing debt and begin work on the Lake Shore Campus.

WILL YOU HELP IN THE WORK?

There is a great educational work to be done here in Chicago. Will you help to accomplish it? $85,000 is needed to lift our debt and $50,000 to begin the Lake Shore branch school. This is the most pressing need at the present time. $135,000 seems to be a very large sum, but we hope to find ten subscribers of $5,000 each, twenty-five of $1,000, and a sufficient number of $100 or less to cover the balance.

No doubt the generous Catholics of Chicago, who have done wonders in building up the Church in Chicago, will be equal to the occasion, and as they have shown an enterprise in the past, surpassed by no Christian community of history, they will certainly take a pride in putting a crown to the work by establishing a great Catholic university in our midst.

A subscription list has been opened and if you feel able to make a contribution kindly communicate with the undersigned. In case you wish further information we shall be glad to call on you.

Chapter 3

New Beginnings in the City

1909–1929

Even before the ink was dry on its 1909 application
for a charter, Loyola University was heralded by the
Chicago Tribune *with the headline "New University
Born in Chicago." The newspaper noted that Loyola
"already . . . has law and medical departments, and
an engineering department will be added next year."
Another headline announced "New School to Be
Liberal." The daily went on to praise the policy of
Jesuit leaders in employing "professors and instructors
without regard to their church association" and
stressed that "liberal and professional education is the
aim of the new institution." Only weeks earlier,
President Alexander Burrowes, S.J., and his Jesuit
consultors had decided to adopt the name Loyola
University—a pragmatic solution to the thorny
question of identity. Chicago's new university would
acknowledge the ancestral home of St. Ignatius, the
founder of the Society of Jesus.*

Dome of Cudahy Science Hall

*"There is much in beginning well, and I make bold
to say that we have done so."*

Becoming a Professional School

Loyola's plans for expansion made it clear that the university was going to continue honoring its past as it planned for the future. The *Tribune* reported that "by keeping the name St. Ignatius for the school of arts and sciences [on Twelfth Street], Burrowes has preserved the identity of the parent school, which has been the desire of all graduates." Not only had the Loyola Academy building, known

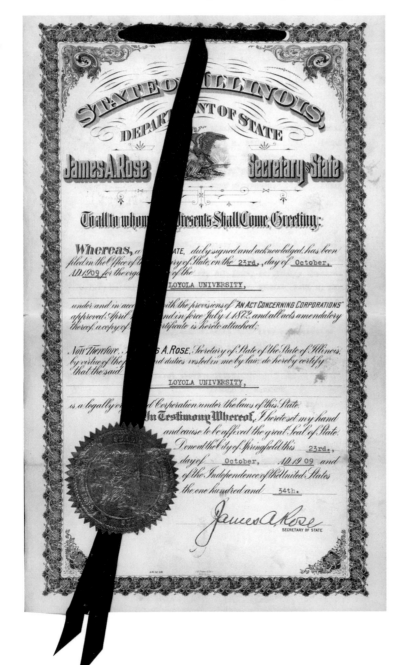

Charter of Loyola
University,
October 23, 1909

as Dumbach Hall, recently opened for classes on the Rogers Park campus, but the professional schools were also off to a promising start. Loyola's Lincoln College of Law, located in the Ashland Block, downtown, enrolled fifty students in its night classes. Also, thanks to the recent affiliation with the Illinois Medical College, eighty-three Loyola students formed the nucleus for a university medical department that was expected to develop into "one of the best institutions of its kind in the west."[1]

In 1909, Burrowes wrote in glowing terms about Loyola's proposed campus. The description appeared in *The Woodstock Letters*, a quarterly journal intended solely for *Ours* (the familiar term used by Jesuits for Jesuits) and widely circulated at that time throughout the United States. He predicted that the property "on the Lake shore, between Devon and Hayes Avenues . . . is considered a beautiful location and although the place is not built up as yet, it will be within ten years." Without mentioning DePaul University in Lincoln Park, he informed his Jesuit colleagues that "the elevated road between Chicago and many suburban towns to the North joins the site [in Rogers Park], and there is no Catholic college between us and Milwaukee, so we expect to draw from considerable territory." In a reference to Loyola's long-standing tradition as a commuter day-school, Burrowes noted that "many of our students come from great distances, 5-6-10-20 miles," and he stressed that the new academy building, one of six to be constructed in the Spanish style of architecture, would alleviate the overcrowded conditions in the original college building on Twelfth Street.[2]

Although Loyola's enrollment in October 1909 ranked behind those of St.

Louis, Marquette, and Creighton universities, there were clear signs of hope for the future. While its old Jesuit rival, St. Louis University claimed 1,169 students, only 464 were registered in arts and sciences, compared with Loyola's 630. With this solid foundation, there was every reason to believe that Loyola's total enrollment would grow steadily. After all, at nearby Marquette University, the affiliation with professional schools brought about during Burrowes's presidency accounted for 579 of its 921 students.[3]

In his address at the first faculty banquet on November 22, 1909, in the elegant Great Northern Hotel downtown, Burrowes seized the opportunity to articulate his vision for Loyola University. Acknowledging that it would take several years until all the departments could be established, he stated, "There is much in beginning well, and I make bold to say that we have done so." The president made it clear to the faculty that the new university must adhere to a recognized high standard of studies and that in the medical and legal departments "it is our intention to carry out exactly what the State laws require, both for admission and for graduation" as well as "endeavor[ing] to meet all the requirements of the American Medical Association of Colleges." Reiterating that Loyola would open its doors to all students, irrespective of religious belief, Burrowes reassured his colleagues that in other Jesuit schools, notably Georgetown, Marquette, and St. Louis universities, "Catholic and non-Catholic professors are teaching side by side . . . and there is generally a spirit of union among our different faculties that is not found elsewhere."

He also did not hesitate to embrace the challenges that lay ahead for a university whose only endowment consisted in "the lives of men devoted purely to

232. Great Northern Hotel, Chicago.

education." He asserted that far from being an isolated institution, Loyola would derive a measure of strength and prestige from its connection with other Jesuit colleges and universities throughout the world, and he denied that it was "rash . . . to build up another university here in Chicago, where already several exist." Although not identifying the University of Chicago and Northwestern University by name, Burrowes nevertheless refuted the idea that these two institutions, by reason of their large endowments, appeared to have pre-empted the field. On the contrary, he argued, "It is not always the most richly endowed college or university that turns out the best products."

A colored postcard depicting the site of Loyola University's first faculty meeting in 1909, Dearborn Street and Jackson Boulevard

Celebrating Lincoln's birthday in 1909 were (1) William Dillon, dean of Loyola's law school; (2) Alexander J. Burrowes, S.J., university president; and (3) Patrick H. O'Donnell, criminal defense attorney.

He reminded the faculty that "most of our ablest men have come from the small colleges." Reflecting his pragmatism and Midwestern sensibility, Burrowes left no doubt that Loyola stood "ready and able to give a suitable return for value received."[4]

Echoing the president's high hopes for the university was Dr. William Rittenhouse, dean of the medical department of the newly reorganized Illinois Medical College at Washington Boulevard and Halsted Street. Since its founding in 1895, the institution had trained nearly 500 doctors in Chicago, many of them students who could attend part-time only during the summer months. Rittenhouse expressed his dream that in addition to becoming "a veritable medical university, embracing all of the cognate branches of medical science and art," Loyola would also establish a high-class hospital. He concluded his remarks by applauding the Jesuits' commitment to teaching Latin and Greek as well as their success in "converting the precious youth of our land into splendid American citizens."[5]

There could be no disputing the university's intentions to prepare young men for professional careers in Chicago—and

to compete vigorously with other Jesuit institutions. At the first law school banquet earlier in the year, Burrowes pointed out that its initial enrollment had exceeded that of Georgetown, Fordham, and other leading universities that started with eight to fifteen students. Consciously embracing the legacy of Abraham Lincoln, the three-year evening program provided young men employed full-time during the day with the opportunity to extend their practical experience with a regular, scientific course in the law taught by some of the best-known practitioners in Chicago. Patrick H. O'Donnell, a criminal defense attorney and one of the founders of the law school, for example, instructed students in common law pleadings and trial practice while Thomas B. Lantry, a former municipal court judge, conducted the popular and successful practice court where students were required to institute, prosecute, and defend the proper proceedings. Guest lecturers included Illinois Supreme Court Justice Orrin Carter; Judge Edward Osgood Brown, an authority on riparian rights; Harry Olson, chief justice of the Municipal Court; and Judge Edward F. Dunne, a former Chicago mayor. Of the thirty-five students who enrolled in

Stained-glass window,
Dumbach Hall

the Lincoln College of Law in September 1909, more than one third had attended St. Ignatius College, with the remainder coming from institutions such as Notre Dame, St. Viateur, De La Salle, and DePaul.[6]

A Leader on Many Fronts

Burrowes's success in transforming Marquette from a small college to a university was due in no small part to his ideas about the future of Catholic higher education. Just weeks after his arrival in Chicago, he hosted a meeting at St. Ignatius College with representatives of eight other Illinois Catholic colleges to discuss changes in requirements that were being considered by the state teachers' association. Elected president of the new Association of Catholic Colleges on April 21, 1908, Burrowes pledged his support and endorsed the idea that these small Catholic institutions "could unite . . . in advancing their interests and protecting their rights."

He strongly believed that the diplomas from Jesuit colleges "will be of little value to the owners" unless the schools met state requirements, and he was not shy about pressing his case for the value of the classics and bachelor of arts

degrees. On April 27, 1909, at a meeting of the Federation of Illinois Colleges in Evanston, the home of Northwestern University, Burrowes presented his arguments in an address entitled "A Liberal Education as the Best Preparation for a Professional and Business Career." He warned his colleagues that emphasizing laboratory instruction to the exclusion of theoretical instruction would produce "a great many mechanics, but very few scientists." In its account of the meeting, the *Chicago Tribune* commented that he

The first building on the Lake Shore Campus, Dumbach Hall housed Loyola Academy until the school moved to Wilmette, Illinois, in 1957.

After Loyola University affiliated with Bennett Medical College at Fulton and Ada streets in 1910, graduates such as Dr. Raymond E. Hillmer (highlighted) transferred their allegiance to the Jesuit university and became Loyola alums.

"took a slap at business colleges which advertise complete courses to be finished in a short time. 'They may turn out stenographers' [Burrowes claimed], 'but not a college educated man or woman.'"[7]

Worthmann & Steinbach's plans for Dumbach Hall on the Lake Shore Campus reflected Burrowes's belief in beginning well. Constructed of reddish-brown brick at a cost of nearly $100,000, the mission-style structure that faced Lake Michigan included such marks of refinement as stained glass, arched windows and doorways, and a tiled roof. Archbishop Quigley, who had given his blessing to the Jesuits' plans for expansion, dedicated Loyola Academy on November 19, 1909, and Edward Joseph Amberg delivered the students' address. The choice of

Amberg, one of the eighty-four students who enrolled in the fall of 1909, was particularly fitting. As the Jesuits had hoped, the academy did function as a feeder school for the university, clearly demonstrated by Amberg, who went on to receive his BA degree from the university and became a loyal alum.

In March 1910, Burrowes and his Jesuit colleagues took another great leap of faith by affiliating with Bennett Medical College, one of the city's oldest medical schools, founded in 1868. Located within walking distance of the West Side medical district, Bennett owned spacious quarters at 1360 West Fulton Street, and its students interned at nearby Jefferson Park Hospital at 1421 West Monroe Street as well as at Cook County Hospital.

16 Cook County Hospital, Chicago, Ill.

Cook County Hospital at Harrison and Wood streets on Chicago's Near West Side, c. 1910, is shown in this colored postcard.

Fighting for Professional Survival

Almost immediately, Burrowes found himself in the public eye, challenging the findings of the AMA's Council on Medical Education. At a meeting at the Congress Hotel, February 28 through March 2, 1910, the AMA group criticized local medical schools, among them Illinois Medical College and its affiliate, Reliance Medical College, as being "operated for profit, limited in equipment and clinical facilities, and maintaining a low educational standard." Bennett did not escape unscathed: the committee described it as a Class B medical college that was "doing fairly good work" but needed improvement.

In a statement to the *Chicago Tribune*, with characteristic even-handedness, Burrowes reminded Chicagoans that the AMA was "a body of physicians who meet annually to voice their opinions concerning the state of medical education in the country" and that they should not be confused with the Association of American Medical Colleges. Unlike the AMA, he pointed out, the association "does not pass a wholesale condemnation on medical schools" but rather examines "each one in particular, and specifies the particular deficiency to the dean of the college." In a March 10, 1910, letter to his provincial discussing the conflict, Burrowes put the matter succinctly: "We had a tilt with the American Medical Association which met here about a week ago [and] of course there was much indignation because our college had not been examined since we got it."[8]

In June 1910, Abraham Flexner turned up the heat on the issue of doctors' training when he lambasted Chicago's medical schools as "the plague spot of the country." Flexner headed a survey funded by the Carnegie Foundation that critiqued 168 medical schools in the United States. The Carnegie report had an immediate impact and resulted in the merger or closing of many small institutions. In his report, which garnered widespread attention in the press, Flexner strongly urged the Illinois State Medical Board to recognize only three medical schools in the city: Rush, Northwestern, and the College of Physicians and Surgeons. He referred to these as the three great universities of the state. Further, he insisted that the modernization of medical education in Chicago demanded tighter entrance requirements, the abolition of night schools, better laboratory and clinical instruction, and smaller class sizes. He believed that "the execution of this plan might set the country at large to thinking on the wisdom and necessity of coordinating our educational enterprises."[9]

As one of the ten schools in Chicago to make Flexner's list, Bennett was criticized for being "frankly commercial" and having inadequate clinical facilities. Burrowes wasted no time in registering a protest, asserting that the recommendations in the Carnegie report "lean toward depriving the poor man of an education." James A. Egan, secretary of the Illinois State Board of Health, asserted that parts of the Carnegie report were maliciously

Abraham Flexner whose 1910 report forced the closing of more than half of the nation's 155 medical schools

Henry S. Spalding, S.J., first regent of Loyola's medical school, 1909–18

Loyola benefactor Michael Cudahy (1841–1910)

false. Dr. John Dill Robertson, Bennett's dean, agreed, noting that "Flexner hasn't been here for a year and a half" and that major improvements already had been made. Robertson told the *Tribune*, "We have a $60,000 laboratory building to be finished September 1" at the corner of Ada and Fulton streets, and he added that Bennett is "now part of Loyola university, the only Catholic institution with a medical department in Chicago. We're up to requirements."[10]

Determined to make Loyola's medical school a Class A institution, Burrowes drew on the support and experience of Henry S. Spalding, S.J., who was appointed regent in October 1909. The two had worked together closely at Marquette University and understood the challenges involved in affiliating professional schools. Spalding believed that "the medical school and the large medical faculty gave [Loyola] university a standing in the city," but he knew that nothing could be taken for granted. It was "a fight for eight years, but in the end, the school won out." In addition to doing battle with the AMA, Spalding found himself challenging the Ohio State Medical Board whose inspectors had ignored Loyola's new laboratories, equipment, and dissecting room that "was larger, brighter and in every way better than Northwestern or the State and nearly as good as Rush." Spalding turned the tables during a stormy session in Columbus that ended with doctors from Columbus Medical School defending their own school rather than attacking Bennett.[11]

Rogers Park Campus Begins to Take Shape

Very little correspondence has survived that documents Burrowes's original plans for Loyola, but one poignant letter, written on January 25, 1910, recounted his experiences in raising the funds necessary for a second building on the new Rogers Park campus. He planned a structure "that would embody what is best in Marquette, Chicago University, & other schools. A brick wall from the foundation to the attic divides the building in two separate buildings so that the fumes & gases of the chemistry will not affect the physical instruments (as they do in Marquette) & inconvenience students of physics."

Burrowes attempted to explain to his provincial in St. Louis, who had questioned, "Why so fast & why the science building?" Burrowes informed Rudolph Meyer, S.J., of a meeting held three weeks earlier in the offices of millionaire meatpacker Michael Cudahy. Loyola's president had described for Cudahy the various buildings he envisioned for the Lake Shore Campus. Cudahy responded by "[asking] the price of each. I told him some would cost one hundred thousand & that [the] faculty building & the science building would require only about sixty thousand. He said he could give the latter figure but one hundred thousand was too much for him." Apparently Burrowes regarded Cudahy's invitation and comments as such a good omen that he promptly hired Worthmann & Steinbach to draw up plans for the Cudahy Science Hall. But, he assured Father Meyer, "of course we shall put up no new building without the money. We have debt enough."[12]

Negotiations with Cudahy continued, and on June 21, 1910, after all twenty-nine graduates of Loyola had received their diplomas, Burrowes made the dramatic announcement of Cudahy's generous gift to the university. According to a *Tribune* report, the crowd in Orchestra Hall erupted in liberal applause. Not only would the building mark the center of the campus literally, but it would also symbolize the university's commitment to science and engineering. Loyola's president went on to express his hope "for the erection of a number of dormitories . . . intended for students from other Jesuit colleges who attend Loyola for the engineering course."[13]

It appeared that the Lake Shore Campus was about to bloom. In June 1910, news of a large bequest to Loyola from Barbara DeJonghe buoyed hopes that before long Jesuit professors would have a new residence on the campus. Like so many of the Midwest Jesuits, the DeJonghes were Belgian-born and the family's hotel on Monroe Street had

introduced Chicagoans to Belgian cuisine, especially the popular garlic-spiced shrimp DeJonghe. In announcing the donation, Burrowes noted that $100,000 would be used to build a residence; $25,000 was earmarked for a new grammar school in St. Ignatius parish; and $10,000 would endow college scholarships. Why the bequest apparently never materialized after Mrs. DeJonghe's death in July 1911 remains unclear, but once again the Jesuits of Loyola were made to realize that the pool of wealthy Catholic donors was small and constantly besieged for donations to charitable and educational causes.[14]

Although construction of the science building was underway when Michael Cudahy died suddenly in December

In 1911, *Life* magazine satirized John D. Rockefeller's contributions to the University of Chicago, founded as a Baptist school.

A Thousand Miles From Broadway

WORTHMANN & STEINBACH,
ARCHITECTS.

KOŚCIÓŁ NAJŚW. MARYI PANNY ANIELSKIEJ
N. HERMITAGE AVE. & CLYBOURN PLACE,
CHICAGO, ILL.
KS. FR. GORDON, C. R., PROBOSZCZ

This postcard shows St. Mary of the Angels at 1850 North Hermitage Avenue. Worthmann & Steinbach received the commission in 1911 after completing the dome of Cudahy Science Building.

1910, equipment for the classrooms and laboratories had not yet been contracted. Remaining optimistic, however, Burrowes informed Meyer, "I have no doubt about the intention of the Cudahys to put up this building as Mr. Cudahy wished it & to make it a fitting memorial of him." He was relieved that Michael Cudahy's widow, Catharine Cudahy, "spoke of the building & how it was progressing & asked if they could work at it in Winter time." Several of the Cudahy children attended a special mass in their father's honor at St. Ignatius Church on December 23, 1910, and "all went after Mass to see the building." Among the contractors involved in the construction of the new science building were the Edward Baggot Plumbing and Fixture Company, whose owners included two generations of St. Ignatius alums, and the Matt Rauen Company, which would put its imprint on the Loyola and Mundelein campuses over the next thirty years.

The Loyola commission proved to be a turning point for Henry Worthmann and J. G. Steinbach. Between 1908 and 1925, they emerged as leaders in the field of ecclesiastical architecture with such important structures as St. Nicholas Ukrainian Cathedral and St. Mary of the Angels Church, whose terra cotta dome was patterned after St. Peter's in Rome.

The plan of Worthmann & Steinbach's firm for Cudahy Hall expanded on its design for Dumbach Hall. The hall's main architectural feature was a massive dome rising 100 feet above the water line of Lake Michigan, large enough for a telescope. Not only did the firm draw up plans, but it also acted as contractor, making sure that the building's solid foundation would be free from vibrations.

Although Loyola never got around to purchasing a telescope, it did succeed in installing a seismograph so that students and professors could register and measure earthquakes. The Loyola seismograph was representative of a larger initiative that had been started by Frederick L. Odenbach, S.J., of the Cleveland Observatory. His program became a distinctive feature of Jesuit colleges and universities throughout the United States and Canada, all of which were generally funded at least in part by loyal alums. In 1909, for example, Loyola law school founder Patrick O'Donnell headed a campaign for Georgetown, his alma mater. Enough funds were raised so that the observatory at Georgetown was one of the very few in the country to include vertical and horizontal seismographs. Loyola's new seismograph soon proved its value: on September 30, 1912, the first recorded earthquake in Chicago was registered by the equipment, located in the basement of Cudahy Hall, and for several decades, this remained the city's only official site.[15]

Exploring New Fields

Loyola's plan to open an engineering school received widespread coverage in the *Chicago Tribune* and was viewed as yet another sign of the university's commitment to science. The new engineering dean, James D. Newton, was a graduate of Cornell University and the Jesuit College of Holy Cross. Newton had distinguished himself earlier by beating out twenty-one other competitors to take first place in a civil service exam that ensured him a position with the engineering corps, and in the summer of 1911, he left the University of Kansas to organize Loyola's engineering school. In announcing the opening of this new department, *The Woodstock Letters* claimed that in terms of equipment and curriculum, students would find "the same advantages that are offered in the old and well endowed colleges." According

Loyola University
=== **EMBRACES** ===

DEPARTMENT OF MEDICINE (Bennett Medical College) Ada and Fulton Streets.

DEPARTMENT OF LAW (Lincoln College of Law) Ashland Block.

DEPARTMENT OF PHARMACY (Central States School of Pharmacy) 1360 Fulton Street.

DEPARTMENT OF ENGINEERING (Loyola College of Engineering) Evanston and Devon Avenues.

DEPARTMENT OF ARTS AND SCIENCES (St. Ignatius College) 1076 West Twelfth Street.

ACADEMIC DEPARTMENT (St. Ignatius Academy) 1076 West Twelfth Street.

ACADEMIC DEPARTMENT (Loyola Academy) Evanston and Devon Avenues.

Ad in 1913 for Loyola University and its academic departments

to the college catalog, Loyola expected to profit by the experience of other institutions, such as Xavier in Cincinnati and Marquette in Milwaukee. Its course of studies would include nine months of theoretical work with field and laboratory exercises and three months' employment in a real shop where students, under supervision, would be able to "observe the application of the theories mastered in the class-room."[16]

For about seven years, beginning in the fall of 1910, Loyola also offered a pharmacy program through an affiliation with the Central States College of Pharmacy. Originally located at 1360 West Fulton Street, the site of the Bennett Medical College, the pharmacy department's lecture halls and laboratories were moved to the north half of Cudahy Hall in 1912. The thirty-five-week program incorporated "Mathematics, Bookkeeping and Pharmaceutical Jurisprudence as an integral part of its [progressive] course" aimed at preparing students to assume the responsibilities of the modern pharmacist. About a year after it relocated to a downtown site in 1916, however, the program was discontinued and professors were transferred to the engineering department.[17]

In 1882, Arnold Damen McMahon, first secretary of Loyola's law school, was baptized and named after Father Damen.

Invitation to Cudahy Science Hall dedication, April 28, 1912

Although enrollment figures continued to increase steadily, it was difficult to promote collegiate spirit among students who were commuting from different areas of the city: the college on Twelfth Street, the law school downtown, and the medical school on the West Side. As a former president of the Loyola Debating Society, Burrowes had been a great supporter of clubs and sports, and one of the first things he did after returning to Chicago as president in 1908 was to compose a school song. According to the *St. Ignatius Collegian*, he realized that students had no common refrain to sing at debates, ball games, and other mass meetings. The song he composed was "Ignatius' Name," which was acclaimed for its lilting march tempo. Without strong sports teams, however, even the best school song would have little effect on school spirit.

In September 1911, Burrowes commended law school secretary Arnold D. McMahon for "the number & the quality of the law students" and predicted that "doubtless we shall reach the hundred mark this year." He confided, however, that it was almost impossible to field varsity football and baseball teams—or a band—without some sort of financial assistance to the players. Burrowes observed that "students of Medicine & Law turn out in the beginning of the season for football & baseball but nearly all disappear before the middle, leaving us in the lurch [with Academy students]. It is not a pleasant state of affairs, but every University offers some inducement & students expect it. If we wish to make any showing at all in football or baseball we shall have to follow suit. But we shall confine it in as narrow limits as possible."[18]

When students gathered in the college building on Twelfth Street on February 3,

1912, "for the reading of the marks," they learned that Burrowes had been appointed to head St. Louis University. Their regret at his leaving was tempered by the knowledge of what he had accomplished for the university, especially the "extensive improvements...in the physical and chemical laboratories" and his unflagging support of "every College activity" ranging from musical and literary events to sports teams and the introduction of senior and junior proms. The first senior prom had been held February 27, 1911, in a North Side ballroom and had been widely hailed as a magnificent social success that gave promise of Loyola's growth.[19]

Cudahy's Legacy

Despite the rain that fell on April 28, 1912, a crowd of more than 500 men and women gathered to watch as Archbishop Quigley blessed the second building on Loyola's new campus. Burrowes returned from St. Louis for the ceremony and delivered a powerful speech in which he emphasized that the new $200,000 Cudahy Science Hall was not only a magnificent gift to the cause of Catholic education but "also a gift to the City of Chicago, because it helps to make Chicago a centre of University education as well as a centre of industry . . . as remarkable in the intellectual world as she is in the business world." He praised the late Chicago meatpacker for building a monument "on the shore of Lake Michigan . . . to 'Religion and Science' and asserted that it "will keep his name sacred long after other monuments shall crumble to dust." He also assured his audience that Cudahy Hall would be "another safeguard to the moral life of Chicago," one that would challenge the growing influence of socialists on college campuses whose "doctrines are destructive of the rights of the individual, of the family, of religion, and of the state."

Applauding the idea of expanding higher education to the people as far as possible, Loyola's former president endorsed the concept that "students should not be compelled to travel far from home, and at great expense to enjoy its benefits." The creation of new universities such as Loyola reflected American faith in higher education, he claimed, reminding his audience that despite the increase in the number of universities over the preceding thirty years, neither Harvard nor Yale nor Cornell nor Princeton "suffered by this western competition."

Burrowes called attention to the role universities could play in improving urban life, and he characterized medicine as a growing field in which to aid the city, state and federal government, noting that more chemists were needed in light of the new legislation regarding pure food and

drugs. To the charge that there were too many lawyers in America, he responded that the study of law would continue to attract students "because of the advantage its study gives them over others in business and in the politics of the country." Further, he used the speech at Loyola to challenge the idea held by the late Chicago industrialist Richard Teller Crane that "academic learning beyond the essentials of the grammar grades in public schools is a waste of time and waste of money for the boy who is to enter commercial life."

As the son of a widowed Irish immigrant, Burrowes knew all too well that the opportunities for skilled and unskilled workers were multiplied a hundred-fold as a result of the knowledge of educated men. Although he did not minimize the difficulties involved in sustaining a Catholic university, he remained adamant that "the call for educated men is growing louder day by day, and the field of each science is broadening out into ever increasing vistas of usefulness."[20]

View of Dumbach and Cudahy halls, 1913

Loyola on the Lake

By the bank of the roaring waters,
    On Lake Michigan's fair shore,
Is an edifice most noble,
    That will live forevermore.
There she stands in all her glory,
    When in the east the day does break;
Proud, magnificent, imposing,
    Is Loyola on the Lake.

Moonlight waters 'round her glisten,
    As her shadows dance and play,
There by solitude encompassed,
    Guardian-like till break of day.
Then her children from their slumbers,
    To a day of toil awake,
And hasten to her waiting shelter,
    Their Loyola on the Lake.

Student poem, 1913, extolling beauty of Loyola's Lake Shore Campus

Throughout the nineteenth century and well into the twentieth, Jesuit college presidents in the United States generally served in one place for only a few years before being assigned to another position or institution. While this tradition ensured that schools would not become identified with a single individual, it also made the carrying out of ambitious building plans quite difficult, as John L. Mathery, S.J., soon discovered when he succeeded Burrowes in 1912. An immigrant from France who had entered the seminary in Florissant, Missouri, when he was eighteen years old, Mathery understood that the construction of a dormitory was "a necessity if we wish to get students for the Engineering Department . . . from different parts of the U.S." and his experience as treasurer at Jesuit colleges in St. Louis, Omaha, and Kansas City confirmed his belief that parents expected their sons "to be under our supervision."

Mathery proceeded with the plans for a dormitory, and in March 1912, he informed his provincial, Father Meyer, that the architectural firm of Hyland & Green had drawn up plans for a $30,000 building that would properly harmonize with the color scheme and general design of Dumbach and Cudahy halls. He said he remained confident that "within 3 years time we will have sixty occupants," enabling the Jesuits to "meet the interest and & pay off part of the loan." Frederic Siedenburg, S.J., also urged Meyer to seek speedy approval for the dorm for the engineering school, arguing that "we lost quite a number of prospective Catholic students because we could not satisfy this demand." Comparing Loyola with Armour Institute on the South Side and the "schools for Jewish students conducted partly on philanthropic lines," Siedenburg pointed out that in addition to being "a truly 'Social Work,'"

Father Siedenburg's 1912 sketch of the proposed dorm also showed the original St. Ignatius church (top), Cudahy Science Hall and Loyola Academy (center), and the future site of Mundelein College (in pink at left).

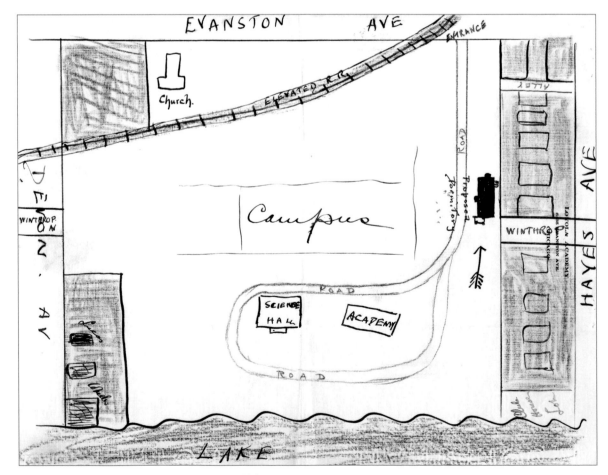

the School of Engineering would help
the university financially and be the only
school on the North Side. He also added,
pragmatically, that the new dormitory
"would be 120 feet long & thus substan-
tially help to shut out the background
views of the Hayes Av. houses."[21]

After filling out the proper Latin paper-
work requiring permission from Rome,
Paul M. Breen, S.J., vice president of the
College of Arts and Sciences, registered a
lone voice of protest against the dormitory.
In a letter to Meyer, he questioned "how we
can possibly carry any more debt than we
have at the present time $210,000.00."
Breen characterized his Jesuit colleagues'
enthusiasm for the engineering department
as praiseworthy but reminded his provincial that it would not pay for a building.
Contrary to Breen's opinion, members of
the alumni association were so convinced
that a dormitory "would help develop the
spirit of mutual assistance among the students," especially with regard to athletics,
that they launched a fund-raising campaign in October 1912.[22]

The unexpected death of Dean Newton in August 1912 came as a great shock
to faculty and students, but Professor A.
A. Neff continued to head the engineering program, serving until June 1914
when William H. Cahill was appointed.

Cahill was born in Kinsale, County Cork,
Ireland; had graduated from the University of Pennsylvania; and worked as an
engineer in Persia, Africa, and Saskatch-
ewan before settling in Chicago. In 1910,
he became the first principal of the Trades
and Vocational Studies program at the
Chicago Hebrew Institute on Taylor Street,
formerly the Convent Academy of the
Sacred Heart. Evidence of Cahill's desire
to make Loyola known the world over as
an engineering college was his consul-
tation with such notable programs as
those at Harvard, Yale, Boston School of
Technology, and the Armour Institute.
In keeping with the tradition of the day,
the university's engineering program
was housed in one wing of the new heating plant.[23]

As Siedenburg, professor and head-
master of Loyola Academy had hoped,
academy graduates enrolled in the engineering school, and their love of sports, especially football and baseball, contributed
to the collegiate atmosphere of the Lake
Shore Campus. Beginning in September
1912, the varsity football team officially
moved to the North Side campus, where
it enjoyed "a large grassy field, with every
facility for scrimmage and for practice
in punting." Westbrook Pegler, who later
became a nationally known sports writer,

James Westbrook Pegler (1894–1969), sports writer,
wearing his Loyola Academy jersey, 1911

Loyola's schools of sociology and law occupied quarters in the Ashland Block, Burnham & Root's 1892 skyscraper at Randolph and Clark streets, shown in this postcard.

Ad in Yiddish for Loyola's School of Sociology

had attended Loyola Academy in 1912 and remembered long walks along the lakefront with Siedenburg, whose commentaries were "more beneficial than an inch of progress in algebra or Greek." Pegler characterized football at Loyola as "pure sport" and recalled that the players "generally bought their own equipment, watching the bargain sales in the sporting goods departments for special opportunities in helmets, pants, pads, and shoes."[24]

Although Siedenburg's hopes for the dormitory designed by Hyland & Green never materialized, his plans for the School of Sociology had long-term positive consequences, both for enrollment and for the university's identity as a progressive Catholic institution. The Loyola School of Sociology was formally organized in

1914 as a department of the university, becoming the first program of its kind in a Catholic institution in the United States. The department was located on the sixth floor of the Ashland Block, the building that housed the law department.

The Catholic Women's League of Chicago wasted no time in giving the School of Sociology its stamp of approval. On March 21, 1914, the group announced plans to endow a free scholarship to the school and encouraged all its members to attend the three ten-week sessions of classes covering "economics and ethics, the history of social reform, social and industrial reorganization, race problems, the church and social service, health and housing, physical and psychic factors in dependency and delinquency, child welfare and the problems of local and national government." Among the most prominent supporters of the new school were Mary Wilson, mother of future Loyola president Samuel Knox Wilson, S.J., and her sister, Sallie Grieves Gaynor.[25]

Loyola Opens Its Doors to Women

The long-standing ban against coeducation in Jesuit universities did not apply to Loyola's medical or law schools, but women were not permitted to enroll as full-time students in the College of Arts and Sciences. However, they could—and did—appear in astonishing numbers as students in the two-year program of the School of Sociology, which led to the bachelor of philosophy degree. Enrollment increased from 400 to 1,689 men and women between 1917 and 1920. These figures did not include the hundreds of teachers who attended the summer sessions at St. Xavier College, St. Mary's High School, the Academy of Our Lady, and Mallinckrodt College

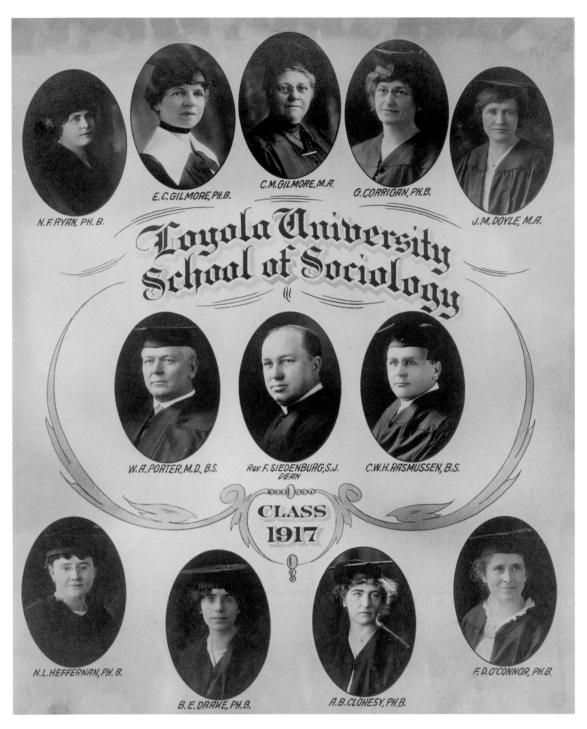

N. F. RYAN, PH. B.

E. C. GILMORE, PH.B.

C. M. GILMORE, M.A.

O. CORRIGAN, PH.B.

J. M. DOYLE, M.A.

Loyola University School of Sociology

W. A. PORTER, M.D., B.S.

Rev. F. SIEDENBURG, S.J. DEAN

C. W. H. RASMUSSEN, B.S.

CLASS 1917

N. L. HEFFERNAN, PH. B.

B. E. DRAKE, PH.B.

A. B. CLOHESY, PH.B.

F. D. O'CONNOR, PH.B.

in suburban Wilmette. For most women religious, the pursuit of a college degree came after a full day of working in a classroom and often required years of amassing credit, one course at a time.[26]

Ads for the School of Sociology "in the heart of a great city" did not specifically mention coeducation but rather stressed the "demand for social workers in the public and private relief work" and the special training required of "modern charity workers."

The ads appeared in not only English newspapers but also the ethnic press. In fact, many of the Loyola students were teachers and principals in the Chicago public schools who knew from personal experience the challenges facing the families of their immigrant and black students. Issues of housing, segregation, child labor, and citizenship took on new meaning as the city continued to increase, growing from 2,185,283 in 1910 to 2,701,705 by 1920.

continued on page 110 ▶

Loyola alumnae presidents Celia M. Gilmore and Agnes Clohesy Mangan eventually became lawyers.

An Early Voice for Social Reform

Once Frederic Siedenburg, S.J., was exposed to the ideas of social progress

championed by several European mentors, there was no turning back.

Summer Course of Lectures

ON

Vital Social Questions of the Day

BY

Rev. Frederic Siedenburg, S.J.
Director of the School of Sociology
Loyola University, Chicago

TO BE GIVEN IN LOS ANGELES

Columbus Auditorium, 612 S. Flower St.

August 3ᴿᴰ to 15ᵀᴴ, 1914

Driven by a deep belief that the Catholic Church had a significant role to play in social reform, Siedenburg not only established the very successful School of Sociology at Loyola University but also became one of Chicago's important public figures.

Siedenburg was born in Cincinnati, Ohio, in 1872 to a Lutheran father and a Catholic mother who had immigrated from Germany. After public school, he graduated in 1893 from St. Xavier College, the Jesuit school now known as Xavier University. He entered the Jesuit novitiate and pursued advanced studies in science and philosophy at St. Louis University.[27]

From 1900 to 1903, he taught physics and mathematics at the original St. Ignatius College, and although urged by his Jesuit superiors to continue his work in chemistry, "Siedie" decided instead to study sociology and economics in Europe. He first attended the University of Berlin and then the universities of Innsbruck and Vienna. During this time, he was deeply influenced by Father Victor Catherin, a moral philosopher and authority on socialism, and by Pope Leo XIII's encyclical "On the Condition of Labor."

Siedenburg returned to Chicago, convinced not only that the Catholic Church must be a leader in social reform but also that Loyola ought to embrace sociology as a discipline. In an address, "The Social Question in Germany," on October 23, 1911, he recounted for Loyola alums his recent audience with Pope Pius X at the Vatican. It didn't take long after this presentation for Siedenburg to become a household name in Chicago.[28]

In addition to his work as prefect of studies at Loyola Academy, Siedenburg in 1912 organized the University Lecture Bureau, which drew on the expertise of Chicago reformers. Among them were Mary Bartelme, assistant judge of the Cook County Juvenile Court; Leonora Z. Meder of the National Conference of Catholic Charities; and Loyola law school professors Municipal Court Judge Michael F. Girten, Michael V. Kannally, and Arnold D. McMahon. Over the next two years, the wide-ranging program of lectures reached a large audience and put the university on the map in terms of social reform. National attention quickly followed. *America* magazine hailed Loyola's Lecture Bureau as "the beginning of a great movement [that ought to] spread over the entire country" and praised its "constructive work . . . covering practically the entire industrial, economic and social field."[29]

Siedenburg continued as one of Chicago's most significant civic leaders over the next two decades, and news accounts consistently stressed his close association with Loyola. He routinely crossed denominational, ethnic, and racial boundaries in his dealings, and he never wavered from his belief that religion could be a progressive force in urban life.

In 1915, the *Chicago Tribune* commented on Siedenburg's role with the American Peace Federation, his appearance with Rabbi Emil G. Hirsch at Sinai Temple, and his visit to Tuskegee Institute as the guest of Jewish philanthropist Julius Rosenwald, along with Jane Addams of Hull-House and the Reverend Jenkin Lloyd Jones, a Unitarian minister, of the Abraham Lincoln Center. In addition to serving on committees such as the National Conference of Catholic Charities and the Illinois State Conference of Charities and Corrections, he served as a director of the Chicago Public Library and helped to organize the Illinois Catholic Historical Society and to establish its journal, now known as *Mid-America*. He also found time to publish ground-breaking articles in the *American Journal of Sociology*, including "The Recreational Value of Religion" (1922), "The Religious Value of Social Work" (1922), and "War and the Catholic Church" (1925).[30]

Siedenburg (center) addresses grievances during the 1924 women garment workers' strike. At right is Ellen Gates Starr, cofounder of Chicago's Hull-House.

Siedenburg's activities took on a variety of forms: from actively mediating the 1924 garment workers' strike to appearing regularly with Progressive reformers and ministers of different faiths. At a time when few Catholic priests ventured outside their own parishes and schools, the dean of Loyola's School of Sociology relished the opportunity to deliver talks such as "Why I Am a Catholic." In October 1928, for example, he was featured in a program at Chicago's Sinai Temple along with defense attorney Clarence Darrow, an avowed agnostic; Rabbi Louis Mann; and Episcopalian bishop Francis J. McConnell.[31]

In August 1932, news spread quickly throughout the city that Father Siedenburg had been transferred to the University of Detroit, where he would serve as executive dean. The outpouring of affection for the founder of Loyola's School of Sociology was undeniable: hundreds of Chicagoans attended a dinner in his honor at the Blackstone Hotel and collected enough money to purchase a Buick Victoria. Like most Chicago Jesuits, Siedenburg had traveled the city by streetcar and elevated road, and he learned to drive only after he moved to Detroit. The bulletin of the Council of Social Work lamented, "What shall we do without Father Siedenburg? He seems as much a part of Chicago as the Public Library." Graham Taylor of Chicago Commons Settlement at Grand Avenue and Morgan Street on the city's Northwest Side, spoke for many when he characterized Siedenburg's transfer as an "irreparable" loss to Chicago and the Midwest. He assured Siedenburg that his twenty-one years "of outstanding public service . . . will long continue to earn returns to us all." He further observed, "I am free, as you are not, to question the loss and the gain of it to the cause of the Common Welfare."[32]

How much Siedenburg's friendship with Progressive Protestant reformers and Jews contributed to his transfer has been the subject of much speculation over the years. In a rare public statement given to the *Chicago Daily News*, Siedenburg commented, "I have tried to interpret the church to the community . . . [and] have tried just as sincerely to interpret the outside world to the

church. I believe I am a better priest when a better citizen and the better citizen the better priest I am." Robert Hartnett, S.J., recalled that when he was a student at Heythrop College near Oxford, England, in 1938, Siedenburg stopped to visit him enroute to the Soviet Union. They remained friends until Siedenburg's death in 1939, and Hartnett maintained that his mentor was "ousted from Chicago in 1932 rather unceremoniously" because of his involvement with the National Conference of Christians and Jews, established when Al Smith ran for president.[33]

Religious Debate Tonight at Emil G. Hirsch Center

Clarence S. Darrow, Chicago lawyer and agnostic. will face representatives of three religions tonight at the Emil G. Hirsch center at Sinai temple, in a discussion of the "Why" of religion. The other speakers will be the Rev. Frederick Siedenberg, dean of Loyola university, on "Why I Am a Catholic"; Bishop Francis J. McConnell of New York, on "Why I Am a Protestant," and Dr. Louis L. Mann rabbi of Sinai temple, on "Why I Am a Jew." Bishop McConnell three years ago debated with Darrow from the same platform.

An ecumenical pioneer, Siedenburg presented an address, "Why I Am a Catholic," at Sinai Temple on October 22, 1928.

FORTY-SEVENTH ANNUAL BANQUET
TENDERED
SENIOR CLASS 1914
BENNETT MEDICAL COLLEGE
MEDICAL DEPARTMENT OF LOYOLA UNIVERSITY
Hotel Sherman   May 7, 1914

Loyola's medical school banquet in 1914 at the Hotel Sherman was regarded as one of the great social events of the year.

▶ continued from page 107

The first three female graduates of the School of Sociology in 1915, Celia Gilmore, Kate Meade, and Ella R. Connell, led the drive to organize the university's alumnae association. Although the sociology graduates were far outnumbered by the medical school and law school graduates, their influence was felt profoundly in the larger city, especially in the public schools and the juvenile court. Several sociology graduates, among them Agnes Clohesy and Celia Gilmore, continued their professional education at Loyola's law school and joined the small but growing ranks of female attorneys in Chicago.[34]

The tremendous growth of Loyola was immediately apparent to John B. Furay, S.J., who succeeded Mathery as president in 1915. Related to the millionaire Catholic philanthropist John A. Creighton, who was instrumental in founding Creighton University, Furay had been one of the first students to enroll in the new Jesuit college in Omaha. He entered the

Jesuit seminary at Florissant, Missouri, in 1891 after receiving his BA degree from St. Mary's College in Kansas. Furay had taught at St. Ignatius College from 1898 to 1902 before going on to other positions. At that time, St. Ignatius had an enrollment of about 450 students, but when he returned to Chicago, Furay found a fully functioning university with 150 professors and 1,604 students.

In his first public address as president of Loyola on January 16, 1916, he expressed amazement at the progress and expansion that had taken place in terms of both enrollment and campus construction. The College of Arts and Sciences accounted for half the university's students (892), followed by the medical school (292); sociology (217); law (104); pharmacy (61); and engineering (38). Furay reminded alums that Loyola was a young institution full of hope and promise and "planning greater things for the future," and he assured them that the buildings to be erected on the North Shore campus would be "a credit to the cause we represent and to the Catholic citizens of Chicago."[35]

Furay immediately had to deal with the problem involved in the expansion of the medical school, a solution that needed to be reached if Loyola was ever to achieve a Class A rating. In 1914, the school had experienced what regent Spalding called the final clash with the AMA when an investigator from that group, using the name W. R. Cowgill, sought admission to Bennett Medical "with the intention of deceiving and misrepresenting" his educational qualifications. Dean Maximilian J. Herzog and fourteen members of the faculty signed a statement refuting charges published in the *Journal of the American Medical Association* and the *Chicago Tribune* that Loyola admitted students to Bennett Medical without proper credentials. Moreover, they reiterated that the officials and faculty of Loyola "have done everything in their power to live up to the requirements of the Educational Council of the American Medical Association" and that every dollar received "has been used for legitimate educational purposes." As Spalding recalled, through the efforts of the legal counsel of Levy, Mayer and Levy, the AMA finally agreed "to work in harmony with us."[36]

A great step forward occurred on April 13, 1915, when Dr. John Dill Robertson, president of Bennett Medical College, formally transferred the school to Loyola University. Spalding, who had been regent for six years, regarded Loyola's future as full of promise, especially since its medical school "not only held its own but has forged to the front rank" at a time when "so many other colleges failed to meet the high standards in medical education."[37]

The medical school building at 706 South Wolcott Avenue, 1917

In April 1916, Loyola took the lead nationally by applying to Washington for instruction in medical field work in anticipation of the United States' entry into World War I. With a graduating class of 150 students, the largest in its history, Loyola was also one of the largest of any medical schools in the country involved in preparing future doctors for the medical corps of the army and navy. The commencement ceremonies on May 29, 1916, began with a valedictory address by Alexander W. Burke and included the awarding of degrees to graduates from the medical school and the pharmacy school as well as to nurses from St. Bernard's and Jefferson Park hospitals.

Shortly after the classes in medical training began in February 1917, Spalding entered into negotiations with the Chicago College of Medicine and Surgery to acquire its buildings and equipment at 706 South Lincoln Street [Wolcott Avenue], just across the street from Cook County Hospital. Since 1902, it had been the medical department of Valparaiso (Indiana) University and was rated by the AMA as a Class B institution. The letters sent by Spalding and Furay to their provincial, Burrowes, did not go unnoticed.

James W. Burke, a graduate of St. Ignatius College, received his medical degree from Loyola in 1918.

Louis D. Moorhead, dean of the medical school 1920–40

As a former president of Loyola, Burrowes understood that the location of the College of Medicine and Surgery "in the midst of the greatest hospital and medical district in the United States" made it especially valuable to Loyola. By combining the two medical schools, Loyola would acquire a new complex composed of four large, well-lighted, steam-heated buildings of brick and stone that included "six large lecture and laboratory rooms . . . [for instruction] in pathology, histology, physics, and operative surgery." Not only would the combined faculties number about 100, but Loyola's medical school could also claim "an active alumni membership of over three thousand physicians."[38]

While the $85,000 purchase price for the Chicago College of Medicine and Surgery, was reasonable, Spalding still needed $50,000. Where would he find the money? Former St. Ignatius College student Eugene V. McVoy, president of the McVoy Sheet and Tinplate Company, who lived at 6363 North Sheridan Road, did not hesitate to offer $33,000 with the remainder pledged by Dr. Lawrence Ryan, first dean of the combined medical schools, and Dr. Alfred de Roulet, professor of gynecology. In his memoir about the origins of Loyola's medical school, Spalding recalled McVoy's "ready response and financial aid" that made possible the merger of Bennett Medical with the Chicago College of Medicine and Surgery and he delighted in the knowledge that as regent he had "done something that the AMA had not been able to do: I had closed out four medical colleges."[39]

The reorganization of the medical school under Regent Patrick J. Mahan, S.J., and Dean Louis D. Moorhead that began "when the country was in the throes of war" soon produced results. Moorhead, a 1913 graduate of St. Ignatius College

who had trained at Rush Medical College where he received the J. W. Freer prize for research in 1917, understood the necessity of a Class A rating. Not only did the school's survival depend on it, but without such accreditation from the AMA, Loyola graduates would be less likely to obtain internships at Cook County Hospital. In 1919, according to statistics gathered from state medical boards, Loyola's graduates outnumbered those of Jesuit rivals Fordham and St. Louis universities, and their pass rate—69 of 72 students—placed them among the largest medical school classes in the country.

Finally, in 1920, all major hurdles had been overcome. Although no records exist documenting the reaction of the Jesuits to news of the school's new status as a Class A institution, the annual report issued by the AMA left no doubt: Loyola had taken its proper place alongside Northwestern; Rush, which earlier had affiliated with the University of Chicago; and the University of Illinois College of Medicine. Despite the dire predications of Abraham Flexner ten years earlier, Loyola had not closed. On the contrary, it had successfully competed and improved its ranking, outperforming Chicago's Hahnemann Medical College and Hospital (Class B) and the Chicago Medical School (Class C).[40]

There was the promise of an even brighter future for Loyola in 1920 when the medical school moved its dispensary to Mercy Hospital at 2526 South Prairie Avenue. The arrangement provided Loyola's medical establishment with senior medics who had extensive clinical experience, and it marked the beginning of a collaboration with the Sisters of Mercy that soon expanded. Enthusiastically, the Jesuit *Province News-Letter* reported that "Loyola has entirely supplanted Northwestern

A Female Medical Pioneer

Dr. Bertha M. Van Hoosen (1863–1952)

If the American Medical Association had gotten its way, Dr. Bertha Van Hoosen would never have advanced as she did in her career.

Instead, as she recalled in her autobiography, *Petticoat Surgeon*, because of the loyalty shown her by three prominent administrators at Loyola—President Furay, Dean Moorhead, and Regent Patrick J. Mahan, S.J.,—she was given the prestigious position of department head at the medical school at the time it received its Grade A standing.

Van Hoosen recounted how, as she was picking up forms in the school office on Harrison Street one day prior to her appointment, she spotted a letter from the AMA. She was astonished to read its recommendation that Loyola "put a man at the head of the Department of Obstetrics." The following day, in a chance encounter with Moorhead during rounds at Mercy Hospital, she learned that she had been appointed head of obstetrics at the medical school.

When a week passed without any official confirmation, however, she became convinced that the Jesuits had changed their minds. Then came a telephone message: she was asked to meet with Furay at 7:00 p.m. in the old St. Ignatius College. Van Hoosen recalled being ushered into "an enormous high-ceilinged, unfurnished room hung with life-sized paintings of Popes and Archbishops." Seated in the only chair, she waited to hear her fate. Suddenly Furay appeared with a smile on his face. He apologized and asked her forgiveness, adding, "It was an old man's weakness. I wanted to tell you face to face that you have been appointed Head of Obstetrics of the Loyola University School of Medicine. We appreciate the splendid work you have done in helping us get an A grade. I know there is prejudice against women, and we are prejudiced too—but it is for you, and not against you."[41]

Before joining the faculty at Loyola's medical school, Van Hoosen had attracted national attention for her 1914 study of scopolamine-morphine anaesthesia. Women about to give birth were injected with the anesthetic and experienced "Twilight Sleep," delivering their babies without pain. At a meeting of the Chicago Medical Society, she informed the 200 male doctors present that labor was dramatically shortened, and quipped, "We call it the eight hour labor law."[42]

University [in teaching at Mercy Hospital]" and that Mercy "has also made application to have its training school for nurses recognized as the training school for Loyola University."[43]

Although sixty-five graduates in the class of 1921 achieved a 100 percent pass rate on state board examinations, the medical department remained in financial straits, mounting an annual deficit of $20,000. Archbishop George Mundelein, who had succeeded Quigley in 1916, shared the Jesuits' concern that the closing of the medical school would be "a catastrophe for Catholic life in and about Chicago." Consequently, he devised a solution that would link Loyola more closely to the city. Beginning on September 18, 1921, and continuing for years, parishioners throughout the Chicago diocese contributed much-needed funds to the medical school as part of the annual collection originally earmarked for Catholic University in Washington, DC. In commenting on the generous response to the appeal, *The Woodstock Letters* predicted

Loyola doctors provided obstetrical care for unwed mothers at Misericordia Maternity Hospital, opened in 1921.

John A. Zvetina (1898–1984) received the first of several degrees from Loyola in 1921. His 1942 pageant at Soldier Field united thousands of Chicagoans of foreign birth in the effort to win World War II.

"Palm" card for democratic precinct committeeman John Zvetina, 1910

that it would enable Loyola to maintain "its present high standard without causing a drain on the general funds of the University." Mundelein's approach proved to be very successful, and over the next six years, the Archdiocese of Chicago was able to advance $120,971 to the medical school.[44]

Throughout the 1920s, the school continued its commitment to urban life by directing its attention to issues of maternal and infant mortality. Not only did Loyola professors such as Dr. Bertha Van Hoosen, Dean Moorhead, Dr. Charles J. Mix, and Dr. Walter McGuire participate in "Mothercraft" lectures about prenatal development, pregnancy and nursing, and the omnipresent dangers of tuberculosis and contagion, but they also played a pivotal role in the new Misericordia Maternity Hospital and Infants' home at 2916 West 47th Street. Operating as the obstetrics department of the medical school, Misericordia provided free care for unwed mothers who were cared for by the Sisters of Mercy. At the dedication of the maternity hospital on November 2, 1921, John W. Melody, S.J., an 1885 graduate of St. Ignatius College, praised the institution as "a needed haven for the protection of the poor and unfortunate women of the Archdiocese." Joining Melody for the occasion were Archbishop Mundelein, President Furay, and Regent Mahan.[45]

Loyola in Wartime

The response of Loyola to America's involvement in World War I was profound. Of the 1,100 students and alumni who served in the war, about 230 undergraduates, mostly freshmen, joined the Students' Army Training Corps (SATC) and lived in barracks that had been set up at several locations: the college auditorium, Sodality

Hall next to Holy Family Church, and St. Joseph School at 13th and Loomis streets. Among the six young men recommended by the faculty for officers' training at Fort Sheridan was future Loyola professor John A. Zvetina. His father had emigrated from Dubrovnik, Yugoslavia, in 1891 and settled in Chicago, where he became a lawyer, concentrating on insurance and real estate matters, as well as a dedicated member of the Democratic Party, helping others to become citizens. Young John Zvetina experienced first-hand the cosmopolitan neighborhood that surrounded St. Ignatius College, where he had attended classes beginning in 1913. His employment as a "Sabbath boy," a job that entailed lighting fires for Orthodox Jewish families on Friday evenings, left him with a deep respect for the Torah and religious tradition. He also shared his father's faith in the self-determination of small nations as outlined in President Woodrow Wilson's Fourteen Points.[46]

In an impressive ceremony on October 1, 1918, (reported on the front page of the first edition of the *Loyola News*), Furay welcomed the college students enrolled in the SATC program and delivered an impassioned speech to the recruits. He emphasized the generosity of the United States government in "giv[ing] you a home, care and education" and reminded them that "Germany is not broken; she is still arrogant in her claims and still brutal in her conduct." Loyola's president encouraged the college students to take advantage of the special officers' training because the world needed them "to strike the decisive blow for human freedom."[47]

Over the next few months, the recruits attended classes and practiced military maneuvers and, thanks to the intervention of medical officer Dr. Edward J. Kiefer, "not a single case of the [Spanish influenza] developed here." When news of the armistice finally reached Twelfth Street on November 11, the khaki-clad students joined in a snake dance "about the campus . . . through store and office buildings and round about street cars." The entire SATC company assembled at the corner of Taylor Street and Blue Island Avenue to march to the Loop, singing popular songs of the day as well as "Loyola U" and the SATC song. According to one Jesuit chronicler, "There was a continuous chorus of sirens, whistles, and every conceivable sort of noise making instrument; the enthusiasm was simply delirious." Following his graduation with some thirty other SATC recruits in 1921, Zvetina's association with Loyola only deepened. After receiving a law degree in 1925 and a master's degree in 1933, he continued to teach constitutional law for forty-three years, during which time he also served as chair of Loyola's business law department and became a widely respected authority on the history and culture of Croatians, Serbs, and Slovenes.[48]

When 543 current and former students of St. Ignatius College gathered at the Hotel Sherman on January 26, 1921, to observe the school's fiftieth anniversary, the focus of the event was on the future, not the past. Members of the alumni association resolved to reinvigorate the organization so that it could "lend wholehearted support to every University activity" over the next five decades. They didn't have long to wait. A new era in Loyola history was about to begin as the Jesuits made plans to move the College of Arts and Sciences to Rogers Park in the fall of 1922. Already a new tradition had begun: commencement exercises were held for the first time on the new

Cassie and Albert Wheeler mansion, 1910, now the Ann Ida Gannon, B.V.M., Center for Women and Leadership of Loyola University Chicago

campus on June 12, 1920, and the imposing academic parade had drawn a crowd of 2,000 from all parts of the city.

The Changing Urban Landscape

In the fourteen years since the Jesuits had purchased property from the Chicago, Milwaukee, & St. Paul Railroad, the neighborhood had experienced dramatic development. Although the Wheeler mansion, built in 1909 at the corner of Devon Avenue and Sheridan Road, remained the local showplace, hundreds of modern steam-heated apartment buildings had been constructed nearby, swelling the population of Rogers Park to 26,857 by 1920. The original location of the Edgewater Golf Club at the northwest corner of Devon and Sheridan was later subdivided for homes. These apartment buildings were especially popular because they assured rental income for resident owners. Also critical to local development

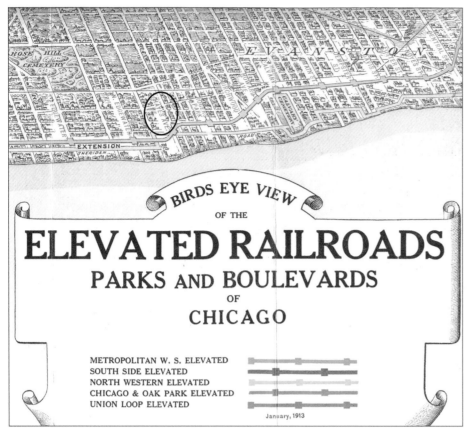

In 1913, Hayes Avenue (highlighted) was renamed Loyola Avenue, reflecting the important role the university had played in the development of Rogers Park.

St. Ignatius Church, Loyola and Glenwood avenues dedicated in 1917, replaced the original frame church on Sheridan Road north of Devon Avenue.

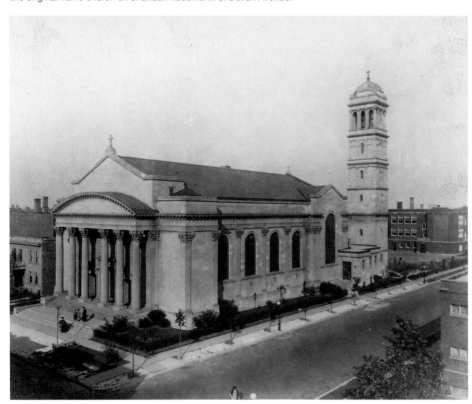

was the extension of the Northwestern elevated road from Wilson Avenue, which provided commuter service from downtown Chicago. Although it took years and cost several lives to build the elevated railroad tracks, by 1920, modern "L" stations were on the drawing board for the stops between Loyola Avenue and Argyle Street.[49]

Catholic families from the Jesuit parish of Holy Family helped to swell the crowds that soon filled to overflowing the original frame church of St. Ignatius on Sheridan Road. To meet the needs of the growing parish, Architect Henry J. Schlacks designed an imposing Renaissance structure at Loyola and Glenwood, modeled after the Jesuit Church of the Gesù in Rome. Amid great fanfare, the new St. Ignatius Church was dedicated on September 16, 1917, by Archbishop Mundelein. This monumental basilica church with its distinctive campanile—a special type of bell tower that could be seen for blocks—constituted a focal point in the Rogers Park neighborhood, and it increasingly played a role in the life of Loyola's North Shore Campus.[50]

By the summer of 1921, motorists on Sheridan Road who had once "turned north at the little white and green frame church" discovered that the quaint landmark had been demolished to make way for business buildings. In announcing the sale of the 1.4-acre triangular plot along Sheridan Road to developer Ralph D. Huszgah for $122,000, the *Province News-Letter* reminded Jesuit professors and priests that the original 20 acres in 1906 "cost $165,000" and that the 300 feet on Devon Avenue purchased later by Father Burrowes had "more than doubled in value."[51]

Loyola was not the only Catholic institution in Chicago making plans for

Aerial view of St. Mary of the Lake Seminary, c. 1934

expansion. Since his arrival in Chicago in 1916, Archbishop Mundelein had hoped to create a great "Catholic university of the West," and in 1920 he purchased property forty miles north of the city in a town known as Area, Illinois. Although only the seminary department became a reality, Mundelein's appointment of Furay as head of the educational department of St. Mary of the Lake in August 1921 marked a great event for the Catholic Church of Chicago. No longer would young men have to leave the diocese to pursue studies leading to ordination. Now all candidates for the priesthood from the Archdiocese of Chicago would share the same academic instruction provided by Jesuit professors.[52]

For more than fifty years, the inauguration of a Jesuit college president had been a relatively private affair, involving a reading of the letter of appointment before or after a community meal. All that changed on November 2, 1921, when William Agnew, S.J., was honored at a special banquet at the Hamilton Club at 18 South Dearborn Street. Offering congratulations to the new president of Loyola were

Illinois State Superintendent of Schools Franklin G. Blair and the presidents of the University of Chicago, Northwestern, the University of Illinois, DePaul, and Notre Dame. The event was regarded as "one of the best [celebrations] of its kind ever held." A Jesuit chronicler noted with satisfaction the spirit of civic cooperation that existed and "the necessity of moral training was specifically mentioned."[53]

The fifteenth president of Loyola University had no illusions about the necessity of relocating the College of Arts and Sciences to Rogers Park. During his years as a professor at St. Ignatius College, the neighborhood surrounding Twelfth Street (renamed Roosevelt Road in 1919) had become a major port-of-entry for Italians, Jews, and Greeks. Agnew had enthusiastically supported the Italian mission of Holy Guardian Angel, and his small pamphlet for catechism instructors had profoundly influenced Mary Agnes Amberg to organize Madonna Center social settlement. He knew, however, that enrollment in the collegiate department on Twelfth Street was not keeping pace with that in the medical and law schools or the School of

RECEPTION AND DINNER

tendered to

REV. WILLIAM H. AGNEW, S. J.

President of Loyola University

by the

FACULTY *and* FORMER STUDENTS

At the Hamilton Club

Wednesday, November 2, 1921

Chicago

Reception in 1921 welcoming William H. Agnew, S.J., as Loyola's fifteenth president

J.A.GAUER, A.B., J.D.

Joseph A. Gauer, who battled the Ku Klux Klan, received his law degree from Loyola in 1925.

Sociology downtown. In fact, only ten of the forty-five undergraduate degrees awarded by Loyola in 1920 were granted to young men from St. Ignatius College, located at 1076 West Roosevelt Road. Still, there was reason to believe the trend could be reversed, especially after the March 17, 1921, accreditation by the North Central Association of Colleges and Secondary Schools, which the Jesuits regarded as a milestone that "means a great deal to this school." Final approval had come following an inspection by Registrar G. P. Tuttle of the North Central Association and the filing of papers that listed the college's resources and income, including its productive endowment of $114,650 and its total indebtedness of $176,000. But as a handwritten note on the application made clear, an even larger debt was owed the Society of Jesus, whose eleven members of the Arts and Sciences faculty "receive no compensation for their services as teachers."[54]

One of the first things Siedenburg did after his appointment as regent of Loyola's

law school was to add "morning classes" in September 1921 and to open both day and evening sessions to women. The good showing of graduates on the state bar exam—nearly 70 percent successfully passed—in 1920 was directly related to tightened admission requirements. Originally, students with a high school diploma had been admitted to law school, but now the three-year day course required "two years of college as an entrance condition." Another significant change involved extending the night-school program to four years. Loyola acquired additional space in the Ashland Block, thus ensuring that students would have ready access to nearby courts, especially Judge Olson's innovative Night Court. According to the *Loyola Quarterly*, night-school law students "are so interested that they gleefully come down on Saturday nights [and] any evening after class a number of students may be observed in [Night Court], taking down copious notes and addresses of bootleggers and others."

Another sign of Loyola students' engagement with urban life was their active participation, along with law school founder Patrick H. O'Donnell, in the American Unity League (AUL). Organized to defeat the anti-Catholic and anti-Semitic Ku Klux Klan, the AUL launched the newsletter *Tolerance* in September 1922, in which were published "the name, address, and occupation of hundreds of area Klansmen." Joseph A. Gauer, who had honed his skills as an undergraduate debater and editor of the *Loyola News*, developed a reputation for fiery anti-KKK speeches at local Catholic parishes, and his classmates described him as "a stronger and stronger pillar . . . of the American Unity League." According to historian Michael Jacobs, by August 1924,

Father Agnew and World War I French hero Ferdinand Foch in a ceremony at Dumbach Hall, 1921

the Klan's power in Chicago was severely diminished. The group "no longer held parades in the city for fear of reprisal," and the exposure of secret Klan membership "led to runs on 18 banks."[55]

Loyola's status as a Jesuit university with international roots was highlighted on November 6, 1921, when French Field Marshal Ferdinand Foch, a former student at the college of St. Clement in Metz, France, accepted an honorary doctor of laws degree from Agnew. Twelve motorcycle policemen "made possible a swift drive up the North Shore Boulevard" and, along the way, the commander-in-chief of Allied Forces in World War I asked questions about Loyola and "the value of the residence property he passed in his drive." A crowd of 3,000 surrounded the steps of Dumbach Hall to greet "the savior of Alsace and Lorraine," an event the *Chicago Tribune* called the most intimate glimpse of Marshal Foch. His whirlwind Chicago tour concluded with the dedication of a public service health hospital in suburban Maywood. For years, Jesuit officials had hoped that Catholic

millionaire lumber merchant Edward Hines would become a Loyola benefactor, but after his twenty-one-year-old son died in a base hospital in France in 1918, he decided to honor his son's memory with a medical facility. Hines donated $1.6 million toward the construction of a "monument of mercy," built on the site of the former Speedway automobile and motorcycle track that the government renamed the Edward Hines Jr. Hospital. It would take several more decades, but finally in the 1960s, Loyola University acquired property near Maywood from the Veterans' Administration and entered into a cooperative arrangement with Hines Hospital.[56]

Agnew faced an endowment shortage just as his predecessors had faced, and, like his predecessors, he nevertheless forged ahead with bold plans: he hired architect Paul V. Hyland to design a $250,000 administration building/faculty residence as well as a modern gymnasium on the Lake Shore Campus. Although the Jesuits worried that the sharp advance in tuition to $175 for the college department

Horses (one shown at left near the shed) provided much of the labor when construction began in 1922 on the university's administration building on the Lake Shore Campus.

View looking south
on Sheridan Road
from the porch of the
Wheeler mansion,
c. 1916

would result in "a disastrous slump in attendance," their fears were allayed when 170 college students enrolled in September 1922 with an additional 425 at Loyola Academy ($150 per year) and 665 at St. Ignatius ($125 per year). This steady increase was part of a larger, nationwide trend in education, as more and more students continued their education beyond high school. With a 1922–23 enrollment of some 340,000 students in college in the United States, Charles Franklin Thwing, president emeritus of Western Reserve University in Ohio, predicted a rosy future for higher education because, he stated, Americans regarded it as "a worthy investment of time money and labor for most young men and women." According to figures compiled in October 1922, Marquette University led the Midwest Jesuit colleges with an enrollment of 3,367, but Loyola with 2,350 students pulled ahead of its long-time rival, St. Louis University, due mainly to the 1,799 students in the School of Sociology.[57]

The Final Move from Roosevelt Road

Relocating the College of Arts and Sciences from Roosevelt Road to Sheridan Road was a massive undertaking. Faculty members such as James J. Mertz, S.J., took an active role in the move, packing up thousands of books and driving load after load in a truck up North Ashland Avenue. Nearly fifty years after the move, the classics professor could still recall his impression of the "private homes on Sheridan Road . . . beautiful homes" as well as the "high grasses and wild trees" that dotted the Loyola property. He remembered that the faculty building and gymnasium were under construction and there was "none of the modern equipment, just an old horse who would pull up the [cement and brickwork] on a pulley." No breakwater had yet been installed, which meant that the "winds from the northeast were bitter cold."[58]

On September 18, 1922, "the [Jesuit] community at the North Side and the college professors from West Roosevelt Road moved into the new faculty building on the lake . . . [which was about] 85 per cent completed." In keeping with the Midwest Jesuit pay-as-you-go philosophy, $163,000 had been "appropriated for this work and as much of the structure will be completed at the present time as this sum warrants."

In November 1922, twelve Loyola alums who called themselves "the bugs," hosted a dinner at the Hotel LaSalle that raised $32,000 in pledges for the new gymnasium, the outlines of which were "beginning to take definite shape above ground" on the Lake Shore Campus. Spearheading the campaign with a donation of $10,000 was David F. Bremner of the Bremner Bakery, who had attended St. Ignatius College in the 1890s. Several of Loyola's female alums, including Celia Gilmore of the School of Sociology and Dr. Anna F. Novak, also made generous contributions to the gym, as did members of the Loyola Academy alumni.[59]

Nationally acclaimed artist Harry McEwen Pettit's 1922–23 color rendering of the Lake Shore Campus captured the hopes and dreams embodied in Agnew's vision for the Greater Loyola. Regarded as the "bird's-eye view king of America," Pettit had won the medal of honor in 1915 from the Pan-American exposition in San Francisco for his twenty-eight-foot panoramic view of the Gary, Indiana, steelworks. He later served as official artist of the Chicago Century of Progress in 1933–34 and

the New York World's Fair of 1939. His design for Loyola's North Shore Campus featured Dumbach Hall, the Cudahy Science Building, the administration building, the heating plant, and the new gym, along with ten more structures, including a medical building and hospital, a law school, and two more academic buildings for the College of Arts and Sciences. Initial plans called for four dormitories, but, Agnew promised, "more will be erected, if needed."[60]

The modernization of the Lake Shore Campus continued even as "an extensive roadway of macadam" was constructed from the Sheridan Road entrance "sweeping around the front of the faculty building and passing north and west to Winthrop Avenue." As part of the plan to promote

continued on page 124 ▶

Sketch of Loyola's future campus by Harry Pettit, the "bird's-eye king of America," as it appeared on a 1922 postcard

LOYOLA UNIVERSITY, CHICAGO (When completed).

▶ *continued from page 121*

Dr. Truman W. Brophy, (1848–1928), pioneer in dental surgery

Loyola's dental school, 1757 West Harrison Street, c.1925

the Greater Loyola and "advertise the University in a dignified way," a housewarming event was held at the new administration building on December 3, 1922, and more than 500 guests "wandered through the corridors, many of them learning for the first time what a Jesuit house looks like above the parlors." The following Saturday, several hundred women religious took the tour and the house was officially blessed on December 14, 1922.[66]

A few months later, the Jesuits of Loyola took an important step to impress upon Chicagoans and visitors to the city that the university was here to stay: a de luxe metal sign, fifty-by-ten feet, was installed at the southwest corner of the property where it could be readily seen by passengers on the elevated and by automobiles going in either direction. In addition to two new clay tennis courts, "the entire area of the campus facing on Devon Avenue has been topped with rich black dirt, twenty

carloads of which were shipped in from out of town. A steam-roller loaned by the City has levelled off the space, and it is now possible to have three standard-size gridirons." Also significant was industrialist Frank J. Lewis's donation of 500 feet of elaborate iron fence from the grounds of the Armour mansion on South Michigan Avenue to enhance the Devon Avenue frontage finally purchased by the Jesuits in 1909. Lewis was one of Chicago's wealthiest Catholics, and by 1925, he was serving as a member of the university's auxiliary board of trustees. His connections with Loyola deepened after World War II, when he and his second wife, Julia Deal Lewis, became the university's most generous donors.[67]

One of the hallmarks of Agnew's presidency was his active role in civic functions such as the dedication of the new medical complex of the University of Illinois on March 6, 1924. Designed by architect Richard E. Schmidt, the new buildings occupied the former site of the old baseball park at Polk and Wolcott where Charles Comiskey's White Sox had beaten the Chicago Cubs in the 1906 World Series. Agnew's presence on the same platform with Illinois state officials and celebrities of the medical profession signaled the Catholic university's elemental role in the city.

Loyola's Catholic Identity

Loyola increased its presence in the medical and health field once again in 1923 when it entered into an affiliation with the Chicago College of Dental Surgery at 1757 West Harrison Street, the largest institution of its kind in the city since its founding in 1883. Dean emeritus Dr. Truman Brophy was known internationally for his pioneering surgery—having performed some 10,000 cleft palate operations since 1886—and had been honored by the French Republic with the Legion of Honor. With its enrollment of nearly 600 students, the Class A dental college contributed to the university's growing reputation for excellence in medicine and, along with the medical school, constituted an important anchor in the West Side medical district.

That the dental college included the highest percentage of non-Catholic professors and students did not worry President Agnew. On the contrary, in a 1927 document entitled "Is Loyola a Catholic Institution?" he informed Father General Wlodimir Ledochowski, S.J., in Rome that in three short years, the increase of Catholic students in the dental college had been "very marked." Of the 625 dental students registered at that time, 300 were Protestant; 250 were Catholic; and 75 were Jewish; and the dental faculty consisted of 44 Protestant, 6 Catholic, and 2 Jewish professors. Statistics also showed that 94.95 percent of the 4,213 students enrolled in Loyola's other departments and professional schools were Catholic; 3.5 percent were Protestant; and 1.44 percent were Jewish. Agnew pointed out that "no noticeable religious prejudice against Catholic teaching and control is encountered in the university," and he quoted several deans who believed that "non-Catholic students are better disposed toward the Church as a result of their attendance at the university."

While a crucifix or sacred picture could be found "in all departments except those of medicine and dentistry," Agnew assured Ledochowski that Catholic medical and dental students had opportunities for religious services as well as "special occasional lectures by distinguished

Catholic authorities upon questions of ethics and morality." Loyola's president also stated firmly that Chicago's Jesuit university "gives prestige to the church by promoting scholarship, especially Catholic scholarship." Although the place of women at Loyola would remain a contested issue for years to come, their presence in the university was undeniable. In his report to Rome, out of a student body of 4,838, Agnew counted 2,938 women, mostly in the School of Sociology and the Home Study/Correspondence Division that had been established in 1922. Dentistry had an all-male enrollment, as did the College of Arts and Sciences, but three departments were regarded as coeducational: medicine with 20 women, law with 15, and commerce with 33.[68]

Loyola's resolve to extend its urban mission was strengthened in June 1926 with the purchase of the four-story Thompson-Ehlers Leather Company at 20-28 North Franklin Street in Chicago's Loop. Enrollment in the university's schools of law, commerce, sociology, and education had overwhelmed the quarters in the Ashland Block, and the new location promised fifteen spacious classrooms as well as space for offices, libraries, and recreation. Moreover, the small shops on the first floor and in the basement would generate much-needed income. Remodeling of the building was designed by architect C. A. Eckstrom and completed by the Matt Rauen Company at an estimated cost of $120,000. In announcing the relocation of Loyola's professional schools in February 1927, the daily newspapers commented favorably on the new site, known as Hearst Square, where the Kent College of Law was also located.[69]

The university had expanded in several directions, reaching a milestone in

In 1927, Loyola's downtown college moved from the Ashland Block to 28 North Franklin Street.

Loyola Shapes *America*'s Voice

Loyola's winning 1927 debate team, Robert C. Hartnett; James C. O'Connor, Jr.; Francis G. Haley; and Francis P. Canary

That Loyola University was rapidly establishing a reputation as a progressive, socially conscious institution was due largely to three of its leaders during the 1920s: President Agnew, Father Siedenburg, and Joseph Reiner, S.J., an 1899 alum and dean of the College of Arts and Sciences from 1923 until 1932. These men encouraged and supported student initiative, as the career of Robert C. Harnett, S.J., (1904–87) made abundantly clear.

Father Hartnett came to the attention of many Americans during the 1950s for his courageous opposition to Senator Joseph McCarthy's anti-Communist activities. As editor-in-chief of *America* magazine, Hartnett challenged McCarthy, a graduate of Marquette. His political commentary in the Jesuit weekly earned him equal shares of admiration and scorn. Interestingly, his tenure as editor came to a sudden end in September 1955, when he was reassigned by his superiors. He returned to Loyola in 1956 as dean of the College of Arts and Sciences and as a teacher in the political science department.[70]

Hartnett traced his strong views of social justice to his boyhood experiences while growing up in Rogers Park. He remembered that "Siedie" stopped by his parent's home at 1222 West Pratt Avenue to discuss politics and Catholic publications, such as "The Condition of Labor" and John Ryan's "Living Wage." And he never forgot Agnew's vote of confidence in granting the first budget for the university debate team—$300 in 1926. Although Agnew had been a great supporter of Loyola's interscholastic basketball tournaments that began in 1924, he insisted that

"debating is closer to the objective of a Jesuit higher education than sports." The investment paid off on April 19, 1927, when Loyola's team emerged victorious against Boston College, thanks to the intensive legal research they conducted on whether the Volstead Act could be amended to permit the manufacture and sale of light wines and beer.[71]

In addition to serving as head of the Debate Club, Hartnett was also the first president of Loyola's Blue Key Fraternity and a successful organizer of student dances and events at downtown hotels that were remarkable for their lack of Jesuit supervision. His greatest accomplishment as a senior was the organization of the first Catholic Student Conference on Religious Activities on May 26, 1927, that brought together nearly 100 young men and women from Chicago-area Catholic colleges and high schools. Hartnett wrote a small piece for *America* (where he would later serve as editor-in-chief) documenting the historic meeting in Loyola's Alumni Gym.

As he and Dean Reiner had hoped, Catholic students left the event convinced that "they could learn from one another new ways and methods of translating the principles of their religion into the practices of their every-day lives." By the 1930s, Catholic Inter Student Catholic Action (CISCA), as his group came to be known, drew more than 3,000 Catholic teenagers from the Chicago area, and Daniel A. Lord, S.J., credited it with giving him the encouragement he needed to continue organizing Sodality Schools and Sodality Unions in all sections of the country. Critics who dismissed CISCA as "all talk" soon discovered that bringing together young Catholic men and women to attend meetings, talk, dance, and think up bright ideas fueled the drive for social justice and equality. From the 1920s on, Loyola students and professors continued to play a key role on the issue of interracial justice, often challenging their own Catholic institutions.[72]

Robert C. Hartnett (second from left) and friends from St. Ignatius grammar school on the beach, c. 1922

1922 with the establishment of a department of commerce and finance modeled after the one in operation at the University of Illinois. According to one Jesuit publication, "The first two years of this course are identified with the general arts course with a few modifications. The last two years will be entirely distinct." Evening sessions, open to men and women, were offered in September 1924. Finally, in 1926, graduate courses were inaugurated, leading to master's degrees in education, law, medicine, psychology, and sociology, fulfilling the promise of the 1909 university charter.[73]

The Perils of Lakefront Property

In keeping with Jesuit custom of the day, after six years in Chicago, Agnew was transferred to Omaha as president of Creighton University. His successor in September 1927 was Iowa-born Robert M. Kelley, S.J., an administrator well known in the Missouri Province. From 1920 to 1926, he had served as president of Regis College in Denver where he expanded the campus, launched a $250,000 fund-raising drive, and financed the first collegiate residence and football stadium, "the largest bowl for sports in the entire Rocky Mountain region." One of Kelley's first initiatives was to create a council of deans and regents as a way of improving communication between Loyola's departments and professional schools. He also organized a lay board of advisors that drew on the expertise of alums such as David F. Bremner, Eugene McVoy, and John A. Shannon as well as prominent businessmen Edward I. Cudahy, William H. Sexton, and Frank J. Lewis.[74]

The new president soon discovered, however, that much of his time was taken

Robert M. Kelley, S.J., president of Loyola, 1927–33

In 1928, Loyola conferred honorary degrees on Teapot Dome investigator Senator Thomas J. Walsh of Montana, Madonna settlement founder Mary Agnes Amberg, Loyola benefactor David Bremner, and Marquette University president William Magee, S.J.

Northwestern University President Walter Dill Scott (1869–1955)

Architect Andrew N. Rebori (1886–1966)

up trying to ensure the very existence of the North Shore Campus. As a result of a rise in the level of the lake, nearly two acres of land had been washed away, and the university could not afford to part with any more of its spectacular Lake Michigan frontage of nine hundred feet. Kelley's response to the problem was to join forces with Northwestern president Walter Dill Scott to explore ways in which both universities could protect and extend their shorelines, a remarkable cooperation across denominational lines. In his diary entry for August 3, 1928, Kelley recorded his meeting with his Evanston neighbor and their joint plan to "present a petition to the State of Illinois legislature for permission to fill and acquire land in front of (east) our present shore line for 2500 feet, at least as far as consistent with the planned outer drive along the Lake Shore." Writing to Northwestern lawyer George P. Merrick on August 4, 1928, Scott expressed his belief that extending the campuses of Loyola and Northwestern "would be in the interests of the two universities [and] in the interests of public welfare," and predicted that approval would "probably be granted by city, park, state or national authorities, in so far as they have jurisdiction."[75]

Kelley discussed the matter with his board of trustees and Loyola attorney Michael V. Kannally, an 1894 alum of St. Ignatius College and one of the founders of the university's law school, and reported to Scott that his "suggestion of presenting this joint petition [is] a very happy one." Charles H. Thorne, who advised Northwestern University on issues related to development in the city of Chicago, praised Kelley's appointment and his interest in riparian rights and declared that "Loyola is altogether too tightly restricted by the size

of its site to permit the growth which will naturally come and which should be anticipated." There was not a moment to lose. Earlier, Kelley had discussed the needs of Loyola with Edward A. Cudahy, chairman of the board of the Cudahy meatpacking company. Perhaps because his brother, Michael, had donated the science building in 1910, Edward Cudahy expressed interest in endowing chemistry fellowships, scholarships, and research.

Architectural Views of the Lakefront Property

Over time, Kelley sensed that Cudahy's "viewpoint was changing from chemistry to helping us where we most need help." By July 1928, Cudahy made it clear that he preferred to build a library in honor of his wife, Elizabeth, rather than providing an endowment for the College of Arts and Sciences. Before leaving for his summer home in Mackinac, Michigan, he insisted that plans be drawn by Andrew N. Rebori, one of Chicago's up-and-coming architects. His investment had long-term effects on the development of the Lake Shore Campus and upon the university's urban identity.[76]

The son of Italian immigrants, Rebori grew up in New York City, where he played baseball and swam in the East River with future governor Al Smith. After his father's death, Rebori helped to support his seamstress mother by working in an architect's office, meanwhile taking evening classes in high school. After finishing his education at the Massachusetts Institute of Technology on scholarship, he became a professor of architecture at the Armour Institute of Chicago in 1911. Two years later, he married Nannie Prendergast, the oldest daughter of the late Judge

Rebori's elegant
1918 design for a
monumental arch
north of the Michigan
Avenue Bridge

Richard Prendergast, one of St. Ignatius College's most famous alums. Although Rebori's 1919 plan for Michigan Avenue as the Gateway to the North had not been built, his innovative designs were widely acclaimed by the city's architectural community and established his reputation as one of the leaders of the City Beautiful Movement.[77]

In the fall of 1928, Cudahy informed Kelley that he would be willing to spend $250,000 on the library, that he wanted it to be "good looking inside & outside," and that he liked Bedford stone. In addition, the meatpacker suggested that the firm of Rebori, Wentworth, Dewey & McCormick, Inc. where his son-in-law, Vaughan Spalding, was employed, "should be given an opportunity to submit plans."

Although Kelley had been trying to develop a comprehensive plan for the North Shore Campus, he found matters further complicated by Father Mertz's dream for Our Lady of the Wayside chapel. Since

1924, the classics professor had written and spoken passionately about creating a 1,000-seat chapel honoring the Madonna della Strada, who was revered by Ignatius of Loyola and later by the Jesuits in their Church of the Gesù in Rome. Mertz developed a variety of fund raising activities

Rebori plans for Cudahy Library, January 19, 1929

SOUTH ELEVATION
PROPOSED MEMORIAL LIBRARY - LOYOLA UNIVERSITY
CHICAGO — ILLINOIS

Father Mertz's map of the proposed Madonna della Strada Chapel, 1924

Breakwaters along Loyola's lakefront campus, 1920s

that brought together Loyola students and their parents for card playing and dancing in such popular venues as the Edgewater Beach Hotel and the Aragon Theater in Uptown. Contributions increased steadily, from $1,600 in 1925 to $160,000 by April 1929. Several architects, among them Paul V. Hyland and Alfred Shaw, had presented plans for the Madonna della Strada Chapel, with the commission finally awarded to Patrick M. O'Meara. The firm's sketches clearly showed the library and chapel facing east toward Lake Michigan and anticipated the new Outer Drive that the City of Chicago intended to build north of Devon Avenue to the city limits.[78]

The only way to safeguard the site of the proposed library and chapel was to install a breakwater; after the necessary federal, state, and city permits were obtained, work began in May 1929. But two months later, the North Shore Park commissioners served notice on Loyola that unless construction stopped immediately, the commissioners intended to "take such steps as may be deemed necessary, to protect and preserve the shoal and shallow waters for park purposes, for the good of the public, and for the use of the people as directed by the legislature." In a legal proceeding filed on August 29, 1929, Loyola claimed that its site on the North Side "has become of very great value, well in excess of four million dollars for buildings and grounds" and asserted that the lack of available land for expansion in any direction made it "absolutely essential to the well-being and . . . existence of the University that the present campus be preserved without loss of ground." Kelley vigorously denied allegations that Loyola was "seeking to add new ground to its Lake Shore Campus." On the contrary, he maintained, the university was merely "attempting to recover the land lost" as a result of high lake levels and to "furnish protection for the foundations and building operations of the library now being erected."[79]

Following the example of President Burrowes, Kelley also publicly challenged the *Chicago Tribune*'s reporting that an injunction had been filed against Loyola. He took pains to set the record straight, pointing out that the wooden retaining wall

built on dry land "to protect the university property from the lake storms" had been destroyed and that "the new breakwater is being built on the site of the old wall as a matter of safety." Vindication came when the Circuit Court ruled that the breakwater was enclosing only land belonging to the university and that Loyola was free to continue construction aimed at protecting the new university library.[80]

Kelley was no stranger to controversy and took it in stride, especially the antivivisection campaign that continued in full force throughout his presidency. He served as an honorary vice president of the Illinois Society for the Protection of Medical Research and joined with his colleagues at the University of Chicago, the University of Illinois, and Northwestern to oppose the passage of an Illinois senate bill that would have barred the medical schools from use of animals for experimentation. The greatest part of the cost of renovating the Loyola medical school building in 1926 had been for the construction of a new doghouse, nearly $3,000. After his public appearance at City Hall on April 15, 1929, to discuss the proposed legislation, Kelley confided to Dr. A. C. Ivy of Northwestern that he had received mail proclaiming him "a disgrace to the Catholic faith and to the Catholic priesthood." But Kelley's Midwestern sensibility came through loud and clear as he insisted, "It is all in a day's work . . . and I am very glad to lend my help to blocking such wild and injurious legislation."[81]

Coming from Denver where he had supervised the construction of a modern stadium, Kelley deeply appreciated the promised financial support from alums for a new athletic field and football stadium but had serious concerns about the proper balance between athletics and scholastics.

Even at an athletic banquet, he informed the crowd gathered at the LaSalle Hotel on December 20, 1928, "I will not hesitate to say that the purpose of attending a college is to gain an education."

Loyola's head coach Roger Kiley, an All-American end when he played football for "Rockne's Ramblers" in 1921, had introduced the aggressive "Notre Dame brand of football" to Chicago. Although Loyola's team could not attract the crowds the Fighting Irish did when they played in Soldier Field while their new stadium in South Bend, Indiana, was under construction, the publicity Loyola's Ramblers received was considerable. During the 1928 season, for example, it was estimated that "6,383 column lines have been devoted to [Loyola's] team, which would have cost $4,468.10 in the form of advertising." Unlike Notre Dame, where football generated substantial revenue, soaring from $235 in 1919 to $529,420 in 1929, however, gridiron competition at Loyola remained a losing proposition. In 1929, the deficit for the season was $24,500, and projected estimates for the next five years indicated similar losses. Still, in May 1929, Kelley endorsed plans for a stadium but warned members of Peter Angsten's committee that Loyola would contribute $25,000 to the project "and no more."[82]

Loyola's greatest football rival since 1912 had been DePaul. Chicago's two Catholic universities competed fiercely for the Little Brown Barrel, a take-off on the Big Ten's Little Brown Jug. Winning—and retaining—the mahogany treasure became a matter of great pride for the all-male student body on the Lake Shore Campus. But at a pregame rally in 1928, enthusiasm exceeded judgment when Loyola fans ripped up a section of the bleachers and used it "as fuel in an already immense

Roger Kiley (1901–74) brought Notre Dame–style football to Loyola in 1923; he later became a judge and served on the United States Court of Appeals from 1961 until 1973.

In 1929, Loyola beat its archrival, DePaul University, 13-0 before a crowd of nearly 50,000 at Soldier Field; as a result of the victory, Loyola retained the "brown barrel."

Seeing Chicago by Airplane: No. 1, the Loyola District

In fewer than twenty years, the neighborhood surrounding Loyola's lakefront campus was completely built up with modern homes, two- and three-story "flat" buildings, and elegant high-rise apartments.

bon-fire." The Inter-Fraternity Council interceded with the faculty and, as a result, students were permitted to make atonement for the loss by contributing between seventy-five cents and two dollars each, depending on their "degree of guilt." When the teams met for a rematch in Soldier Field on November 3, 1929, before a crowd of more than 50,000, the largest in their history, the Ramblers won a decisive 13-0 victory over "the very Blue Demons" and the city's daily papers were extravagant in their praise of Loyola's defense and the "unstoppable, unconquerable" trio of Les Molloy, Robert Burke, and Tommy Flynn.[83]

The New Neighbors on Sheridan Road

Ironically, the proceeds from Loyola's greatest football victory in Chicago's most prestigious venue went to the Sisters of Mercy, not Loyola's B.V.M. neighbors who had just broken ground for a fifteen-story "skyscraper" college at Devon and Sheridan! In a stunning act of faith in the future, the Sisters of Charity of the Blessed Virgin Mary forged ahead with their plans to build even as the Depression of 1929 deepened. Sister Mary Justitia Coffey, B.V.M., was appointed supervisor of the building on Sheridan Road, and in 1930, she became the college's first president. As a former superior at Immaculata High School from 1921 to 1927, she understood the aspirations of young women, many of whom were the daughters of immigrants. Also, she had predicted, correctly, that this first Catholic day-college for women in Chicago "is a novel idea that will attract girls. It is the modern way of living."

But no one understood better than Mother Isabella Kane, B.V.M., how much appearances mattered. After all, she had grown up in Holy Family parish when St. Ignatius College was under construction and knew that the new Catholic college for women "should open on a scale that

"The Phoenix typifies Chicago rising up from the plains after the fire in 1871 . . . I would rather have a phoenix than two wolves like Loyola University."

will attract the attention of the city." Not only did Mother Isabella work closely with Dubuque architect Nairne Fisher in the design of the Art deco college and the choice of marbles for the walls and floors, but she also expressed her preference for symbols. "The Phoenix," she reminded members of her community "typifies Chicago rising up from the plains after the fire in 1871, shortly after our coming to Chicago . . . I would rather have a phoenix than two wolves like Loyola University." Yet as the Jesuits and B.V.M.s soon discovered, keeping alive two Catholic institutions in the depths of the Depression would require more than the legendary bird of rebirth and the hospitality provided by wolves at the kettle.

LOYOLA NEWS

MUNDELEIN COLLEGE FOR WOMEN

Picture of the fifteen story Mundelein College for Women which is under construction on the north side of Sheridan road—at Devon avenue extended—just west of the lake and overlooking the campus of Loyola university. Designed by Joe W. McCarthy of Chicago and Nairne W. Fisher of Dubuque, the structure will give to Chicago another notable example of modern architecture. F. W. Jackson is the delineator.

MUNDELEIN COLLEGE FOR WOMEN GOES UP NEAR ARTS CAMPUS

$1,500,000 Is Cost of New 14-Story Structure; Ready in 1930

By ROBERT J. HEALY

Mundelein College for Women, a university skyscraper of modern design being erected at a cost of $1,500,000, points out the architectural thought trend of the colleges of today. Situated on Sheridan Road near Devon Ave., overlooking our north campus, it will be affiliated with Loyola University though conducted by the Sisters of Charity of the Blessed Virgin Mary. Its unique modern mode is brought out in bold significance by sweeping vertical lines characterized in set-backs and terraced roofs, both on the street and side elevations. Indeed, the entire bulk of the building is broken up in such a way as to give the onlooker, glancing at it from a perspective, a number of varied effects. The fire escapes will be encased in the building thus eliminating the unsightly element.

Opens in September

It is believed that work on the institution will be completed in August, and the opening is therefore scheduled for the beginning of the 1930-1931 school year. Four-year courses will be offered in liberal arts and sciences. There will be departments in history, philosophy, mathematics, sciences, languages, journalism, education, and music.

Site of the new educational building fronts 250 feet on Sheridan Rd. and 254 feet on Devon Ave.; the building, however, will take up 173 feet on Sheridan Rd. frontage, and 205 feet of the Devon Ave. frontage. The building will rise to the limit allowed by the zoning ordinance, 198 feet, and the roof structures will be set into the fifteenth floor in order to beautify the top.

Will Accommodate 1,000

The basement and first eight floors of the building will be given over for school purposes, while the upper

Loyola welcomes its B.V.M. neighbors at Mundelein College, December 11, 1929

Chapter 4

Surviving Hard Times in Chicago

1930–1957 |

The balmy temperatures of January 6, 1930, came as a welcome surprise for the few Loyola students who gathered for the cornerstone laying of Cudahy Library. Dressed in cassocks and accompanying President Robert Kelley, S.J., were student council president Charles Boyle, Sodality prefect Emmett Meagher, and Sodality officer Joseph Kearney. During the preceding weeks, the brisk winds off Lake Michigan had buffeted them as they hurried to classes in the science building. Once inside, enveloped by steam heat, they could hear the unmistakable sounds of construction. Although the Depression had cast a long shadow on the rest of the city, in Rogers Park, workmen were busy creating a new library for Loyola University and a fifteen-story skyscraper for the new Mundelein College next door. These two major projects signaled hope for the future of Catholic higher education in Chicago—on a grand scale.

Sundial of Cudahy Library

Embracing Art Deco

Elizabeth Murphy Cudahy at the dedication of the library named in her honor, 1930, with husband, Edward; and Robert M. Kelley, S.J.

Kelley had adopted architect Andrew Rebori's modern design for the library, which was donated by Chicago meat-packer Edward Cudahy, Sr., in honor of his wife, Elizabeth. At a time when prominent universities such as Harvard, Brown, Yale, Dartmouth, and Notre Dame were returning to traditional Gothic or American colonial styles in their new construction, Loyola looked to the future. Rebori had been a leader of the City Beautiful movement that aimed to make Chicago "the most convenient, attractive, and healthful city in the history of the world." He also advocated modern architecture and materials such as reinforced concrete. Rebori regarded the ceiling and roof above the main room of Cudahy Library as "a worthy achievement and a real contribution to the science and art of building construction." He explained to Kelley that because the ornamental surface of the ceiling "could be treated with paint . . . a truthful use of materials will be achieved at a lower cost than would be possible otherwise."[1]

Despite the economic downturn, there had been no attempt to scale back Rebori's design by reducing the size of the stacks from five floors to two. On the contrary, Kelley rejected Dean Siedenburg's view that "it will be fifty years or more before 250,000 volume space may be needed." The president also dismissed the idea that the "great height of the reading room"

"... a worthy achievement and a real contribution to the science and art of building construction"

Cudahy Library, featured in *Architectural Forum*, June 1931

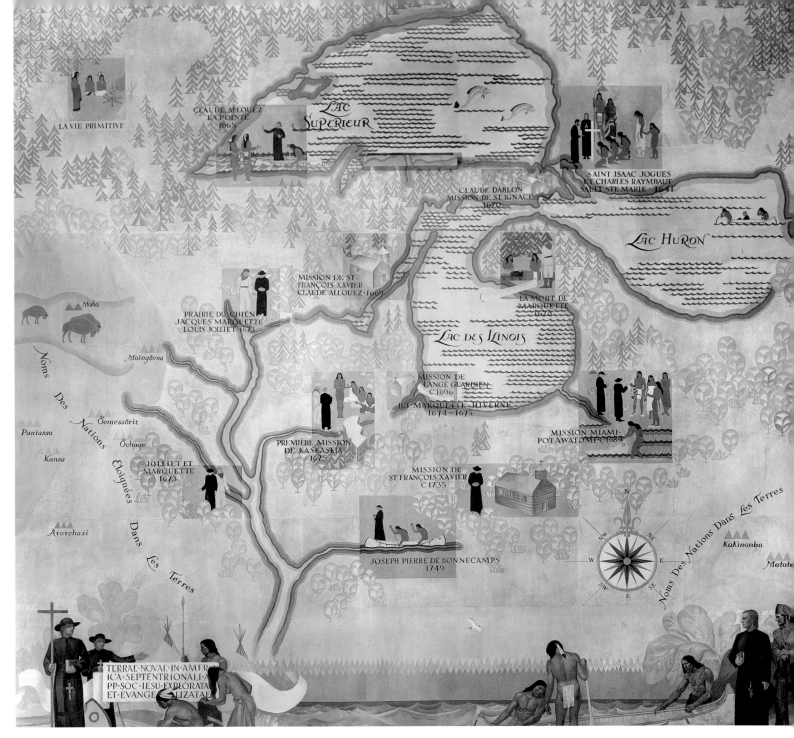

John Warner Norton's mural in Cudahy Library celebrated the role Jesuit explorers played in opening up the Middle West. Annually, beginning in 1924, Loyola students on December 4 held a celebration to honor the memory of Jacques Marquette, S.J., one of the earliest Jesuits to arrive in the area. Marquette spent the winter of 1674–75 along the banks of the Chicago River near what is now Damen Avenue.

with its distinctive geometric pattern was out of proportion. Construction on the limestone edifice with its interior walls of Mankato stone and stained glass windows by Giannini & Hilgert proceeded through the spring of 1930. Before long, students could read the nineteen Latin inscriptions carved on the frieze around the exterior that symbolized the Jesuit commitment to liberal arts education, from "Philosophia to Physica."

The library designed by Rebori echoed plans he had made for a monumental arch on North Michigan Avenue, one that was never built. Now its tower would stand as one of the most distinctive features of Loyola's Lake Shore Campus as well as a reminder of the Cudahy family's generosity. Edward Cudahy, Sr., (1860–1941) was the younger brother of Michael, who had financed the science building before he died in 1910; Edward A. Cudahy, Jr., served as one of

the first members of the university's administrative council.[2]

At the dedication of the library on June 8, 1930, Kelley thanked Rebori for the personal interest he had taken in the project, praising his talents as an artist and as an engineer. Then, in keeping with a long-standing Loyola tradition of announcing important news at public events, Kelley told the assembled crowd that Edward Cudahy had made generous

George Cardinal Mundelein (1872–1939)

This construction photo of the new Mundelein College offered a rare view of Loyola's campus as it looked on March 12, 1930.

provisions for a $100,000 trust, the interest on which would be "devoted to the maintenance and development of this library." Plus, there was more good news: Cudahy had authorized $5,000 for the artist John Warner Norton to paint a mural featuring Jesuit explorers of the Midwest.

Norton (1876–1934), Chicago's best-known muralist, had been born in Lockport, Illinois; studied law at Harvard University; and volunteered as a member of Teddy Roosevelt's Rough Riders. Norton then decided to dedicate his life to art, becoming a teacher at the Art Institute of Chicago, where he nurtured the talents of artists such as Archibald Motley, Sr. Among his many commissions in Chicago that received widespread acclaim were the 180-foot-long ceiling of the concourse of the Chicago Daily News building at Madison and Canal streets; the Ceres mural in the trading room of the new Chicago Board of Trade; and the Tavern Club murals, for which he was awarded the gold medal by the Architectural League of New York.

The artist drew on the remarkable scholarship of Gilbert J. Garraghan, S.J., the foremost Jesuit historian of the Midwest. Garraghan had been born in Holy Family parish in 1871 and entered the Society of Jesus following his graduation from St. Ignatius College. Thanks to Garraghan's extensive research, Norton was able to incorporate fourteen Jesuits who played key roles in the development of Catholic life in the Great Lakes region and the Upper Mississippi Valley during the seventeenth and eighteenth centuries.

In collaboration with two of his students, Tom Lea and June Knabel, Norton produced a colorful installation that measured thirty-five by thirty-eight feet for the west wall of the Cudahy Library reading room. Adapted from Father Jacques Marquette's historic holograph map that documented the Jesuit's travels with Louis Joliet in 1673–75, the mural depicts "New lands in North America explored and evangelized by the Society of Jesus."[3]

New Life on Sheridan Road

At the same time Cudahy Library was nearing completion, the Sisters of Charity of the Blessed Virgin Mary were putting their own imprint on the urban landscape with an Art Deco skyscraper. As spelled out in the 150-page building contract, the B.V.M. Sisters expected that "all workmanship and finish must be first class in every particular and strictly in accordance with the best practice." Although the new college was to be named after Cardinal George William Mundelein, and designed by his favorite architect, Joe W. McCarthy, Mother Isabella did not share their enthusiasm for American Colonial architecture. She rejected McCarthy's plan for a brick exterior as "beyond our means" and

returned three versions of his plans as unsuitable. A compromise was reached: Nairne Fisher of Dubuque, Iowa, would draw up the plans, and McCarthy would serve as supervising architect.[4]

Motorists turning the corner on Sheridan Road at Devon could not miss the sign announcing that the college would be "ready to accept students September 1930." For Carol Jegen, who became one of Mundelein College's leading social justice activists, her first glimpse of the women's college left an indelible mark. She remembered taking a Sunday afternoon ride with her family when suddenly her father "stopped the car as we came to Sheridan Road and Kenmore Avenue." The Jegen family operated a successful florist business on Chicago's North Side, and her father especially was "mindful of the tremendous financial challenges brought about by the Depression." Although more than seventy years have passed, Sister Carol Frances can still recall her father's deep concern and his exclamation of genuine anguish, "I don't know how those Sisters are ever going to pay for that building."

How did they finance a $2.5-million-dollar skyscraper? By mortgaging their community's property in Dubuque, Iowa, a great act of faith in the future of women's education. Just as there had been an outpouring of support for the Sisters of Charity of the Blessed Virgin Mary after the Great Fire of 1871, self-denial offerings for Mundelein College totaling $14,489.42 poured in from B.V.M. schools throughout the United States. Twenty of the B.V.M. grammar schools in Chicago contributed more than $9,000, one of the largest individual contributions coming from St. Agatha School in Lawndale, named for B.V.M. Sister Agatha Hurley. With jobs in short supply, tradesmen welcomed the oppor-

Sister Justitia M. Coffey, B.V.M., president of Mundelein College, at her desk on the first floor of the Art Deco skyscraper.

tunity for employment on the skyscraper, and, as a result, the Sisters were able to keep construction crews working around the clock for months.[5]

Mundelein College's first president, Sister Justitia Coffey (1875–1947) understood the critical role the college would play in the life of Chicago. The daughter of Irish immigrants, Alice Marie Coffey had grown up in North Hadley, Massachusetts, not far from Mount Holyoke and Smith colleges. These elite Protestant institutions did not welcome working-class Catholic girls like Coffey, and she became a public schoolteacher in 1893 after her graduation from high school. As one of the first B.V.M.s to study at Catholic University in Washington, DC, Coffey was a pioneer in higher education for women religious, inspiring many of her Chicago colleagues at St. Mary and Immaculata high schools. Sister Justitia referred to the lakefront college that opened in

AW, THERE AIN'T NO SANTA CLAUS

Joe Loyola's 1930
Christmas wish?
A dorm on the Lake
Shore Campus

September 1930 as "a temple of classic beauty in the heart of a great city" and emphasized its proximity to streetcar lines and the elevated road. A young woman who enrolled could expect to receive a liberal arts education "in harmony with the exterior of the college, thoroughly modern, complete, and efficient." Moreover, she would be prepared to "maintain her place in the economic world [as she claimed] the place that is rightfully hers as a Catholic social and civic leader."[6]

Loyola students welcomed the idea of having female students nearby and published articles in their newspaper praising the college's unique design and modern classrooms, lecture rooms and laboratories, a thoroughly up-to-date cafeteria, gymnasium, swimming pool, auditorium, and library. One editorial suggested, wryly, that Loyola's housing problem could easily be solved—if only the B.V.M.s would give over two or three floors to the men! Twenty-five more years would pass before the first men's dorm was built on the Lake Shore Campus. However, long-standing concerns about lack of collegiate spirit deepened on December 4, 1930, when Father Kelley abolished intercollegiate football.[7]

The Battle Against the Gridiron

Kelley's decision was not made lightly. Coach Dan Lamont and Peter Angsten had led the drive for a new stadium, and plans were underway to complete it in 1930. As expected, the new floodlights had increased attendance, and the season turned out to be a financial success.

But many wondered, was the investment worth it? During football season, professors routinely dismissed evening classes early, with the result that law students did not complete the full casebook assigned. Kelley's diary and correspondence document payments made to repair the damage the football squad had inflicted on their rented quarters. A report he filed with the North Central Association of Colleges and Secondary Schools [NCA] confirmed that when it came to scholarships "athletic ability had been taken too much into account." In his public statement, Kelley asserted that intercollegiate football no longer served the best interests of the students, and he lamented the fact that, in order to survive, teams were now "competing with entertainment agencies for the patronage of the public."[8]

Editors of the school newspaper hailed Kelley's decision, claiming that it had made Loyola "the most talked-of major university in this country." By abolishing football, Chicago's Jesuit university had become the first school in the nation "to grapple with a corrupt system." Many students disagreed, asserting that the games had brought much-needed publicity to the university and contributed to school spirit. Also unimpressed by Kelley's reasoning was Notre Dame president Father Charles O'Donnell, C.S.C. In a letter to Father Kane, Loyola's librarian, he confided that critics of intercollegiate football "would do well to give a little more attention to the doctrines taught by their professors, and bother a little less about the menace of college football."[9]

From 1875 on, the debating society had been one of Loyola's most honored clubs, with students competing vigorously against teams from other Jesuit colleges and universities. Now they faced a new rival, Mundelein College. Debate coach William Conley used the skills he learned at Loyola to prepare young women for the great debate of April 22, 1931: "Resolved, that the emergence of women into public life is to be deplored." When debate day arrived, approximately 200 Loyola men marched "proudly in phalanx formation through the main portals of [Mundelein College], singing their school songs . . . and in other ways showing their utter fearlessness of the foe." The forensic flare up that began with junior Joseph A. Walsh's "eloquent plea" to restrict the role of women in public life was challenged by freshman Mary Jane Sullivan. She argued that "it was due to the interest which women took in public life that so much good had been accomplished in the past." In her account of the debate, Alice Durkin noted, "The final decision . . . was received with as much good humor and sportsmanship as a man can exhibit when he is beaten by a woman."[10]

continued on page 146 ▶

On the issue of the day—women's role in public life—Loyola debaters in 1931 lost to their Mundelein rivals. From left to right: James F. Rafferty; Joseph A. Walsh; Leonora Stahr, chairperson; Mary Jane Sullivan; and Katherine Brennan.

A Women's World on Sheridan Road

From its opening day on October 3, 1930, Mundelein College attracted ambitious and talented young Catholic women from throughout the Chicago area. Thanks to its location near the elevated railroad and the city's streetcar lines, the commuter college was a success from the very beginning.

Like the B.V.M. Sisters who taught them, many of the students were the daughters or granddaughters of immigrants. Often the first in their families to attend college, they were attracted by the promise of successful professional lives. In addition to the standard courses of a four-year liberal arts program, the college offered music, art, and speech, as well as preparation for pre-law and medicine, library science, journalism, commerce, home economics, and physical education.[16]

Among the staff members who brought distinction to the college was Sister Mary Therese Langerbeck, B.V.M., who trained hundreds of young women for careers in science. As chairman of the physics department, in 1938, she supervised the installation of a Foucault pendulum in an empty elevator shaft, a display that drew scientists from around the country. The first woman to receive a PhD in astrophysics from Georgetown University in 1948, Sister Langerbeck was an invited guest at the launch of *Apollo 9* in 1969.

Sister Mary Therese Langerbeck (1902–93)

In 1934, the Sisters acquired the Wheeler mansion on Sheridan Road for much-needed library space. During a visit in 1936, the Wheelers' daughter predicted to the Sisters that her childhood home "will always be inspirational and cultural to your students." The building was restored to its original beauty in 2005 and is now known as Piper Hall, which houses the Ann Ida Gannon, B.V.M., Center for Women and Leadership of Loyola University Chicago.

Despite the fact that the B.V.M. Sisters built Mundelein College with funds from their own community and sustained it by their labor, on dedication day, they sat six rows behind Jesuit professors and lay teachers of Loyola University. From his throne at the left, George Cardinal Mundelein pressed a button that illuminated the Kilgen organ (beneath the stage at the right), his only gift to the college.

When Mercedes McCambridge, class of 1937, received an Academy Award for her performance in *All the King's Men*, she returned to Mundelein College to celebrate with Sister Mary Leola Oliver, B.V.M.

Players in Loyola's popular National Catholic Interscholastic Basketball Tournament (NCIBT) celebrated at a banquet in 1934. Future Ramblers coach George M. Ireland had played in Alumni Gym in the 1932 tournament as a member of the team from Campion Academy in Prairie du Chien, Wisconsin.

Loyola's short-lived boxing team (1936) benefited from the expertise of students who had participated in the Catholic Youth Organization (CYO) and the Golden Gloves tournaments sponsored by the *Chicago Tribune*. Top row, left to right: Charles Mullenix, manager; Louis Benedict; Al Cornille; Denis Molloy; Charles Eulo; bottom row: William Herlihy; Francis Corby; Edward Maciejewski; Robert Denkewalter; not pictured: Arthur Baptist; Charles Jasiel; Emmett Molloy; Carlos Morrison; Fred Lindenfeld

▶ *continued from page 141*

Although Loyola's enrollment had increased steadily, from 407 in 1920 to more than 6,000 in 1930, not all Jesuit professors regarded this as progress. In his diary, Father Kelley recorded a long talk he had had with Father Kane, who argued that the university "should return to the traditional classical courses which have been from the beginning proper to our colleges and academies." In the librarian's view, Loyola's professional schools were "appendages" and that the university was "striving to maintain too many of them." Moreover, he criticized the Downtown College with its coeducational classes as "doing us harm" and suggested that "we should effect much more good if we limited our field to, say 1000 boys," and emphasized Latin, Greek, history, and philosophy.[17]

While Jesuits had long debated what constituted a classical education, in March 1930, the North Central Association (NCA) nearly "dealt a knockout wallop" to the university's interscholastic basketball meets. Ironically, the tournament had been formed in 1924 because Amos Alonzo Stagg of the University of Chicago had excluded participation by Catholics! Now both schools were threatened by expulsion from the NCA if they continued to host or promote a national meet. For Loyola, the annual March tournaments that brought together the best Catholic high school teams from across the country drew crowds of nearly 50,000 spectators and generated national publicity. Since the event benefited Catholic education in terms of "increased enrollment and enhanced prestige for the participating schools," Loyola was loathe to discontinue it. The solution? Quietly, in 1935, the university handed sponsorship over to Loyola Academy, and the event continued until 1941.[18]

A New Role for Sports

Although varsity basketball continued to grow in popularity, Loyola students devoted time and energy to other sports as well, particularly boxing and track. Throughout the 1930s, the Catholic Youth Organization (CYO) provided working-class boys with opportunities to learn the "manly art

of self-defense" and to participate in the *Chicago Tribune*'s Golden Gloves competitions. The sectional tournaments in Alumni Gym provided many Chicagoans with their first glimpse of Loyola University, and a few young men such as Arthur Baptist returned as scholarship students.

Beginning in 1931, the deserted football field was put to good use by the newly organized cross-country team. Although track didn't formally start until that year, Loyola had gained national attention when it hosted relay races at Grant Park Stadium (now Soldier Field) on April 19, 1925. Billed as the First Annual Relay Carnival of Loyola University, the event featured Olympic star Paavo Nurmi, "the superman from Finland," as well as "top notchers from colleges and universities around the country." As the 1925 Loyola yearbook exulted, the Loyola Relay provided Chicagoans with the opportunity "of seeing the makers of track history perform in their own municipal museum."[19]

Loyola's three-and-a-half-mile course attracted competing runners from DePaul University, the University of Chicago, Illinois State Normal, and Wheaton, Elmhurst, and Monmouth colleges. An indication of how important the sport had become was the heavy recruiting of Olympic and Notre Dame track star Alex Wilson, who became the team coach in 1932 and stayed until 1950. Although it wasn't until 1940 that Loyola won its first tournament, captain Max Lenover and his teammates played a key role in popularizing the sport.[20]

The Depression notwithstanding, young men and women who commuted to Loyola took advantage of the social and cultural attractions available in Chicago. Many were the first members of their families to aspire to college degrees, working a variety of jobs to pay their tuitions. As

1940 track stars Charles R. Beauregard, Thomas L. Layden, William O. Elson, and Max Lenover

they proceeded to organize social events away from campus in downtown venues, they received a blessing of sorts from the Academic Council, which adopted a series of rules in 1930. When it came to student conduct, the watchword was responsibility. Acknowledging the prohibition of alcohol that was then national policy, students were reminded not to use "intoxicating liquor" and to seek the "cooperation of hotel managements." Dances were "to be confined as far as possible to Loyola students," but if students took liquor to the events and offered it to someone else or drank it themselves, they "are to be disciplined."

Loyola's First Chicago-born President

Although Loyola traced its beginnings back to 1870, not until 1933 did the school claim one of its own as president. Father Samuel Knox Wilson, who succeeded Father Kelley, was also Loyola's first Chicago-born leader. His city roots ran deep. Baptized at Holy Family in 1882, he attended St. Ignatius College,

Samuel Knox Wilson, S.J. (1882–1959), served as president of Loyola from 1933 until 1942.

perceived as a "Catholic bloc . . . voting as a unit in all questions of policy." A far more valuable and practical approach, he believed, was for Catholic law schools to participate in the deliberations of the Association of American Law Schools and "utilize the power of personal persuasion."[25]

Although Loyola's trustees continued to be Jesuits, Wilson also relied on the expertise of the Administrative Council organized by Father Kelley in 1930. This eleven-member group of prominent Chicago businessmen that provided advice and recommendations for investing university funds included executive Edward A. Cudahy, Jr.; coal magnate Stuyvesant Peabody; Loyola alum and financier Matthew J. Hickey; and bakery owner David F. Bremner. Wilson joined a long line of pragmatic Jesuit presidents, and so it was no surprise that Loyola had incurred "no new debts" in 1934 and that the university had actually succeeded in paying

down some of its indebtedness. No bequests had been received, but Wilson hoped that condition would change "with the expected return of better times." He believed that yet more needed to be done to improve the image of the university.

Surveys conducted in the summer of 1935 for Thomas A. Egan, S.J., dean of the College of Arts and Sciences, revealed that word had gotten out about the success of Loyola students in passing the Illinois bar exam. Nevertheless, many recent Catholic high school graduates believed, mistakenly, that all sports had been abolished. Some cited the lack of "real, genuine college spirit at Loyola" and pointed out that, unlike Notre Dame, Northwestern, or the University of Chicago, "we have no distinctive song [and] we never have school banquets, ceremonies, or activities broadcast over the radio." Recommendations included more help from alumni in recruiting students and announcing the $50

Expanding Jesuit Education

The Chicago Province of Jesuits received a stunning windfall in 1934 when Edward Ballard donated the opulent West Baden Springs Hotel in Indiana for use as a seminary college.

The hotel, designed by noted architect Harrison Albert, was built in 1902 by Lee W. Sinclair. The resort's atrium boasted a dome that was 208 feet in diameter and 150 feet high with more than 18,000 square feet of glass in the skylight. It was said to be the largest dome in the world, inviting comparisons with those of St. Isaac's Cathedral in St. Petersburg, the capitol in Washington, DC, and St. Peter's in Rome.

Easily accessible from Chicago by the Monon railroad line, West Baden was popularly known as the Carlsbad of America for its mineral springs. With more than 700 rooms, two golf courses, and modern recreational facilities, it provided Jesuit seminarians with ample living quarters during their three years at the college.

Among those attending the school was Raymond C. Baumhart, S.J., who later served as Loyola University's president from 1970 to 1993. Baumhart, born and raised on Chicago's North Side, had entered the Society of Jesus after a tour of duty in the navy. He recalled his first impression of West Baden as a "little town . . . on the way to nowhere." The only neighbors were "mostly farmers," and the seminary was "by far, the biggest building in West Baden." Several generations of Jesuit scholastics shared the timely and magnanimous gift from a man who was not Catholic. Sold at auction in 1966, the complex has recently been restored to its former glory, and the West Baden Springs Hotel is once again a tourist attraction, along with nearby French Lick Springs Resort.[26]

partial scholarships "as closely to the first of September as possible in order that the high school graduates may be allowed to know where they stand."[27]

Loyola Weathers the Depression

In a surprising demonstration of unanimity, the presidents of Northwestern, the University of Chicago, the University of Illinois, and Loyola all claimed that the Depression had done their students "a great deal of good" and that professors were much more satisfied with their students than they had been during "the luxury years" of the 1920s. Wage-earning students at Loyola were not uncommon, especially those who attended classes downtown, and an estimated 10 percent of the 517 students on the Lake Shore Campus were paying some or all of their tuitions in 1934. William Finnegan, S.J., explained to *Tribune* reporter James O'Donnell Bennett that "the depression has

steadied [Loyola students]. Many of them come from homes of moderate means where there is a real spirit of sacrifice. The spiritual and disciplinary value of sacrifice is . . . [also] impressed upon them here in their classes on religion and economics, in their annual retreats, at their weekly masses, and in frequent conferences with their advisers on the faculty. We emphasize to them that these are serious times and that they must get down to serious business."[28]

The fact that Loyola's medical and law schools functioned during the Depression was nothing short of remarkable. Loyola graduates continued to secure the prestigious internships at Cook County Hospital and, in 1931, James D. Glynn and Michael M. Morrissey placed among the top ten students nationwide of those who took the National Board of Medical Examiners test. The competition among the 439 candidates had been tough, but Loyola's record against Harvard and Northwestern was regarded as

New West Baden Springs Hotel, West Baden, Ind., Carlsbad of America.

Loyola University's West Baden College, where Jesuit scholastics studied philosophy and theology from 1934 to 1964.

Loyola journalism instructor Clement Quirk Lane (1897–1958), who became city editor of the *Chicago Daily News*

so valuable as in the newspaper business." In his experience, one trustworthy reporter was rewarded with "a full story, whereas another reporter calling the same person on the same story but lacking his acquaintanceship and confidence may well be thrust off with a few meager details." The lesson for aspiring reporters? In Lane's view, "the higher the person, the more important the story, the greater necessity there is for that friendship and trust." In 1958, Loyola honored Lane with an honorary doctor of laws degree for his many years of service as a journalism professor, his role as a founding member of Chicago's Cana Conference, and his tireless work on behalf of Alcoholics Anonymous.[40]

Throughout the 1930s and 1940s, the relationship between Loyola and Mundelein ranged from cooperation to antagonism. Although Jesuit professors did provide much-needed services at Mundelein College, Wilson's correspondence confirms that the president preferred to keep the school at arms' length. When workmen made necessary repairs on Mundelein College in November 1936, they apparently parked their cars on Loyola's property near the Sisters' back gate. Wilson fired off a letter to Sister Justitia reminding her that he was "most willing to grant permission to

outsiders to use the grounds" but that "this preemption of our territory should not be made without due consideration for Loyola University."[41]

While the B.V.M. Sisters enjoyed the support of women who had graduated from St. Mary and Immaculata high schools, it would be years before they could have a network of alums comparable to Loyola's. For example, Loyola's graduates were able to demonstrate their increasing visibility in Chicago at the alumni association banquet at the Stevens Hotel downtown on May 24, 1937: their guest speaker was Postmaster General James Aloysius Farley, who delivered a stirring address on behalf of President Franklin Delano Roosevelt. Addressing a crowd of more than 2,000 Loyola alums and friends, Farley reminded his Chicago audience that the Democratic president had two social objectives, "the conservation of natural resources and above all the conservation of human needs." Adding to the significance of the event, Farley's speech was broadcast on a nationwide NBC radio hookup.[42]

Just a few months later, Loyola staged an even greater event when President Roosevelt's son James addressed a crowd of 20,000 Catholic students in the university's stadium. It was a remarkable event

CISCA rally at Loyola, 1937, featured Mayor Edward Kelly; James Roosevelt; Bishop Bernard J. Sheil; William J. Campbell; and Jack Elder, master of ceremonies.

THE LOYOLA NEWS

VOLUME XIV, NO. 7   CHICAGO, ILLINOIS, TUESDAY, NOVEMBER 9, 1937   FIVE CENTS

20,000 Cheer Roosevelt

It's North vs. West in Della Strada Game

St. Mel Invades Loyola Academy for Benefit

North will meet West next Sunday afternoon when Loyola academy meets St. Mel's high school on the gridiron of Loyola stadium. The game, which begins at 2:15, is sponsored by the Fathers' and Mothers' clubs of Loyola university.

The proceeds of this contest will go towards the Madonna Della Strada (Our Lady of the Wayside) chapel fund. After years of patient and earnest campaigning by Rev. James Mertz, S. J., work on a student-faculty chapel will begin on the South side of the Arts campus.

2 Spirited Squads

This game brings together the two most spirited squads in the Catholic league. Loyola is coached by Leonard Sachs, for many years a successful mentor on the north side. The Maroon and Gold have lost two and won one. Their defeat at the hands of the St. George team, which at the present is one of the strongest aggregations in the city, was the first in nine years that they failed to defeat the Evanstonians.

Speakers' Stand Personalities

Prominent personalities present at the Cisca rally last Friday were left to right: The V...   James Roosevelt, secretary and eldest son of the President; The ...   Bam Campbell, Illinois N.Y.A. director, and ...

Hails Cisca In Address At Loyola

President's Eldest Son Delivers Peace Plea

"Catholic Youth, trained in devotion to the Prince of Peace" must take the initiative in the crusade to bring everlasting peace to the world and to preserve the democratic ideals of America, James Roosevelt, eldest son of the president of the United States, told some 20,000 Ciscans assembled in Loyola stadium last Friday morning.

Chicago Inter-Student Catholic Action representatives from eighty-two Catholic universities, colleges, and high schools in the Chicago area jammed the Loyola Arts campus to hear the scion of America's first family proclaim that we cannot accomplish real peace "unless we are wise enough to follow the teachings of St. Paul that we are members one of another, who cannot live and achieve apart from one another."

Preserve Human Dignity

The Church long ago learned as truths, Mr. Roosevelt said, "that the human dignity...

on several levels. Not only did the rally highlight the deep connections between Roosevelt's New Deal and the city of Chicago, but it also acknowledged the important role Loyola University had played in founding and developing CISCA. A Loyola student had served as president of this organization since its first meeting on the Lake Shore Campus in 1927, and its astonishing growth was not lost on Chicago's newspaper editors. According to the *Chicago Tribune*, the Chicago transit lines ran thirty-five specials over the elevated system alone to transport students from Catholic high schools and colleges in the metropolitan region to hear Roosevelt.[43]

Planning for the event had been meticulous, and Wilson took an active role, specifying that each Catholic college and high school represented was to have a definite place in the stadium. Girls were "to occupy seats in permanent stands—about 6000" and "additional girls and all boys and men [were] to stand on field, facing east, toward lake." In his public remarks, broadcast on CBS radio hookup, Roosevelt exhorted young Catholic men and women "to take the initiative in the crusade to bring everlasting peace to the world and to preserve democratic ideals of America." Privately, in an interview with *Loyola News* reporter Norbert Hruby, he asserted that the responsibility of the American Catholic college student "is one of leadership in the solution of the economic and social problems of the United States." Further, he characterized the "militant" CISCA as having "a definite place in the modern American educational system."[44]

As news photos of the CISCA rally made clear, Loyola alum William J. Campbell (1905–88) had emerged as one of President Roosevelt's most trusted young advisors. Campbell was born in St. Agatha's parish on Chicago's West Side in 1905, the son of a Scottish wool merchant who headed the commercial tailoring department at Sears Roebuck and Company. His mother, a Dane, was lovingly described by Campbell as "a deep sea hard shell salt water Baptist [who] never joined the holy Roman Irish Catholic Democratic Church." Like so many of Loyola's students, Campbell in 1926 received his law degree after four years of night school and continued in 1927 to study for a master of laws degree. His experience at Loyola proved invaluable in his career as a trial lawyer, and he credited professors Payton Touhy and Joseph Elward with making sure students "knew our way very well [to the courthouse]."[45]

Campbell worked closely with Bishop Bernard J. Sheil, the founder of the Catholic Youth Organization (CYO), and in his travels to New York he drew the attention of Governor Franklin Delano Roosevelt. When Roosevelt ran for president in 1932, against the wishes of Chicago's Democratic bosses, Campbell successfully organized the Young Democrats in forty-six states and ran interference for Roosevelt. When the city refused a permit for the New York delegation to march into town, Campbell solved the problem by having Sheil bring the CYO band to accompany the delegation. One police officer after another waved the band and the rest of the entourage through, stopping traffic so that Roosevelt could be taken in his wheelchair to the Stevens [later Hilton] Hotel. In 1935, Roosevelt, then president, appointed Campbell the Illinois director of the National Youth Administration and praised his successful efforts at analyzing employment opportunities in Illinois and advising "young people setting out in their job careers."[46] *continued on page 160* ▶

William J. Campbell, Illinois director of the National Youth Administration, c. 1935

Loyola's First Best-selling Author

Dr. Leo J. Latz (1903–94)

When Dr. Leo J. Latz picked up the phone on a hot August night in 1931 and heard the voice of a former professor at Loyola University, he had little way of knowing how this conversation would change his life and the lives of hundreds of thousands of American Catholics.

Since his graduation from Loyola's medical school in 1930, Latz had been investigating theories of natural birth control. On the phone was Father Reiner, former dean of Loyola's College of Arts and Sciences and founder of CISCA (Chicago Inter Student Catholic Action), urging him to publish his findings. The need was great. Adhering to the Church's prohibition against contraception was difficult under the best of circumstances but especially so during the Depression.[47]

Chicago's George Cardinal Mundelein had waged a vigorous campaign against birth control clinics, and in 1932, he used the commencement at Mundelein College to lash out at "pagan women . . . neurotic busy-bodies [who] are clamoring before the legislatures of the land for the right to desolate the population of this nation [through birth control]." The cardinal deplored the plummeting birth rate in Chicago and reminded the fifty graduates seated on the stage that their college had been built

By 1950, *The Rhythm* had sold 400,000 copies in twenty-two printings.

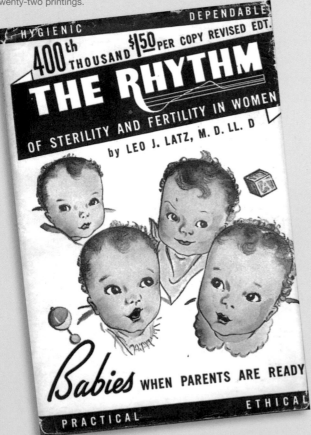

"not as a monument in stone, but to prepare women leaders with a Catholic conscience." Now, thanks to Dr. Latz's book *The Rhythm*, young—and older—married couples found step-by-step instructions on how to calculate the days on which a woman was likely to conceive. The book offered women the hope that they could plan for the birth and spacing of children.[48]

In addition to its scientific information, Latz's book emphasized the sacramental nature of marriage and challenged the idea that the only purpose of marriage was reproduction. Not only did he insist that sexual relations deepened married love, but he also argued that parents had duties to their children extending beyond giving them life. Latz acknowledged that "economic burdens, the burdens of poverty, of inadequate income, of unemployment . . . make it impossible for parents to give their children and themselves the food, the clothing, the housing, the education and the recreation they are entitled to as children of God."[49]

Father Reiner praised Latz's discussion of married life as a sacrament and asserted that couples who read *The Rhythm* would derive benefits "for their minds and hearts, for their bodies and souls." He further claimed that "no physician, no nurse, no social worker, no clergyman, can afford to disregard the information contained in this book."[50]

Sales of the thin blue volume rocketed. The first edition of 3,000 copies sold out within a month of its first printing in October 1932, and 60,000 copies were in circulation by August 1934, when it was reissued in a fourth edition. Yet, far from receiving the thanks and gratitude of Loyola University, Latz was dropped from the faculty of his alma mater without any explanation.[51]

Latz had been caught in a Catholic crossfire. In February 1933, the cover of the Jesuit weekly *America* denounced *The Rhythm* as a "commercial racket." Even Loyola's medical bulletin anonymously took a swipe at his book, claiming that Latz had "rushed into a premature popularization of a highly controversial theory stressing natural methods of birth control." On the other hand, the Catholic lay journal *Commonweal* hailed his book as "New Light on Birth Control."[52]

Shortly before his death in October 1934, Reiner wrote an impassioned letter to Loyola president Wilson defending *The Rhythm* and pleading with him to reinstate Latz. He recounted the many obstacles the doctor had endured. Among these, Reiner pointed out, was the fact that, even after the book was already in print, Loyola had urged Cardinal Mundelein to withdraw his imprimatur "on the ground that the rhythm theory was not reliable." Undaunted by this last-minute retraction, which many viewed as censure, Latz had paid for another printing with the preferred wording "published with ecclesiastical approbation."[53]

Reiner pulled no punches: he informed Wilson that Latz was now "the most talked of member of the faculty, whose book is read in every part of the English speaking world" and that *The Rhythm* enjoyed the confidence of doctors as well as "thousands of priests and married couples." Moreover, Reiner argued, Loyola University ought to honor Latz's initiative and courage and acknowledge his scientific accomplishments in "collecting evidence which establishes one of nature's most beneficent and most important laws."[54]

Despite Latz's contributions to the science—and theology—of birth control, he was never honored by his alma mater. Still, *The Rhythm* continued to sell, and before long, thousands of copies had found their way into the homes of American Catholics. The upshot was that Wilson received so many letters asking how to buy the book that he finally wrote Latz, complaining that the requests "are now getting burdensome."[55]

Latz remained a devout Catholic who never wrote publicly about the controversy over his book and waived all royalties from its publication. For the next forty years, he devoted his energies

to his work as a heart specialist at St. Elizabeth and Alexian Brothers hospitals. His son, Leo Latz II, recalled that on weekends his father would make the long trip to Techny, Illinois, to give free physicals to Divine Word missionaries.

Although the Latz family was deeply wounded by the reaction of Loyola to the publication of *The Rhythm,* their service to the Catholic Church continued. In 1934, Dr. Leo Latz's father, Dr. Peter Latz, was honored as a Knight of St. Gregory for his charitable work, and three of the seven Latz children joined the convent. Also, in 1949, the author of *The Rhythm* generously contributed to Loyola's fulfilment campaign, proceeds of which were earmarked for the medical school.[56]

Although the rhythm method of birth control had fallen into disfavor by the 1960s, historian Leslie Tentler acknowledges that Latz's best-selling book "vested the laity with an unprecedented moral autonomy" and led to new understandings of the role of sex in marriage.[57]

Dr. Leo Latz's pledge to the university's fulfillment campaign (1949) that benefited the medical school

The Latz family on a Sunday visit to Techny, Illinois: left to right, top row, Dr. Norbert Latz, Alphonse Latz, Marie Latz Thometz, and Dr. Leo J. Latz; front row, Mathilde Latz (Sister Norbert, S.C.C.), Anna Latz (Sister Mathildis, S.S.N.D.), Dr. Peter Latz, Mathilda Hug Latz, Elizabeth Mary Latz (Sister Deodata, O.S.B.)

Chapter 5

Loyola Reaches Out

1958–1970 |

After a century of service to Chicago, the Jesuit mission was about to experience its most dramatic expansion. Planning for the future of Loyola's Lake Shore and Water Tower campuses, as well as for the medical and dental schools, was absolutely crucial if the university was to meet the demands of the post– World War II baby boom. For the first time in Loyola's history, a floodtide of students sought admission to the College of Arts and Sciences—with more to follow. Equally significant, young men and women who graduated from Loyola and its professional schools tended to remain in the Chicago metropolitan region. To a degree unmatched by their contemporaries at Northwestern University and the University of Chicago, they were becoming a compelling force in the city and the fabric of urban life.

Beatitude windows in the Paul V. Galvin Chapel, Loyola University Hospital

Within the stained glass windows:

BLESSED ARE THE MEEK

FOR THEY SHALL POSSESS THE LAND

BLESSED ARE THEY THAT MOURN

Playing cards in the Lewis Towers lounge, 1958: left to right, Thomas Split, Merrill Sauriol, Thomas Kolin, Roxane Slaski Fox, Mary Alice Nebel, John Lenart, and Flora Morelli Doody

▶ *continued from page 181*

premium. Students also spent precious time waiting in line for food at the snack bars, especially before evening classes.

Loyola Union president and future White House correspondent William Plante, a member of the class of 1959, led the charge for modern quarters. Through such popular events as the Loyola Fair, homecoming, and the Fall Frolic, members of the Union had worked tirelessly to raise funds to pay the annual fee of nearly $9,000 to use the Lewis Towers lounge. Every penny counted, including the proceeds from the snack bars and the bookstore. Moreover, as Plante reminded faculty members at a meeting of the Student Activities and Welfare Committee in March 1959, student parties were held "in inexpensive locations [in order to] make money and not spend much on overhead costs." Despite long-standing arguments that the physical appearance of the lounge would benefit current students as well as "attract . . . future students of this university," several years would pass before Loyola acquired enough property on which to build Marquette Center.[7]

For all its drawbacks, the Lewis Towers lounge did have some lasting effects and benefits, such as that involving Terese Mulkern, a theater major, and John Terry, a business major. The couple met there in 1959 and remembered it as a lively—but spartan—place. All the more reason, then, that in 2006 they donated $5 million toward the construction of a state-of-the-art student center in the new Baumhart residence hall on Pearson Street.[8]

Building on the academic record attained by returning servicemen, Loyola continued to make significant gains in attracting high-achieving students. Of the 971 incoming students in the Arts and Sciences class of 1959, nearly 200

had received aid in the form of scholarships, most from the State of Illinois. The $330 semester tuition nevertheless represented a significant cost for students from working-class families, and many Loyola undergraduates held part-time jobs to pay their way. Men outnumbered women 649 to 322 in the freshman class of 1959, all coming for the same reasons: "the quality of the teaching" and the university's "location in a major urban area."[9]

Although Loyola remained predominantly a commuter school, fraternity and sorority life enjoyed newfound prestige among undergraduates in the late 1950s and early 1960s. The university's oldest fraternities, Phi Mu Chi (1922), Pi Alpha Lambda (1924), and Alpha Delta Gamma (1924) now found themselves in competition with other Greek chapters such as Alpha Kappa Psi, Tau Kappa Epsilon, and Sigma Pi Alpha. Alpha Delta Gamma and Tau Delta Phi provided living quarters in their substantial residences on Kenmore Avenue, and in 1958, the Tekes became the third Loyola fraternity to acquire a house, at 6229 North Winthrop. Delta Sigma Pi enjoyed the distinction of maintaining

Future White House correspondent William M. Plante (Arts & Sciences, 1959)

Alpha Delta Gamma fraternity, 1959: front row, left to right, Frank Konicek, Richard Krezo, James Gmelich, James Bayley, Tom Eberly; second row, Joseph Ferretti, John Divane, Edwin Biesinger, William Pederson, Emmett Burns, Robert Bielinski, Norbert Slowikowski; third row, William Devine, Robert Von Kaenel, Peter Amberson, Vitas Alekna, John Fournier, Robert Murray, Larry Bernier, Robert Mison, William Gould, Brian Shutts; back row: Jerome Atwood, John Kean, Maurice McCarthy, Michael Colandrea, and Frank Paulo

Loyola Coed Club, 1959: seated on the floor, Clare Hayden, Stella Stasulaitis; seated in the next row, left to right, Virginia Zitnan, June Antonucci, Joan Taylor, Karen Kerns, Dolores Zablotny, Mariette LeBlanc, Joan Vaccaro, Jan Hamilton, Mary Lou Kelly, Judy Altendorf, Ellen Bernacki, Anna Marie Strauss, Barbara O'Brien, Nancy McCarthy; standing, Diana Pallasch, Carolyn Mattern, Mary Lee Cullen, Mary Kay Loess, Christine Kaub, Judy Wolfgram, Mary Gill, Mary Donohoe, Joan Kwiatkowski, Ginny Szigeti, Joanna Hosteny, Ann Shannon, Mary Martin, Teri Mulkern, and Lu Anichini

Tau Kappa Epsilon fraternity house, 6229 North Winthrop Avenue

a key club at 115 East Chicago Avenue, where members could study or socialize. The Veterans Club, founded in October 1956 with seventy members, offered older Loyola students a range of social activities, and the Reserve Officer Training Corps (ROTC) increasingly attracted undergraduates interested in military life. As a smaller proportion of Loyola's enrollment, women had fewer social options than their male counterparts had. However, they formed groups such as the Coed Club (1949) and sororities, among which were Theta Phi Alpha, Kappa Beta Gamma, Sigma Alpha Rho, and Alpha Tau Delta, an organization for nursing students on the Lake Shore Campus. Chi Theta Upsilon, approved in 1958, drew new members from both campuses.

Competition from the State

Planning Loyola's future was complicated by the announcement in 1959 that the University of Illinois would institute four-year undergraduate degree programs in the city. Since 1946, a branch of the state university had offered a two-year program in makeshift quarters at Navy Pier, a short distance east of Lewis Towers. Although the Chicago site of the proposed state university campus was yet to be determined, Loyola's president, James F. Maguire, S.J., and the university trustees immediately realized the implications for Loyola. How could Chicago's Jesuit university compete with a taxpayer-funded state school that would offer a college education at minimal cost?

Father Maguire outlined several of his concerns to Nelson Forrest, executive director of the Greater North Michigan Avenue Association, which represented institutions on the Near North Side. In Maguire's view, the very survival of private institutions that had struggled for decades to provide higher education for Chicagoans was at risk. He acknowledged "the solid merits of tax-supported colleges and universities [as] essential to this nation" but argued that they should not undermine privately funded institutions.

He did not think that schools such as Loyola posed a threat to the proposed Chicago campus of the University of Illinois, but he did worry that "the people of Chicago may, in the future, be deprived of the excellent opportunities afforded them" by the privately funded institutions. His solution? If the State of Illinois provided more scholarship funds that would pay the actual cost of a student's education, Loyola and other private colleges and universities could then invest in building additional facilities they needed to accommodate "the greatly increased enrollments of the near future."[10]

As a native Chicagoan, Maguire believed that the city could become a model for the dual system of higher education, with the new, publicly supported University of Illinois campus "complementing a network of vigorous private colleges and universities." But Chicago's Jesuit university could not—and would not—relinquish any turf. Loyola forged ahead with its plans for a four-story classroom building at the southwest corner of Rush and Pearson streets. Dedicated in 1962, the modern $2.75 million Marquette Center, designed by Barry & Kay, was linked to Lewis Towers by an enclosed skywalk, one of the few in the entire city. Surrounded by the bright neon lights of Rush Street, Loyola students enjoyed the neighborhood's cosmopolitan atmosphere and crowded its legendary meeting places—the Interlude, Armando's, Younker's, Mr. Jones's, Charmet's, and DeMars.[11]

As it had in the past, Loyola responded pragmatically to the competition posed by the construction of the new $150 million campus of the University of Illinois on the Near West Side at Harrison and Halsted streets. Throughout the 1962–63 school year, a faculty committee met regularly

to explore the possibility of consolidating the College of Arts and Sciences on the Lake Shore Campus. Also discussed were moving the Graduate School, in stages, to Rogers Park; reorganizing the University College program; and providing for more library space at Lewis Towers. With remarkable unanimity, the committee agreed that the university's long-term goal must be academic excellence and that convenience of location was secondary. While conceding that many Loyola students preferred classes at Lewis Towers because of its proximity to their jobs downtown, the committee nevertheless envisioned the day when future construction would be shifted to the Lake Shore Campus.[12]

The Mercy Alliance Shatters

Since its incorporation as a university in 1909, Loyola had sought to balance the needs of undergraduate education with those of its professional schools. The Stritch School of Medicine had survived the threat of closing in 1945, but the

Marquette Center, built in 1962 at Rush and Pearson streets, was demolished in 2005 to make way for the Clare at Water Tower, an innovative high-rise, community-living structure for senior citizens.

subsequent $12 million fund-raising campaign had fallen lamentably short, reaching only a third of its goal. It didn't help that the Sisters of Mercy announced plans to build a new $6 million hospital near Northwestern University on the North Side. In the words of Loyola's trustees, the situation was really critical. Faced with the loss of its teaching hospital and staff, Loyola determined to stay on the West Side and purchased a freestanding 145-bed hospital at 432 South Wolcott Avenue. It proved to be a windfall of sorts. In 1948, the city of Chicago condemned the hospital for the construction of the Congress

Dr. John Sheehan, dean of the Stritch School of Medicine, 1950–68

Street (now Eisenhower) Expressway, and the university was able to sell the building for $275,000. Loyola selected another site nearby for a medical-dental building and entered into an affiliation with Loretto Hospital in the Austin neighborhood. On June 15, 1948, the school took on a new identity as the Stritch School of Medicine, the name it bears today.[13]

As Richard Matre details in his history of the medical center, the existing relationship between the Sisters of Mercy and the Jesuits of Loyola did not always mean congeniality. On the contrary. Although Mercy had been the teaching hospital for the university, Jesuit administrators of the medical school had no control over the appointment of physicians or the full-time clinical teachers. According to Matre, both religious communities were "caught between groups of doctors who . . . controlled the admission of patients." Still, Dr. John Sheehan, who was appointed dean of the medical school in 1950, worked diligently to maintain affiliation with Mercy and to continue relationships with Cook County, St. Francis (Evanston), Loretto, and Resurrection hospitals. A native of New England and an alum of the Jesuit College of the Holy Cross and Georgetown's medical school, Sheehan had joined Loyola in 1936, and he knew the institution inside and out. Regarded as brilliant but strong-willed, he served as chairman of the pathology department from 1940 until his appointment as dean in 1950.[14]

In much the same way that the university expanded its mission in Chicago by acquiring property at Devon and Sheridan in 1906, Loyola announced plans in 1954 to purchase a fifty-acre tract for the Stritch School of Medicine, the dental school, and a new Mercy Hospital. Because tremendous growth of Chicago's Northwest

Side appeared certain, the site chosen was undeveloped property located near Touhy and Carpenter avenues in suburban Skokie. Plans called for the site to be annexed to the city of Chicago and rezoned for the construction of a new medical center. Tension over the terms of affiliation, however, continued to escalate, and even the intervention of Samuel Cardinal Stritch in August 1957 did not resolve the long-standing issues of autonomy.

Then, as Matre writes, "the bombshell exploded." The university suffered a serious blow. In March 1958, the Sisters of Mercy informed the cardinal that they had decided to build a new Mercy Hospital on the South Side at 26th Street and Prairie Avenue, effectively withdrawing their support for the new Loyola site. The cardinal's unexpected death several months later was the second blow, and the third occurred in March 1959. At a meeting with the new archbishop, Albert Cardinal Meyer, Father Maguire learned that the archdiocese no longer felt "an obligation to support Catholic medical education in view of the more pressing needs on the primary and secondary [schools]." Since 1947, Loyola had been receiving $50,000 each year from the collections at Chicago Catholic parishes, and any remaining medical school deficit was generally satisfied by proceeds from the annual dinner honoring Cardinal Stritch.[15]

On the same day that Maguire and a group of trustees met with the cardinal, representatives of the AMA were inspecting the Stritch School of Medicine. The group stated that the lack of a teaching general hospital was regarded as acute and critical, and Loyola was warned that if substantial improvements were not made, the school might lose its accreditation as of June 8, 1962. As Robert W. Mulligan, S.J., dean of Faculties and Philosophy

chairman, noted, however, the committee headed by Dr. John E. Deitrick provided some hope. Deitrick, dean of Cornell University Medical College, was a nationally respected expert, and his survey of medical schools in the United States for the Association of American Medical Colleges had been published by the AMA. In addition to declaring that the Loyola student body "constitutes excellent academic material," the survey team praised the amazing progress made by Sheehan and his "remarkable staff" in the basic science program.[16]

Notably, graduates of the Stritch School of Medicine accounted for nearly one-fourth of all physicians in Chicago. Moreover, despite inadequate facilities, the school's teaching staff annually provided "solid medical education to some 340 future physicians." In a rousing address to faculty members in the spring of 1959, Sheehan reminded them that "there is much at the Medical School worth fighting for," and he remained optimistic that Loyola would continue to attain excellence. While the problem of hospital affiliation cast a long shadow over the medical school, it may have been a blessing in disguise that funds were not immediately available for construction of a new teaching hospital. Instead, it prompted the university to turn its attention to acquiring government property near suburban Maywood for a proposed medical center.[17]

Just as Loyola had publicly challenged the findings of the Flexner report in 1910, the university steadfastly refused to be intimidated by criticism from a group known as Protestants and Other Americans United for Separation of Church and State. In the summer of 1961, Illinois senators Everett Dirksen and Paul Douglas had introduced a bill that would deed land at Hines Veterans Hospital in suburban

The dream of generations of Loyola doctors and dentists was finally realized.

the university's new medical center, was absent from the celebrations. He had resigned in late October 1968 after Father Maguire appointed him Special Assistant to the President for Medical Center Affairs with an office at Lewis Towers. Angered at the decision, Sheehan vacated his office one weekend, and as Father Baumhart recalls, "When I arrived at the office on Monday, all the records I found were in a single, thin manila folder."[53]

Aerial view of Loyola
University Medical
Center, Maywood, 1970

Loyola Joins the National Debate on Minority Education

There was no question that Loyola and Mundelein College had played a major role in the education of the children of Catholic immigrants. Now their mission deepened in the 1960s as both institutions reached out to African American and Hispanic students. In 1965, several of the B.V.M.s and their students had marched in Selma, Alabama, with Dr. Martin Luther King, Jr.

Twenty-eight Mundelein College students and eight faculty members marched with Dr. Martin Luther King, Jr., in Selma, Alabama, in March 1965 in support of the Southern civil rights movement. Shown en route: left to right, Sister Mary Irene Meyer, Sister Mary Georgia, Sister Mary Irma Corcoran, and Sister Mary Ignatia Griffin

As part of the national War on Poverty, Loyola and Mundelein participated in the federally funded summer program known as Upward Bound. Beginning in 1966 and continuing for nearly eight years, minority high school students associated with Chicago's Urban Progress Centers experienced their first taste of university life. Not only did they take classes at Loyola and Mundelein but, like earlier generations of students, they encountered close-up the beauty of the lakefront campuses.[54]

Already committed to increasing the number of African American students in the School of Nursing, Dean Kiniery and her staff welcomed the two-year grant provided by the Sealantic Project in 1966. A subsidiary of the Rockefeller Foundation, the Sealantic program aimed at preparing disadvantaged students for nursing careers. Across the nation, the ready availability of federal and state funds meant that students were now being admitted to

colleges with only minimum requirements for admission. Beyond the question of how Loyola was to maintain its high standards was another, equally compelling, challenge for a Jesuit Catholic university: how to help high-risk students reach the academic proficiency necessary for graduation. In 1969, for example, Dean Virgil Boyd of Loyola's School of Business Administration applied to the Ford Foundation for a grant to establish a program for freshmen at high risk. While conceding that the goal was laudable, the Ford Foundation program officer informed Boyd that without massive funds for this purpose, there was little that individual colleges and universities could do "to correct the substantial under-representation of blacks and other minorities in higher education."[55]

As correspondence and reports confirm, Father Maguire and Loyola professors, administrators, and students took seriously the challenge of balancing the university's long legacy of academic excellence with the growing demands for a more diverse student body. Donald Hubert (1948–2006) chairman of the Afro-American Student Association (LUASA), and Richard Norman, head of Loyola's championship water polo team, were among many students who challenged the university to increase minority enrollment and recognize the problems they faced on campus and especially in the Rogers Park neighborhood. Building on their goal of securing "supportive academic assistance for black students on campus," LUASA waged a vigorous but ultimately unsuccessful campaign to use a university-owned frame building at 1128 West Loyola Avenue as the group's headquarters. In addition to covering this controversy, the *Loyola News* and its successor, the *Phoenix*, also cast a spotlight on the experience of black students who found it almost impossible to obtain housing in Rogers Park. As Norman reminded Loyola students, problems of social justice extended beyond the escalating war in Vietnam and deserved as much of their attention as efforts to eliminate comprehensive examinations and the student "cut" system.[56]

In the seven years since the march around Lewis Towers, Loyola students continued to take an active role in the fight for civil rights and, increasingly, the antiwar movement. Joining them were Jesuit seminarians and priests, including law professor William C. Cunningham, S.J., who, in February 1971, would be part of a legal team representing the Harrisburg Six. Among those accused of conspiring to blow up heating tunnels in Washington, DC, were well-know antiwar activists Philip Berrigan, S.S.J., and Sister Elizabeth McAlister, R.S.H.M.

The Vietnam War remained a divisive issue for Loyola's student body as it did for students across the nation. Unlike students at Fordham, who burned the campus center in New York after the Kent State tragedy, however, students at Loyola reacted with what might be characterized as Midwestern sensibility. How to mourn— and protest—the killing of four students by national guardsmen? Loyola undergraduates gathered by the thousands on the Lake Shore Campus to debate the moral and philosophical implications of their overwhelming vote to join the nationwide student strike. Part of the debate was a consideration of the ramifications of leaving school without taking final exams. But as photographs taken on May 11, 1970, attest, Loyola's mass protest began with that most Catholic ritual, the mass, and ended with a prayer service on the lakefront.

Loyola Students Protest the Vietnam War

▲ Jesuit priests concelebrating mass during the protest over the killing of students at Kent State

Chapter 6

Deepening Loyola's Urban Identity

1971–2000 |

One of the significant events of Loyola's centennial in 1970 was an official name change. In an effort to distinguish itself from the nation's other Loyolas—in Baltimore, New Orleans, and Los Angeles—the local university changed its name to Loyola University of Chicago. With a renewed sense of identity and legacy, over the next three decades, Chicago's Jesuit university further embedded itself in the life of the city and the metropolitan area. Loyola's faith in its urban mission remained unshaken by dramatic ethnic and racial change in Chicago. Yet keeping an institution alive and healthy was no small feat, as the Sisters of Charity of the Blessed Virgin Mary learned through painful experience. Mundelein College's affiliation with Loyola in 1991 marked the end of the last women's college in Illinois. It did, however, represent new life and direction for the Jesuit university in Rogers Park.

Archangel Jophiel, Mundelein College

The Passing of an Era

When founded in 1870, the university was one of several Chicago-area institutions of higher learning with deep religious roots. The first University of Chicago, for example, was financed by Baptists, and Northwestern University drew strength from its Methodist benefactors. But by the turn of the twentieth century, these schools no longer regarded their religious origins as fundamental dimensions of their identity. Loyola, on the other hand, continued to celebrate its Jesuit traditions and its longstanding association with the Society of Jesus. After all, the unpaid labor of Jesuit professors had constituted the school's living endowment for more than a century.

When Raymond C. Baumhart, S.J., succeeded Father Maguire as president in the summer of 1970, Loyola, with 16,000 students, had become the largest private university in Illinois. How to maintain this hard-won achievement? One of the most important initiatives was the Progress for Loyola University in the Seventies (PLUS) campaign. In September, Baumhart announced that $47 million of an ambitious $100 million campaign had already been raised, thanks to government grants and the generosity of Chicago corporations, individuals, and foundations. Proceeds of the campaign were to be used for constructing new campus buildings and dormitories; increasing the number of books in the library; and providing financial assistance

Aerial view of Loyola's lakefront campus, c. 1970s

1 Madonna della Strada Chapel

2 Damen Hall

3 Wilson Hall

4 Cudahy Science Hall

5 Jesuit Residence

6 Dumbach Hall

7 Cudahy Library with addition

8 Centennial Forum Student Center and Mertz Hall

9 Alumni Gym

President Raymond C. Baumhart, S.J. (center), at kickoff of Loyola's $100 million campaign, 1970; former president James F. Maguire, S.J. (at left); and Joseph B. Lanterman, chairman of the lay board of trustees and president of Amsted Industries (at right)

for students, faculty development, and new academic programs. The need was great: fully one fourth of the school's enrollment could be found on the Lake Shore Campus, now home to the School of Nursing, as well as Niles College, the undergraduate seminary department affiliated with the Archdiocese of Chicago.[1]

Although Baumhart followed several Loyola presidents who had been Chicago natives, he was the first to have earned a doctorate in business administration from Harvard University. While growing up in St. Benedict's parish on Chicago's North Side, he debated whether to attend St. Ignatius, the Jesuit high school on Roosevelt Road, but one glance at its old gymnasium helped him decide. Instead, he accepted a scholarship and enrolled at DePaul Academy in Lincoln Park and, upon earning his bachelor of science degree from Northwestern University, became the first in his family to graduate

from college. Baumhart joined the Society of Jesus in 1946 after serving as an officer in the US Navy during World War II. He was awarded an MBA by Harvard in 1953 and a DBA in 1963.[2]

The forty-six-year-old Baumhart was well known to Loyola students and faculty from his days as professor and dean in the School of Business and for the role he had played in opening the new hospital near Maywood. As executive vice president, he had been a familiar presence during the tumultuous student protests of May 1970. Historically, Loyola's president had also served as chairman of the board of trustees and as spiritual rector of the Jesuit community. Now Father Baumhart would function more as a chief executive officer, albeit one with deep roots in the Society of Jesus.

Baumhart felt so strongly about lay involvement that he made it a condition of his accepting the presidency of Loyola.

John F. Smith, Jr. (highlighted left), was Loyola's first lay chairman of the board of trustees. Other members: seated, left to right, Brian McGrath, S.J.; Francis X. Quinn, S.J.; Vincent Horrigan, S.J.; John V. Mentag, S.J.; William C. McInnes, S.J.; David Clarke, S.J.; standing, Walter P. Krolikowski, S.J.; Felix P. Biestek, S.J.; Stewart E. Dollard, S.J.; Raymond C. Baumhart, S.J., president (highlighted right); Charles F. Donovan, S.J.; John Bieri, S.J.; Joseph Small, S.J.; Daniel L. Flaherty, S.J.; and Edward J. Drummond, S.J.

He believed that the Jesuit mission would benefit from the expertise of lay men and women, especially in the field of business. After all, the university was now operating a hospital, in addition to its medical school, nursing school, and dental school. In a dramatic break with tradition, the Jesuit trustees elected John F. Smith, Jr., to the previously all-Jesuit board of trustees in January 1971. Smith, the former president of Inland Steel, had not come from a privileged background. Like so many other children of the Great Depression, he had gone to work after graduation in 1930 from Tilden Technical High School, a public school. He began his career as a clerk in the Indiana Harbor plant of Inland Steel and rose through the ranks, eventually serving as company president from 1959 to 1969. Smith had been a member of Loyola's lay board of trustees for ten years, but now he would be an equal among Jesuits, entrusted with the mission of the university.[3]

New Blood for the Medical Center

The opening of Loyola's multimillion dollar hospital in May 1969 had sorely tested the faith of the Jesuit mission. Not only did the hospital account for fully half of the university's $6 million deficit in 1970, but the number of unoccupied beds meant that it was impossible to break even. Still, in January 1971, a visiting team representing the AMA's Liaison Committee on Medical Education acknowledged the hospital's "excellences as a teaching facility." It also predicted that the new Loyola Medical Practice Plan that required a percentage of doctors' incomes from their care of men, women, and children would soon make a difference. But an essential goal for the new hospital, noted the committee, should be the forging of closer relationships within the community. Its status as a suburb notwithstanding, Maywood with its changing ethnic and racial make-up in the 1970s mirrored that of Chicago's urban neighborhoods. In fewer than ten years, Maywood had become a predominantly African American community with a shrinking economic base. Although Loyola's medical center remained an important source of employment for local residents, the community never recovered from the loss of manufacturing jobs at the Canada Dry Company and the American Can Company.[4]

By far the most positive development for the medical center had been the recruitment of talented doctors from Cook County Hospital, beginning with Dr. John R. Tobin, Jr. A Notre Dame grad who received his medical degree from the University of Chicago, Tobin was appointed chairman of the Department of Medicine in 1969. Thanks to his influence, several former colleagues joined Loyola, including Dr. Leon Love as chair of radiology, Dr. Adel El-Etr as chair of anesthesiology, and Dr. Roland Cross as chair of urology.[5]

Another significant event was the arrival in August 1970 of Dr. Robert Freeark, who had won acclaim at Cook County for his pioneering role in establishing a trauma and burn center. Freeark, as medical director of that 2,500-bed hospital, had waged a spirited battle in 1968 against political interference in Cook County's health care system. He called public attention to the urgent need for adequate funding for the historic institution on Harrison Street—where so many of Loyola's doctors had received clinical training—and he advocated the construction of a new facility. Freeark brought that same passion to Loyola, a fact that was immediately apparent in 1971 to the visiting medical committee, which praised his "aggressive leadership" as well as Dr. Tobin's "imagination and . . . substantial record of accomplishment."[6]

The medical school staff included many new full-time professors who were considered "truly outstanding," such as Dr. Herbert Rubinstein, former chief of rheumatology at Hines VA Hospital. The student body also was regarded as "well-qualified and well-motivated." By 1972, Loyola was able to select its incoming class of 130 first-year students from a pool of more than 4,200 young men and women. The student body also gave witness to the school's commitment to diversity: its freshman class included twenty-nine women, eleven African Americans, one Native American, and two Hispanic students.[7]

A New Vision for an Old Chicago Neighborhood

The area around the Water Tower had emerged as one of Chicago's finest neighborhoods in the years since Frank J. Lewis purchased the skyscraper at 820 North Michigan Avenue for Loyola. The so-called Gold Coast stretched north of Chicago Avenue along Michigan Avenue and Lake Shore Drive. While property values in this district were on the rise, just a few blocks west was another story. During the 1920s, the area near Chicago Avenue and Clark Street had developed a reputation for its "bright lights . . . dancing, cabareting, drinking, gambling and vice." Forty years later, urban planners still considered it a slum. They regarded its dilapidated buildings and taverns as evidence of blight and expressed concern that the sordid conditions would spread eastward.[8]

In 1966, Loyola University had joined forces with nearby Henrotin Hospital at Oak and Clark streets in an unusual cooperative venture, which they called

continued on page 226 ▶

Loyola University Medical Center

I was ill and you cared for me.

Loyola's commitment to health care has been a defining feature of Chicago's Jesuit mission since Alexander Burrowes, S.J., signed the university charter on October 23, 1909. Against overwhelming odds, the medical department gained a solid reputation for educating Chicago doctors for generations.

David Csicsko's window with Luke, the patron saint of doctors; Saint Frances Cabrini; and Mother Teresa

The move in 1968 from 706 South Wolcott Avenue on the city's West Side to a modern complex near Maywood, Illinois, had been a long time coming but well worth the wait. In 1915, when Henry S. Spalding, S.J., was waging a fierce battle for the survival of Loyola's medical school, he could not have envisioned that the former Speedway Race-track, where Italian driver Dario Resta set a world's record for a 500-mile race, would evolve into one of the largest academic medical centers in the nation—or that Loyola would become the only Jesuit university in the country to own its own hospital.[9]

The foundation of Loyola's hospital was built over the site of the former Maywood Speedway. Dario Resta's world record at the track in 1915 established Chicago as "first place in the field of international motor racing."

In much the same way that Loyola medical students had benefited from clinical training at Cook County Hospital in Chicago, they would now have opportunities to learn at Hines Veterans Administration Hospital in Maywood and the adjoining Madden Mental Health Center.

Hailed as one of the most important initiatives in the university's history in the twentieth century was the opening of the 451-bed hospital on May 21, 1969. When it was renamed the Foster McGaw Hospital in June 1972, there were clear signs that Loyola's hospital would soon enjoy full capacity. By 1975, the hospital was finally "in the black," and administrators could begin to implement plans for the future. Among them was a 14-bed burn center and a neonatal facility. By 1984, Loyola's hospital enjoyed national acclaim for its heart-transplant program, and in the years to come, it would remain the only Level 1 trauma center in Illinois, as designated by the American College of Surgeons.[10]

Aerial view of Loyola's medical center, c. 1998, looking east across First Avenue. In the foreground are buildings of Hines Veterans Hospital.

Wolcott to Maywood: A Personal View

By Anthony Barbato, MD

As Dr. Anthony Barbato, former president and chief executive officer of the Loyola University Health System recalls, the dedication of the new medical school was a turning point in the university's history.

In 1966, I began my medical education in the Wolcott Avenue building as a member of the last Stritch class at that location. To describe the building as modest would be too kind. It was cramped, having only a few classrooms. The library was a converted classroom with no useable seating because journals, texts, and periodic volumes were stacked everywhere—on shelves, floors, tables, and chairs. The building was not air-conditioned, making the six- month gross anatomy course memorable for reasons other than curriculum content. There were no lounge areas or exercise facilities, and the cafeteria consisted of a coffee vending machine and half a dozen tables in the building's basement.

The school was part of the West Side Medical Center and Cook County Hospital, facilities that Loyola students shared with students from Illinois, Rush, Northwestern, and Chicago Medical schools. Loyola's basic science faculty was small and dedicated, but the clinical faculty consisted of County residents and attending physicians. There was little research, and our education was very much hospital-centric and hands-on. "See one, do one, teach one" was the operative reality, and it encouraged student teaching. We learned quickly to minister to the needs of each other as well as the patients.

The relocation of the medical school to Maywood in 1967 was truly a transforming event. The new building was spacious and well equipped: many lecture rooms; modern, multidisciplinary labs; a large, well-staffed, and inviting library; a student lounge; a hospital cafeteria available even before the hospital opened in 1969; and more faculty offices and basic science research labs than there were faculty members. Enrollment grew rapidly from 88 to 130, and the students' training stage shifted from Cook County to Hines VA Hospital. For a few years after the hospital's opening in 1969, there were more students than patients. (In fact, when I became a patient during my senior year, the number of patients was so small that I think I was examined by most of my classmates.)

Tremendous change occurred at the medical school and center in 1970 and 1971 as the result of a mass resignation of Cook County Hospital's most senior and nationally prominent attending physicians. Loyola acquired this "new" faculty, which brought

with them a legacy of dedication to patient care, education of students and residents, long-standing commitment to clinical research, and the entrepreneurial spirit that had made County a premier teaching hospital. This became a time for Loyola to build new departments and programs and to rethink such critical issues as curriculum, research, and Loyola's mission and expectations. In what seems now to have been the natural order of things, the medical school and the medical center have gone on to gain national prominence.

The legacy of excellence in educating doctors that Loyola has established over the years continues today at the Stritch School of Medicine, built in 1997 and named the John and Herta Cuneo Center in 2001.

Dr. Barbato is the former president and chief executive officer of the Loyola University Health System.

Students in the atrium of the new medical education building for the Stritch School of Medicine, August 1, 1997

Looking to the Future:
Loyola's Cancer Center and Children's Hospital

The university's commitment to cancer research deepened in 1994 with the construction of a freestanding facility devoted to the care of patients through research, diagnosis, treatment, and prevention. This innovative approach underscored the Jesuit ideal of treating the soul as well as the body, combining state-of-the-art research with attention to the physical and spiritual needs of patients.

Joseph Cardinal Bernardin blesses Loyola's Cancer Center in his last public appearance before his death in 1996. At right are John J. Piderit, S.J., and Cardinal Bernardin's doctors, Ellen Gaynor and Anne McCall.

Chicago's archbishops characteristically had welcomed the efforts of the Loyola medical establishment to educate Catholic doctors and provide health care for families, especially the poor. In 1995, Joseph Cardinal Bernardin experienced first-hand these guiding principles when he became a patient at the cancer center. Earlier, he had consulted doctors at Mayo Clinic about his aggressive form of pancreatic cancer, and, without qualification, they recommended Loyola. Bernardin had become well known as the leading advocate of the Catholic bishops' pastoral statement on war and peace and promoted the idea of a consistent

ethic of life, from conception through death. He was also a tireless advocate of Catholic health care. Now he would become an inspiration to other cancer patients.

During his visits with Doctors Ellen Gaynor and Anne McCall for radiation and chemotherapy, Bernardin soon realized that all Loyola's cancer patients received the same special treatment he did. With renewed appreciation for all the stages of life, Bernardin encouraged the patients he met and those who sought his blessing "to have faith, to see the redemptive value of suffering, to look beyond the present moment."[11]

Exterior view of the Cardinal Bernardin Cancer Center

Interior view of Ronald McDonald® Children's Hospital, Loyola University Medical Center, located on the fourth floor of Loyola University Hospital

On a beautiful spring day in May 1996, Loyola renamed its cancer center in honor of Cardinal Bernardin. Dr. Anthony Barbato hailed the momentous event as "rais[ing] the visibility of Loyola and its important work in cancer to new heights." Five months later, on October 29, 1996, in a gesture that epitomized his faith in "the God of all healing and compassion," Cardinal Bernardin made his last public appearance to bless the cancer center. He died on November 14; thousands of mourners attended his wake and funeral.[12]

On November 22, 1996, nearly 1,500 Loyola alums gathered to celebrate the memory of Cardinal Bernardin at the dinner held annually to support the Stritch School of Medicine. That year's recipient of the Sword of Loyola, the university's highest honor, was Sister Helen Prejean. Her book, *Dead Man Walking*, had focused new attention on the lives of prisoners on death row and had been made into a movie. Sister Prejean accepted the award,

In 1991, Loyola president Raymond C. Baumhart, S.J., (center) presented Eunice Kennedy Shriver and R. Sargent Shriver with the Sword of Loyola.

stating, "I'm here tonight for [Cardinal] Bernardin." In his last public statement, published four days before his death, the cardinal had urged the US Supreme Court to abolish capital punishment.[13]

Of all the children's hospitals in the United States, only Loyola's bears the Ronald McDonald® House Charities name. That this would be, in 1996, the first facility in the country renamed the Ronald McDonald Children's Hospital of Loyola University Medical Center was due in no small part to the dedication of Loyola alum Michael R. Quinlan. A 1966 graduate of Loyola, he had begun work for McDonald's as a Loyola sophomore, earning $2 an hour in the mailroom of the old headquarters at 221 North LaSalle Street. Quinlan rose through the ranks of the company, earning a Loyola MBA along the way and, in 1980, became president of the US branch of the company. Two years later, at the age of 37, he was named president of the corporation. In 1996, the $10 million McDonald's donation to Loyola represented the largest of its kind in the university's history, and it enabled the hospital to expand its innovative pediatric care and neonatal health program.[14]

Michael R. Quinlan presents a $10 million check for Loyola University Medical Center, October 4, 1996.

Loyola's law school neighbors in 1966 included Whisky a Go Go discotheque at Rush and Chestnut streets.

▶ *continued from page 221*

the Washington Square Project, after the small city park bordering Newberry Library. Both institutions needed room to expand, and they hoped to persuade the city of Chicago to declare an urban renewal district bounded by Chicago Avenue and Division, Wells, and Rush streets. With the approval of Loyola's trustees, John M. Ducey, president of the university's new Institute of Urban Life, outlined bold plans for the project, which, he declared, might become "a model for the nation" because it would not result in the relocation of families. Rather than pushing for luxury high-rises like Carl Sandburg Village along Clark Street, the project would include "extensive middle-income housing." Moreover, Loyola and Henrotin Hospital would promote the formation of a community organization along the lines of the successful Rogers Park Community Council or the Hyde Park–Kenwood organization.[15]

University records do not explain why the Washington Square Project failed to materialize. Meanwhile, however, attention was drawn to other parts of the city in the aftermath of the riots that followed the assassination of Dr. Martin Luther King, Jr., in April 1968.

Loyola's administration realized that in order to expand the Water Tower Campus, it would have to buy property piecemeal, a costly and time-consuming proposition. The university's academic "blueprint for greatness," drafted in 1965, included plans for a law center costing $2 million; a social sciences building, $3 million; and residence halls, $3 million—all in the vicinity of Lewis Towers. But, as State Senator John J. Cullerton recalls, law students in 1974 took matters into their own hands and challenged the university to invest in their future.[16]

How Loyola Got a New Law School Building

By State Senator John J. Cullerton

In 1974, when I was president of the Loyola Student Bar Association, we threatened legal action against Loyola University because our law library did not meet the standards set by the Association of American Law Schools. We got the idea from students at another Jesuit law school, the University of San Francisco. They had claimed breach of contract because a law school brochure advertised that their library met AALS standards. After examining the USF complaint, we realized Loyola's 191-seat library was not in compliance and that we could actually sue our own law school.[17]

We organized a sit-in on May 1, Law Day, to show that Loyola's students could not all fit into the library in the small building at the southeast corner of Pearson and Wabash. Channel 7 reporter Jim Gibbons interviewed me at the law school—my first time ever being interviewed on television. Next, Robert T. McAllister drafted a complaint. A former editor-in-chief of the *Phoenix* (1970–71), Bob was secretary of the Loyola Student Bar Association.[18]

Unfortunately, when we called a press conference at the Daley Center to put pressure on the university, nobody showed up. It was now late spring and time for us to graduate and start studying for the bar exam. However, incoming student bar president Thomas V. McCauley had an idea. Why not contact Loyola's most famous alum, attorney Philip H. Corboy. Very quickly, Tom, Bob, and I found ourselves—not yet lawyers—sitting in the office of one of the nation's top plaintiffs' attorneys. To say the least, it was very intimidating. After reading the complaint, Mr. Corboy said, "Well, the last two paragraphs are anticipatory, but other than that, it is an excellent complaint." Bob McAllister's face was beaming. Mr. Corboy then inquired, "Do you mind if I call Father Baumhart to see if he would like a meeting before I decide to represent you and sue Loyola University?" Well, of course we said no. He picked up the phone and dialed Father Baumhart, who took the call right away. Mr. Corboy explained about lack of space in the library, our concerns about faculty salaries, and our demand to meet with the board of trustees. This had never been done before in the 100 years of Loyola's existence, but under the circumstances and with Mr. Corboy's clout, the trustees agreed that we could meet with the board's executive committee.[19]

On May 15, we laid out our case. If we agreed not to file the lawsuit against Loyola, a blue-ribbon committee would be formed to study the feasibility of building a new law school. We followed our esteemed counsel's advice. Not only did the blue-ribbon report corroborate our original complaints, but on March 18, 1977, Loyola's trustees passed a resolution that there was "no higher priority than to provide expanded, renovated, or new space" for the law school.[20]

Instead of acting as our attorney in a lawsuit against Loyola, Phil Corboy became one of the most generous benefactors for the new facility. While the original law school building on Pearson Street is now only a memory, I can't forget that my real legal practice began at Loyola even before I passed the Illinois bar.

Illinois State Senator John J. Cullerton received his BA from Loyola in 1971 and his JD in 1974.

When awarded the Medal of Excellence on February 28, 2002, Cullerton became the youngest law school alum to have achieved that distinction.

Philip H. Corboy (JD, 1949) at the Drake Hotel luncheon following the dedication of the new law school building, 1980

227

On June 12, 1978, a large crowd gathered at the southeast corner of Pearson and State streets to witness the groundbreaking for Maguire Hall, named after Father Maguire. In its seventieth year, Loyola's law school had earned a reputation as "the little giant." From its modest quarters at 41 East Pearson Street, it had educated a significant number of attorneys who had left their mark on Chicago, especially in politics, government, and the judiciary. Loyola's tradition of excellence in training students for trial work would now find physical expression in a $5 million building designed by the noted architectural firm of Graham, Anderson, Probst & White. Of special interest was the elegant courtoom with its state-of the-art videotaping system donated by Corboy in memory of his late son, Robert J. Corboy. The first two floors of the red-brick building were designated for classrooms and seminar rooms; a library was on the third and fourth floors; and faculty and administrative offices occupied the fifth floor. On dedication day, May 27, 1980, university officials acknowledged that although "people, not

Architect's rendering of Loyola's law school, 1 East Pearson Street

Among the properties demolished to make way for Maguire Hall was a favorite law school meeting place, the Emerald Isle, formerly known as the Red Garter.

bricks and mortar, make a good law school . . . there comes a point at which inadequate physical facilities can hinder the educational effort." The historic event concluded with a luncheon in the Gold Coast room of the Drake Hotel, where hundreds of law school alums gathered to celebrate.[21]

Growing Pains on the Lake Shore Campus

Most likely as a reaction to the nation's space exploration program of the preceding decade, student preferences had changed by the early 1970s; in greater numbers, they now chose to study science. Biology ranked as the most popular undergraduate course, followed by psychology and political science. An estimated one in four students planned on a career as a physician or dentist; classroom space on the Lake Shore Campus, where the science

courses were taught, was at a premium. Fortunately, Loyola could now respond to the pressure for more facilities. Although the university still did not have a large endowment, the value of its land and buildings had increased dramatically, from $10 million to more than $100 million between 1950 and 1975. It now enjoyed its fourth consecutive balanced budget and could make plans for a much-needed $3 million science building.[22]

Students and alums who turned out in great numbers for the annual Spring Carnival could not help but notice the transformation of the Lake Shore Campus that had begun in earnest with the construction of Damen Hall (1966) and Centennial Forum (1969). From the top of the Ferris wheel, they could see across the campus into the densely populated surrounding neighborhood. That there was precious room for expansion became abundantly

Spring Carnival, Lake Shore Campus, May 1972

229

▶ *continued from page 245*

Reaching Skyward on Pearson Street

While the closing of Loyola's dental school was one of the most difficult decisions in Baumhart's twenty-three-year presidency, the construction of the 25 East Pearson Street building fulfilled long-held dreams for the expansion of the Water Tower Campus. After many years of careful acquisition of property along Chicago Avenue and Pearson Street, the university finally obtained the FlapJaws' Saloon at 810 North Wabash Avenue. Among the colleges most in need of modern quarters was the business school, where enrollment had grown steadily after an MBA program was established in 1966. It was time to think big, and the architectural firm of Holabird & Root did just that with a sixteen-story limestone-and-glass skyscraper. Not only did this facility provide much-needed space for classrooms, libraries, and offices, but its spectacular Kasbeer Hall evoked the feeling of "a cathedral in the sky."

Architectural drawing by the firm of Holabird & Root for Loyola's 275-foot skyscraper at 25 East Pearson, dedicated on June 3, 1994

FlapJaws' Saloon, 810 North Wabash Avenue

The four-story ceiling of the Virgil S. Kasbeer Hall, 25 East Pearson Street, was modeled after the Cathedral Hall of University Club of Chicago at Michigan Avenue and Monroe Street.

entered the Society of Jesus right out of high school, he continued to be fascinated by economics. At Fordham University, he concentrated on mathematics and philosophy before pursuing advanced studies in sacred theology in Frankfurt, Germany. Mathematics won out, however; Father Piderit earned a master's degree in economics from Oxford University in 1974 and a doctoral degree in economics from Princeton University five years later. Although he had spent more than a decade at Fordham, Loyola's twenty-second president came to Chicago from Milwaukee, where he had been corporate vice president of Marquette University.[53]

Loyola Welcomes Its East Coast President

From the outset, Piderit resolved to strengthen the university's Jesuit and Catholic heritage, following Ignatius of Loyola's conviction "that if you search and you consistently pursue truth, it will eventually lead you to God." He asserted that at Loyola this would mean finding God in law, economics, medicine, social work, and education. One of his first efforts was to familiarize himself with Chicago, which he did by walking through the neighborhoods. Piderit commented to *Tribune* reporter Bill Jauss that exploring Chicago's changing ethnic landscape "was like walking around the world." Before long, he was joined on his exploratory walks by groups of students, all wearing distinctive Loyola T-shirts. These experiences, he told alumni, gave him an opportunity to reflect "on what Loyola University Chicago means to our city, our region, and our nation and the people it touches in so many ways every day."[54]

By the time it was dedicated on June 3, 1994, the university had a new president, John J. Piderit, S.J., whose high hopes for Loyola matched the soaring heights of 25 East Pearson.

Piderit was born in New York City in 1944, the second of twelve children of Mary and Frederick W. Piderit, a senior vice president of the Federal Reserve Bank. Although Loyola's new president

Chapter 7

Loyola's Next Century of Service

2001–2008

Continuing its dynamic transformation on four campuses, Loyola is poised to start its second century of service as a university on October 23, 2009. The dream of a residential campus on the Lake Shore has been realized with 3,600 students living in dorms and another 3,000 in apartments. Expansion continues at the medical center and plans are underway to purchase a home for the John Felice Center in Rome. The School of Education has returned to the Water Tower Campus and a new high-rise on Pearson Street houses undergraduates and graduate students who devote much of their time to part-time work or internships. The School of Communication, the first new school in decades, promises to become the second major undergraduate program at Water Tower. Loyola's bright future remains intimately connected with its mission of educating students to be ethical leaders with real-world experience and a passion for service.

View of Lake Michigan from the doors of Madonna della Strada Chapel

on the Law and Justice, and all students can take a variety
of professional skills classes that include live-client clinics,
externships, and practicums. The school, home to three nationally renowned Centers of Excellence (in health law, child and
family law, and business law) also sponsors a growing array of
international programs

Stritch School of Medicine
by John M. Lee, MD

Within recent years, a strategic
plan for the Stritch School of
Medicine (SSOM) has been completed, and a strategic planning
process for the Loyola University
Health System (LUHS) campus
has gotten underway. Because
Stritch is a Catholic Jesuit institution, service and ethics play an
important role in its mission of
education, research, and patient care. For example, a majority of
the medical students participate in some type of service program.

Recent highlights for the school include increasing the number of
first-year students—and thus the overall enrollment—in response
to a major report stating that by 2017 there will be a significant
physician shortage in the United States. The staff now includes
648 full-time faculty members, of which 81 are research intensive; 585 residents and fellows who also participate in student
education; and 119 doctoral students and 32 master's students
on the campus.

Curriculum changes have been extensive, including such initiatives as more genetics and genomic studies and a greater
number of third- and fourth-year students who rotate in a wider
variety of programs. Training and research opportunities for undergraduate medical and graduate students have increased, and
an intranet aimed at greater faculty use of Web-based teaching
and research resources will be implemented.

Students are now allowed to personalize their educational experiences to meet individual career goals. Each student is encouraged to look at his or her education as a personal challenge and
to pursue the path that can ultimately enhance his or her career,
whether it be research, health law, bioethics, public health, or
some other specific area of interest.

In general, medicine in this century will be very personalized at both
the student education and the patient care levels. Through the
genomic/molecular revolution, medicine has become increasingly
personal—now we can design a treatment for each patient based
on an individual molecular profile. Boundaries between the art and
science of medicine will continue to blur and become less distin-
guishable; therefore, our education program will have to be very dynamic and cutting edge to ensure the best training of our students.

School of Nursing
by Mary K. Walker, RN, PhD

Founded in 1935, the Marcella
Niehoff School of Nursing has educated over 6,900 nurses. It was
the first baccalaureate nursing
program and the first accredited
collegiate nursing school in Illinois.
The school initially provided p:
lic health nurses for the c'
Chicago and award fza-
science d

Not only d sound—ap-
to take c'e Campus as
Dean G heavy machin-
Damen of planning, the
pand t
of ser
divisi
Scie
do
fro
also
Besid
well-qua
bachelor
The gradu nit
seventeen
World Rep(
all graduate
the Niehoff
in the count

 us

ig began to
r Mundelein
January 2005,
igned by the firm of
uenz provided Loyola
a state-of-the art facility.
few months, there was more
ws: the opening of Regis Hall
...ntory on Winthrop Avenue just south
of Devon.

An institutional self-study prepared
for the North Central Association of Colleges and Schools in 2005 captured the
renewed sense of Loyola's identity and
mission. "We are a good university moving deliberately and in a focused way
toward greatness," claimed the report, acknowledging that this Chicago institution
was not about to change its core values.
There was no question that Loyola's student body had become much more diverse
than it was when the school was founded
in 1870: it was now coeducational and
welcomed young men and women of all
faiths. Moreover, the university remained
unapologetically Jesuit and Catholic and
promised its students that during the
years they spent at Loyola, they would be
prepared to lead extraordinary lives that
reflected "attention to virtue, justice, and
professional excellence."[7]

Another sign of Loyola's belief in its
urban mission was the relocation of the
School of Education from the Wilmette

currently boasts eighty-two graduates, and in 1995, the school added non-nursing programs in health systems management and dietetics and recently added a master's program in dietetics. It is also offering opportunities for students at all levels to explore global health issues.

charism of seeing God in all things and the university's promise to prepare people to lead extraordinary lives.

School of Social Work
by Jack Wall, PhD

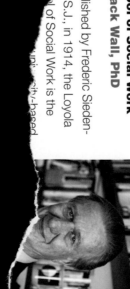

Established by Frederic Siedenburg, S.J., in 1914, the Loyola
... of Social Work is the
... ...ity-based

titute of Pastoral
ies

ert A. Ludwig, PhD

...e of Pastoral Studies,
...tion during the
...n Council, has
...for ministry in
...Chicago, the
...the inter-
...tional
...rn-
...mation. Son

Quinlan Life Sciences buildir
rise just west of the forme
skyscraper. Dedicated in
the modern facility des
Solomon Cordwell P
students with
Within just a
good ne
dorr

oc-
tal
ns
he
d,
d-
e
e

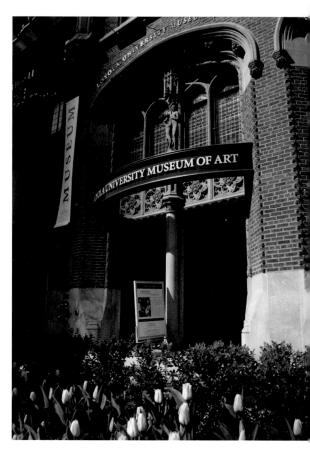

Loyola University Museum of Art, 820 North Michigan Avenue, permanent home of the Martin D'Arcy collection of Medieval, Renaissance, and Baroque art

campus to the Water Tower Campus in 2002. The sale of the Mallinckrodt campus provided Loyola with much-needed revenue and the resources to begin planning for new programs. In 1979, Loyola had become the first Jesuit institution of higher learning in the nation to establish a multidisciplinary women's studies program. The university's commitment deepened in July 2005 with the restoration of Piper Hall, which had served for many years as the library of Mundelein College.[8]

Now housing the Ann Ida Gannon, B.V.M., Center for Women and Leadership, the distinctive white mansion on Sheridan Road includes the Women and Leadership Archives. Established in 1994, the archives collects and makes available to researchers primary source material relating to the history of women and women's organizations in Chicago and the Midwest. It also continues to preserve the history and records of Mundelein College, the last women's college in Illinois. Efforts are now under way to endow a chair honoring Sister Carolyn Farrell, B.V.M., who, as president of Mundelein College, coordinated the affiliation of Mundelein with Loyola in 1991. As founding director of the Gannon Center and its scholars program, Farrell led the $4 million restoration of Piper Hall.[9]

Another momentous event in the Fall of 2005 was the opening of the Loyola University Museum of Art (LUMA). The museum, which occupies the second and third floors of Lewis Towers at 820 North Michigan Avenue, is the permanent home of the Martin D'Arcy collection of art organized in 1969 by Donald A. Rowe, S.J., and originally housed in the Cudahy Library. Made possible through funding from the State of Illinois, LUMA has quickly joined the ranks of the city's art museums. Under the leadership of Pamela E. Ambrose, Loyola's cultural affairs director, LUMA plays a major role in introducing Chicagoans to the beauty of sacred art, a tradition that extends back to 1857 and the Jesuit parish of Holy Family.[10]

In December 2005, the university received its largest single donation to date, a commitment totaling $20 million from the Arthur Foundation and from Loyola trustee William J. Hank and his wife, Joan Los Hank. When Joan's father died, money set aside for her tuition went to pay hospital bills and the undertaker. Scholarship money enabled Joan to graduate from Loyola's School of Education in 1954. In 2007, the university named the Joan and Bill Hank Center for the Catholic Intellectual Heritage in their honor.[11]

William J. Hank and his wife, Joan Los Hank

James J. Mertz, S.J., at groundbreaking for Madonna della Strada Chapel, with architect Andrew N. Rebori behind

Interior view of Madonna della Strada Chapel renovation, 2007

New Life for a Loyola Landmark

When James J. Mertz, S.J., turned the first shovelful of ground on June 6, 1938, for Madonna della Strada Chapel, he had complete faith that it would become the spiritual center of life on the Lake Shore Campus. And it did. It succeeded in bringing together not only the students taking undergraduate classes in Rogers Park but also those from Lewis Towers. Now, nearly seventy years later, the interior of the chapel honoring Our Lady of the Way would shine with a new brilliancy.

From 2004 through 2007, a team of architects and contractors collaborated with artist Meltem Aktas and architect Marvin Herman to breathe new life and beauty into one of Loyola's most cherished buildings. How could they renovate Madonna della Strada to meet the worship needs of post–Vatican II Catholics and,

Marvin Herman, architect for the renovation of Madonna della Strada

at the same time, respect the original vision of architect Andrew Rebori and artist Melville Steinfels? A guiding principle for the team was, in the words of Aktas, to "build a bridge between the past and the contemporary."[12]

The Turkish-born artist had grown up in Mardin, a city on the border of Syria and Iraq, where she was surrounded by the gorgeous iconography of Orthodox monasteries and Muslim mosques.

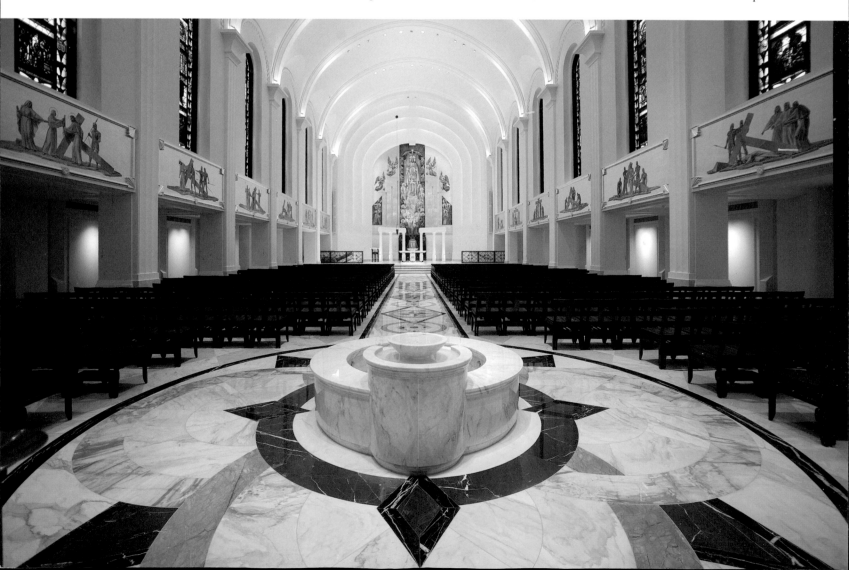

Melville Steinfels's mosaic of Madonna della Strada occupies a prominent place in the chapel on the Lake Shore Campus.

Detail of stained glass, Madonna della Strada Chapel

A resident of Chicago since 1989, Aktas studied at the Art Institute and became an iconographer, painting luminous images of saints. Now a practicing Catholic, her Byzantine-style depictions of the saints have found their way into Catholic churches and monasteries throughout the city and suburbs. In Madonna della Strada, Aktas's patience and skill in layering gold leaf on the background of the Stations of the Cross effectively brought out the richness of Steinfels's al fresco paintings, as did her use of silver leaf on the plaster frames. She also created cloisonné enamel doors for the tabernacle, working with a master craftsmen in Beijing; seven icons depicting the sacraments; the processional gospel book and candleholders; and the presider's chair.[13]

One major decision governing the Madonna della Strada renovation was to raise the new marble floor by twelve inches so that worshipers were ensured an unobstructed view of the main altar. The most significant element of the renovation, however, was Aktas's treatment of the entire west wall of the chapel as an icon. She created four new angels that flank the fresco of Jesus crowning his mother as the Queen of Heaven and Earth and of the

Society of Jesus. The result has been to illuminate—and unify—the figures Steinfels depicted in 1945.

For Lucien Roy, the university's vice president of mission and ministry, this holy place remains a powerful symbol of Loyola's commitment "to strive for the greater glory of God, both now and in the years ahead." While Madonna della Strada remains the primary worship space for Loyola's Catholic students and faculty, men and women of all religious faiths are welcome.[14]

Meltem Aktas designed the cloisonné enamel doors for the Madonna della Strada tabernacle.

Francis Cardinal George, O.M.I., archbishop of Chicago (wearing mitre), presided at the rededication of Madonna della Strada Chapel, September 13, 2007.

On February 22, 2006, ground was broken for The Clare, a project of the Franciscan Sisters of Chicago Service Corporation (FSCSC). The fifty-two-story high-rise designed by Perkins and Will architects will house Loyola's new School of Communication.

Growth on the Water Tower Campus

When Frank J. Lewis purchased the Tower Court building at 820 North Michigan Avenue in 1945, he and the Jesuit community could not have envisioned the profound changes that, over the next sixty years, would affect Loyola—and its surrounding neighborhood. From its prominent location on the city's Magnificent Mile, the university had expanded west, block by block. Ten years after the dedication of the 25 East Pearson Street building in 1994, ambitious plans got underway to reconfigure student facilities on the Water Tower Campus. In 2005, as part of the Pearson Street "flip," the business school moved to Maguire Hall and the law school relocated to the university's sixteen-story skyscraper. As had happened on the Lake Shore Campus, improvements to the urban landscape were palpable, and students were the beneficiaries. Father Garanzini has noted that it has occurred at a pace and scope one might expect in a city as dynamic and forward-thinking as Chicago.[15] On the drawing board for the business school are a new

At the groundbreaking were, left to right, Steve Bardoczi, FSCSC vice president for development; Campbell Paulfrey, sales director of The Clare; Sister Diane Collins, FSCSC provincial; Len Wycozki, FSCSC past president; and Wayne Magdziarz, vice president and chief of staff for the president's office at Loyola.

facility at the northeast corner of Pearson and State streets and plans for Maguire Hall to take on a new identity as the Water Tower Campus library.

That the university's investment in its neighborhood had finally begun to pay dividends was especially evident to older generations of Loyola students. Trustee Frank Covey remembered attending law school classes in the "new" building at 41 East Pearson in 1954. Loyola law students would now occupy the sixth through the fifteenth floors of the skyscraper at Pearson Street and Wabash Avenue.

More progress of a kind that Frederic Siedenburg, S.J., could never have imagined was being made. Years before social security was enacted, the founder of Loyola's School of Sociology had written passionately about the need for old-age pensions. Now Siedenburg Hall, home to the School of Social Work since 1980, and Marquette Center were being replaced by a new kind of residential community. Developed by the Franciscan Sisters of Chicago, the fifty-two-story high-rise known as The Clare at Water Tower would provide assisted living for men and women who wanted to live in close proximity to the city's cultural attractions. Beginning in 2009, the structure would also be home to Loyola's School of Communication, the first new school authorized by the board of trustees since 1969. Headquartered on the first three floors of The Clare, plans call for classrooms, facilities, and offices as well as a media lab where students may train for live studio production work.[16]

Perhaps the most significant change impacting the Water Tower Campus in recent years has been the construction of a residence hall at the northwest corner of Pearson and Wabash. Designed by the

The new building "located in the center of this great city is cause for family rejoicing."

View along Pearson Street, looking east toward Lewis Towers

Raymond C. Baumhart, S.J., Residence Hall and the Terry Student Center, 26 East Pearson Street, were dedicated on September 7, 2006.

architectural firm Solomon Cordwell Buenz and named for Raymond C. Baumhart, S.J., president of Loyola from 1970 to 1993, the building provides juniors, seniors, and graduate students with modern living facilities and, equally important, a convenient meeting place. Not only does the $5 million student center donated by John and Terese Terry reflect the Jesuit tradition of hospitality, but it symbolizes in brick and mortar a friendship that began in the old student center in Lewis Towers. Graduates of the class of 1959, Terese Mulkern and John Terry remembered with great fondness their student days at Loyola and wanted to replicate that experience for a new generation.

On dedication day, September 7, 2006, Terese Terry regaled the crowd gathered in front of the new residence hall, reminding them just how far the university had come in its care of students. As one of the first residents of the girls' dorm at Seneca Street and Delaware Place, she recalled that "we had one telephone for each floor. . . . We had to be in at 11 o'clock

every night or be campused. Weekends it was 1 a.m. Once a month we got to stay out until 2 a.m. But being Jesuit-educated girls we were always thinking about alternatives to accepted patterns of behavior." How to get around "hours" at the dorm? The co-eds were dropped off right at 2 a.m. on Sunday morning, but their dates returned thirty minutes later for the "3 a.m. Printers' Mass at Old Saint Pat's down on West Adams Street." Remembering the excitement of living downtown, Terry expressed hope that "this center in such a convivial atmosphere will foster many life-long friendships such as John and I have enjoyed."[17]

"Pleased and grateful" that Loyola's dorm was named in his honor, Father Baumhart thanked Father Garanzini and the trustees for the "surprising development." As a fourth-generation Chicagoan, he assured them that the new building "located in the center of this great city is cause for family rejoicing," and he thanked the men and women "who decided that this tall rectangular building should be named for this short round man."[18]

Terese Terry and Father Garanzini prepare to cut the ribbon on Loyola's new high-rise dormitory. At the right are Father Baumhart and John Terry.

Loyola's all-digital library, the Richard J. Klarchek Information Commons

Students at a computer work station in the Information Commons, 2008

Loyola Embraces the Digital Age

Loyola once again proved itself to be on the forefront of educational innovation when, on December 7, 2007, it dedicated the Klarchek Information Commons. Not only did the university open its new facility for study and research to Loyola students, but, in keeping with its deep Chicago bond, it threw open the doors to the Rogers Park-Edgewater community. In announcing that this open-door policy would become effective on January 14, 2008, Robert A. Seal, dean of Libraries, said that this extraordinary policy is "one way we can give back to our neighbors."[19]

Loyola's new center is named for Richard J. Klarchek, founder, chairman, and CEO of Capital First Realty, who committed $10 million toward the construction of the Information Commons. Klarchek regarded his gift as a way of honoring his immigrant Italian family's belief in "using one's talents and gifts to follow their dreams" and recognizing the city where he has lived and worked for the last thirty-five years.

Richard Klarchek and Father Garanzini

At the time of its dedication, the Information Commons had already received international recognition by the Leading European Architects Forum (LEAF) in London for its "best use of technology." The first Loyola building constructed according to "green standards," the library has been designated as a silver-level LEED (Leadership in Energy and Environmental Design) building.

The glass exterior of the 72,000-square foot structure designed by Solomon Cordwell Buenz (SBC) provides students with dramatic views of Lake Michigan. Yet as principal architect Devon Patterson has noted, it also reflects the university's commitment to sustainability. Built to withstand Chicago's tremendous range of temperatures, the double-skin façade of the Information Commons functions as a ventilator to reduce energy consumption by as much as fifty percent.[20]

The Information Commons, through its design and innovative use of technology, continues Loyola's tradition of embracing the modern. Its distinctive arches reflect and complement Andrew Rebori's Art Deco design for the original Cudahy Library, which broke with tradition in 1930. Chiseled in the facade are the names of leading female and male intellectuals of the Catholic Church, such as Saint Terese of Lisieux, Saint Jerome, Saint Catherine of Siena, and Saint Robert Bellarmine, S.J.

As Dean Seal told the audience gathered for the dedication, a new chapter in Loyola's history began on December 7,

2007. He emphasized that the Information Commons, as the academic nucleus of the Lake Shore Campus, illustrates the dramatic changes that have taken place in higher education "toward more interactive, collaborative learning in which libraries and technology play an increasingly important, indeed vital role." In pointing out the many progressive features of the building, Seal said Loyola's administration had responded to the students: "They wanted computers and Internet access . . . to eat and drink . . . without being hassled . . . to talk and study together with friends and . . . [to have] more online services." The center represents collaborative efforts of the library and technology sectors plus a cafe where students can meet and work together. In this way, he commented, the university is striving to meet the needs of the "so-called millenials, students who were born after the PC was invented."

Robert A. Seal, dean of Libraries

With its stupendous view of Lake Michigan, the Information Commons is the first new building on the Lake Shore Campus since 1996.

US Senator Richard Durbin at the dedication of the Loyola University Chicago Granville Police Station, 2006

Congresswoman Jan Schakowsky, Father Garanzini, and US Senator Barack Obama at Loyola's Town Hall Meeting, April 10, 2006

Loyola on the Rise

An integral part of the city of Chicago since 1870, Loyola's Jesuit mission has continued to define the university's growth and development. One of the great challenges facing Arnold Damen in 1857 was to counter the prevailing sentiment that the Society of Jesus and its schools were a threat to American life. By building Holy Family Church and St. Ignatius College on a grand scale, Damen and his congregation of working-class immigrants provided incontrovertible evidence that Catholicism was a progressive force in the city. Although at times their faith in urban life was shaken by dramatic economic and demographic changes, members of the Society of Jesus continued to dream big, and there was no talk of giving up turf or leaving the city. The *Chicago Tribune*, which had once disparaged Damen's bold plans, was forced to acknowledge the Jesuits' commitment to the city. Indeed, in 1909, the newspaper praised the new Jesuit university that was "Born in Chicago."[21]

Loyola's engagement with urban life in its many dimensions has intensified for every university president from Alexander Burrowes in 1909 to Michael J. Garanzini one hundred years later. At the turn of the twentieth century, the major challenge was to create the Lake Shore Campus and establish professional schools of law and medicine. Now the phenomenal growth of the university to three campuses has increased Loyola's presence in the metropolitan region and, with it, the responsibility to be a good neighbor.

In the 1980s, Loyola played a major role in the Rogers Park area through its Walk to Work program that enabled faculty and staff members to purchase homes. As confidence in the future of the university returned in recent years, the institution renewed its promise to enhance neighborhood life. Central to this effort was Loyola's participation in the Lakeshore Campus Advisory Council, begun in 2001 over concerns about student parties and noise. By 2004, the university had taken the lead in creating a Tax Increment Financing district (TIF) for the Devon-Sheridan area. Earmarking city funds for a private university remains controversial, but Loyola's fidelity to the neighborhood remains unshaken as does its determination to be a good neighbor. Scheduled for completion in 2011 is the renovation of the landmark skyscraper built for Mundelein College in 1930. As a performing-arts center open to the community, it will provide students and residents with cultural facilities as well as meeting space.[22]

In 2006, the university opened a police station just east of the Granville "L" stop as part of its initiative to promote safety for students and residents alike. Dedicated in memory of Eric Solorio, a Loyola University graduate and Chicago police

officer who died in the line of duty, the station represents an impressive public-private partnership between Loyola, the Chicago Police Department, and the Chicago Transit Authority.[23]

As vice president of capital planning since 2002, Wayne Magdziarz (BA, 1982 MBA, 1987) spearheaded the master plan for the Water Tower and Lake Shore campuses. Now the vice president and chief of staff to the president's office, Magdziarz also has played a critical role in the development of Loyola Station. This innovative project combines new residential and commercial units on five acres of land along Sheridan Road near Arthur Avenue. Not only does the university continue to shape the urban landscape, but its long-range plans for the redesign of the Loyola "L" station and plaza promise to enhance the quality of neighborhood life.[24]

The transformation of Loyola University Chicago has been very visible in the new construction on the Lake Shore Campus, the Water Tower Campus, and the Medical Center in Maywood, as well as new initiatives for study in Beijing and at the John Felice Center in Rome. This progress has gone hand-in-hand with renewed attention to the university's historic service to the larger community. In his report on the university in April 2008, Garanzini observed that, much like Loyola students of fifty years ago, "forty percent of our students are the first in their families to attend college." This remarkable accomplishment continues, he noted, because Loyola regards scholarship money as an investment in the future of its students and as a fundamental part of Loyola's Jesuit mission.[25]

As the largest Catholic research institution in the United States, Loyola attracts students from around the country to its programs and professional schools. But it also continues its tradition of educating Chicago's leaders in medicine, nursing, business, law, government, education, social work, and pastoral studies. Indeed, the Loyola University Heath System, under the direction of Paul K. Whelton, MD, president and CEO, is known nationally for its private teaching hospital and its commitment to research in cancer, neurological disorders, neonatology, and heart disease. The Center, in a series of bold moves, greatly expanded its facilities and services with the dedication on April 6, 2008, of a $120 million tower at its Maywood site. Besides 64 new patient rooms

The new Loyola University Hospital Tower includes twelve state-of-the-art operating rooms designed with the input of nationally-acclaimed surgeons. A new patient-centered model of care better enables Loyola health professionals to *also treat the human spirit.*

Architectural rendering of Loyola Station, a mixed-use commercial and residential development on North Sheridan Road

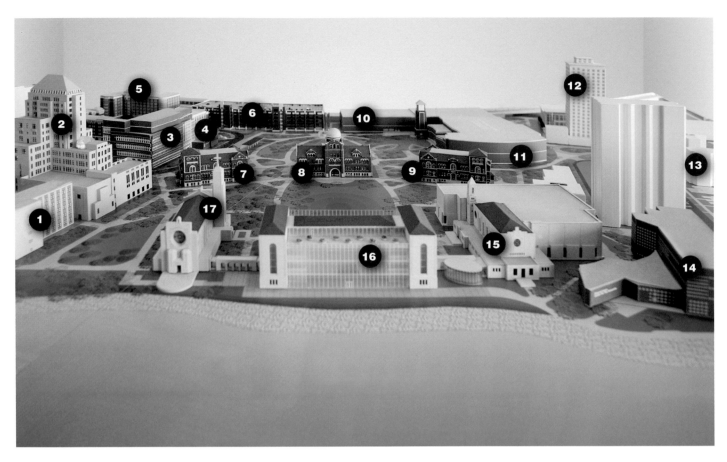

Part of Loyola's master plan for the Lake Shore Campus features a new classroom building to replace Damen Hall. Its architecture will replicate the design of Dumbach Hall.

1 Coffey Hall

2 Mundelein Center for the Fine and Performing Arts

3 Michael R. and Marilyn C. Quinlan Life Sciences Education and Research Center

4 Thomas U. Flanner Science Hall

5 Simpson Living Learning Center

6 Garage

7 Proposed classroom building

8 Cudahy Science Hall

9 Dumbach Hall

10 George Halas, Jr., Sports Center

11 Joseph J. Gentile Center

12 Centennial Forum and Mertz Hall

13 Loyola Hall

14 Edward Crown Center for the Humanities

15 Cudahy Library and addition

16 Richard J. Klarchek Information Commons

17 Madonna della Strada Chapel

and additional labs and operating rooms in Maywood, Loyola inherited 250 beds and other services through a merger with Gottlieb Memorial Hospital in Melrose Park, Illinois. The Medical Center has also created a children's health center in Oak Brook Terrace, Illinois, and twenty-two clinics in the western suburbs.[26]

The university has drawn strength and identity from its long and deep connections

Sister Mary Pat Haley, B.V.M., at the mass celebrating the 175th anniversary of her order, at Madonna della Strada, March 25, 2008

to the city, or as Father Garanzini put it, "Loyola is a product of Chicago and a gift to Chicago." Among the gifts Loyola has received is the "living endowment" provided since 1870 by hundreds of Jesuits and B.V.M.s. Their labor, often unpaid, made possible the university's continued existence and laid the foundation for its current $360 million endowment.[27]

Loyola begins its second century of service as a university with not only a renewed appreciation of its history and traditions but also an understanding of the challenges involved in preparing students to lead extraordinary lives in an ever-changing global world. Among the hopeful signs of Loyola's commitment to fund undergraduate education as well as raise the resources for a high-level research university are its strategic Centers of Excellence and newly endowed chairs. While the city of Chicago—and the university—have experienced dramatic growth and change since Arnold Damen, S.J., arrived in 1856, the Jesuit dedication to education and excellence continues.

"Loyola is a product of Chicago and a gift to Chicago."

Michael J. Garanzini, S.J.

Information Commons and Madonna della Strada at sunrise

279

Mr. Edward W. Elliott
Vice Chairman and CFO,
Franklin Enterprises, Inc.

Rev. Michael J. Garanzini, S.J.
President, Loyola University Chicago

Dr. Louis J. Glunz III
Chairman, Regis Technologies

Rev. Andrew M. Greeley
Professor of Social Science,
the University of Arizona

Mr. John F. Harris
Chief of Staff,
Office of Governor Blagojevich

Mr. Marvin Herman
Architect, Marvin Herman & Associates

Ms. Leslie S. Hindman
President, Leslie Hindman Auctioneers

Mr. Richard H. Hunt
Artist

Mr. Richard J. Klarchek
(Former Chairman)
President & CEO,
Capital First Realty Incorporated

Ms. Merrillyn Kosier
Executive Vice President,
Ariel Capital Management, LLC

Mr. John C. Lahey
Managing Principal,
Solomon Cordwell Buenz & Assoc., Inc.

Mr. Ramsey Lewis
Pianist / Composer / Radio & T.V. Host

John A. LoGiudice, MD
Retired Gastroenterologist

Mr. Steven J. Lombardo
Principal, Gibsons Restaurant Group

Mr. Richard Mancuso
President & General Manager,
Lake Forest Sports Cars, Inc.

Ms. Donna Marzano
President, DOM Foundation

Rev. Daniel G. Mayall
Pastor, Holy Name Cathedral

Mr. Barry McCabe
President Emeritus, Hometown America

Mr. Michael S. McCarthy
Chairman and CEO, Parkside
Management Services, LLC

Ms. Diane T. O'Connell
Partner, Private Investment Group

Mr. David Orr
Cook County Clerk,
Cook County Clerk's Office

Mr. Richard Parrillo
Chairman & CEO,
United Automobile Insurance Co.

Mr. Manuel Sanchez
Founder and Managing Partner,
Sanchez Daniels & Hoffman, LLP

Dr. Patricia Schostok-Reese

Rabbi Byron L. Sherwin
Vice President Emeritus,
Distinguished Service Professor,
Spertus Institute of Jewish Studies

Dr. Carolyn H. Smeltzer, RN, MSN
Partner, Advisory Healthcare Practice,
PricewaterhouseCoopers

Ms. Joan E. Steel
Senior Vice President,
Capital Guardian Trust Company

Mr. Theodore R. Tetzlaff
Partner, Ungaretti & Harris

Governor James R. Thompson
Senior Chairman, Winston & Strawn LLP

Mr. Michael A. Todman
President, Whirlpool North America
Whirlpool Corporation

Hon. Judy Baar Topinka
Former State Treasurer

Mr. Philip Wolin
Attorney, Wolin, Kelter & Rosen

Loyola University Health System

2008 Board of Directors

Mr. Frank W. Considine
Chairman and CEO (retired),
American National Can Company

Mr. William T. Divane Jr.
Chairman and CEO, Divane Bros.
Electric Co.

Mr. James C. Dowdle
Executive Vice President (retired),
Tribune Company

Mr. Thomas Fitzgerald
Managing Partner,
Winston and Strawn LLP

Rev. Daniel L. Flaherty, S.J.
Assistant for Business and Finance,
Chicago Province of the Society of Jesus

Dr. Richard Gamelli
Professor and Chairman, Department of
Surgery, Loyola University Health System

Rev. Michael J. Garanzini, S.J.
President, Loyola University Chicago

Dr. Ellen R. Gaynor
Professor, Division of Hematology/
Oncology, Loyola University
Health System

Mr. Jordan M. Hadelman
Chairman, Witt/Kieffer

Mr. Michael E. Kelly
Chairman of the Board, FBOP Corporation

Mr. Patrick J. Kelly
CEO, Resource 1

Ms. Nancy W. Knowles
President, Knowles Foundation

Mr. John C. Lahey
Managing Principal,
Solomon Cordwell Buenz & Assoc.

Mr. Michael R. Leyden
Corporate Senior Vice President (retired),
First Chicago

Dr. Terry Light
Professor and Chairman, Department of
Orthopaedic Surgery and Rehabilitation,
Loyola University Health System

Mr. Michael R. Quinlan
Chairman, Board of Trustees,
Loyola University Chicago

Dr. Steven Slogoff
Dean Emeritus, Stritch School of Medicine

Mr. Daniel J. Walsh
President, The Walsh Group

Dr. Paul K. Whelton
President and CEO,
Loyola University Health System
Vice President for the Health Sciences,
Loyola University Chicago

2008 Endowed Chairs

Academic Administration

Jesuit University Professorship

Carolyn Farrell, B.V.M., Chair in Women's Studies

College of Arts and Sciences

Edward Surtz Professorship in Medieval Literature

Arthur J. Schmitt Professorship in Philosophy

John Cardinal Cody Professorship in Theology

Helen Houlahan Rigali Professorship in Political/Social Science

Maude C. Clarke Professorship in Psychology

School of Business

Ralph Marotta Professorship in Free Enterprise

Raymond Baumhart, S.J., Chair in Business Ethics

Frank W. Considine Chair in Applied Ethics

Walter F. Mullady, Sr. Chair in Business Administration

Charles Kellstadt Professorship

John F. Smith Professorship in Finance

Marcella Niehoff School of Nursing

Marcella Niehoff Professorship

School of Law

Wing-Tat Lee Professorship in International and Comparative Law

A. Kathleen Beazley Chair in Child Law

Raymond and Mary Simon Chair in Constitutional Law

Stritch School of Medicine

William M. Scholl Professorship

Coleman Professor of Oncology

Anthony B. Traub Professorship

Michael I. English, S.J., PhD, Professor of Medical Ethics

Mary Isabelle Caestecker Professor of Obstetrics and Gynecology

Ambrose & Gladys Bowyer Professor of Surgery

Dr. Lucian & Irene Dyba Matusak Professor of Ophthalmology

Robert J. Freeark, MD, Professor of Surgery

Dr. John P. Mulcahy Professor of Ophthalmology

Dr. John P. & Therese E. Mulcahy Professor of Ophthalmology

Ronald McDonald House Charities Endowed Professorship in Pediatric Oncology

John P. Igini, MD, Professor of Surgery

William B. Knapp, MD, Professor of Medicine & Physiology

Albert J. and Claire R. Speh Endowed Chair in Urology

Robert C. Flanigan, MD, Professor of Urology

John W. Clarke Professor of Medicine

Joseph R. & Louise Ada Jarabak Chair

Maude C. Clarke Professor of Pediatrics

Helen M. & Raymond M. "Burley" Galvin Professorial Chair in Pathology

George M. Eisenberg Professor of Cardiovascular Sciences

James R. DePauw Professor of Physiology

Rolf and Merian Gunnar Professorship in Medicine (Cardiology)

John M. Krasa Professor of Ophthalmology

Notes

Frequently Used Abbreviations

ARSI Archivum Romanum Societatis Iesu

BAUMHART Raymond C. Baumhart, S.J. papers, LUCA

CMM Consultors' Meeting Minutes, 1891-1930, LUCA

CT Chicago Tribune

Diarium Vice-president's diary, LUCA

HUSSEY James T. Hussey, S.J. papers

KANE William T. Kane, S.J. papers

LN Loyola News

LUCA Loyola University Chicago Archives

MAGUIRE James F. Maguire, S.J. papers

MJA Midwest Jesuit Archives

NW New World

SIC St. Ignatius Collegian, LUCA

SICP St. Ignatius College Prep

WILSON Samuel Knox Wilson papers

WL Woodstock Letters

Chapter 1

1. *Chicago Times*, Aug. 9, 1856; *Daily Chicago Times*, Aug. 3, 8, 9, 10, 12, 13, 1856.

2. A. T. Andreas, *History of Chicago* (Chicago: A. T. Andreas Company, 1884, 2:262, 580; "Progress of Chicago," *Chicago Tribune* (hereafter cited as *CT*), January 4, 1856; *Chicago Daily Journal*, May 27, 1857.

3. *New World*, April 14, 1900 (hereafter cited as *NW*); Van de Velde to Archbishop John B. Purcell, January 10, 1849, cited by Gilbert J. Garraghan, S.J., *The Jesuits of the Middle West* (New York: America Press, 1938), 2:129.

4. Van de Velde's first pastoral, June 4, 1849, in James J. McGovern, ed., *Souvenir of the Silver Jubilee in the Episcopacy of His Grace the Most Rev. Patrick Augustine Feehan, Archbishop of Chicago* (Chicago: Privately printed, 1891): 106; itinerary, 102-3.

5. D. J. Riordan, "University of St. Mary of the Lake," *Illinois Catholic Historical Review 2*, no. 2 (October 1919): 138, 143.

6. *Life of Mary Monholland* (Chicago: J. S. Hyland & Company, 1894): 43; Garraghan, *Jesuits*, 2:133

7. Van de Velde to Archbishop Blanc, February 24, 1853, and to Rev. Stephen Rousellon, May 18, 1853, quoted in Garraghan, *Jesuits*, 2:131.

8. Garraghan, *Jesuits*, 2:130

9. *CT*, March 20, 1856; *Daily Chicago Times*, August 28, 1856.

10. M. Dillon quoted in Garraghan, "Beginnings of the Holy Family Parish, Chicago," *Illinois Catholic Historical Review* (April 1919): 438-39; Dillon to Arnold Damen, S.J., September 8, 1856, Midwest Jesuit Archives (hereafter cited as MJA); Garraghan, *Jesuits*, 3:116.

11. Philip A. Conley to Damen, September 4, 5, 25, 1856; December 8, 1856, MJA; "Appointments by the Senate," *CT*, August 15, 1856; "Philip Conley," *CT*, December 19, 1884.

12. Andreas, 1:297-299; *Daily Chicago Times*, August 17, 1856.

13. Anthony O'Regan to Damen, September 16, 1856, MJA.

14. O'Regan to Damen, October 2, 1856, MJA; John Etheridge, S.J., to Father Provincial, October 30, 1856, MJA; Peter Beckx, S.J. to John Druyts, S.J., January 7, 1857, MJA; translation by Raymond J. Heisler, St. Ignatius College Prep (hereafter cited as SICP).

15. Andreas, 1:159; Walter Nugent, "Demography," *The Encyclopedia of Chicago*, eds. James R. Grossman, Ann Durkin Keating, Janice L. Reiff (Chicago and London: University of Chicago Press, 2004): 233.

16. Translation of Damen excerpt, MJA, by Monique and John Brinkman; Garraghan, *Jesuits*, 2:78; Joseph P. Conroy, S.J., *Arnold Damen, S.J.: A Chapter in the Making of Chicago* (New York: Benziger Brothers, 1930): 25-31, 46.

17. O'Regan to Damen, September 16, 1856; October 2, 1856, MJA; Damen to Druyts, March 10, 1857, MJA; *CT*, "Washington's Birthday," February 22, 1856; "The Execution of Jackson To-Day," June 19, 1857; "Old Bull's Head Tavern," January 30, 1887.

18. Damen to Druyts, March 10, 1857, MJA.

19. O'Regan to Damen, March 21, 1857, MJA; Vice-provincial's instructions on occasion of Fr. Damen's going to Chicago, n.d., MJA; Damen to Joseph A. Miller, May 8, 1857, MJA; Damen to Druyts, May 27, 1857, MJA.

20. *Chicago Daily Democratic Press, Chicago Daily Journal*, May 19, 1857; *CT* editorial, "Proposals for a Jesuit College," May 25, 1857. See also, *CT*, "Riots and Riot Makers," December 23, 1853; "Catholicism and Slavery," February 11, 1856; and "An Irish Relief Society, November 23, 1857.

21. *CT*, December 23, 1853; "Irish Missions in Ireland and America," *Northwestern Christian Advocate*, June 3, 1857.

22. *Daily Chicago Times*, August 23, 1857; Robert Emmett Curran, *The Bicentennial History of Georgetown University* (Washington, D.C.: Georgetown University Press, 1993),1:270.

23. "The New Church of St. Ignatius," *Baltimore Catholic Mirror*, August 23, 1856.

24. *CT*, December 29, 1857.

25. *Daily Chicago Times*, August 23, 1857; December 24,1857; *Chicago Daily Democratic Press*, August 25, 1857; Damen to Druyts, October 7, 1857; June 6, 16, 1858, MJA.

26. The cornerstone of St. Patrick's Cathedral was laid on August 15, 1858. When work stopped in 1860, the walls had risen less than eighteen feet high. Katherine Burton, *The Dream Lives Forever: The Story of St. Patrick's Cathedral* (Dublin: Clonmore and Reynolds LTD, 1962):35-39.

27. James W. Sheahan, "Church of the Holy Family," in Otto Jevne and Peter M. Almini, *Chicago Illustrated* (Chicago: Jevne & Almini, 1866).

28. "Holy Family Church Alight," *CT*, March 13, 1899.

29. "Church of the Holy Family," *Chicago Republican*, October 16, 1865; *CT*, March 5, 13, 1899. According to his contract with Anton Buscher, February 1, 1863, Damen "reserved the right to determine what the statues shall represent." Article of agreement, SICP Archives.

30. For biographical information on Anton and Sebastian Buscher and Louis Wisner, see chapter 15, "The Church Beautiful," in Bro. Thomas M. Mulkerins, S.J., *Holy Family Parish Chicago: Priests and People* (Chicago: Universal Press, 1923):282–315.

31. *CT*, October 11, 21, 1870; concert program in Mulkerins, *History of Holy Family*: 98, 100; Bernard Mulaire, "David and his harp: An historic Canadian organ case in Chicago," *Canadian Collector: a Journal of Antiques and Fine Arts* 19, no. 3 (May-July 1984): 44-48; September 14, 1869 invoice declaration and November 29, 1870 testimonial regarding $3,690 in gold duties, SICP Archives.

32. Damen to Beckx, August 1858, Pr. *Missouriana* 1006 xxv I, lv, lvv, Archivum Romanum Societatis Iesu (hereafter cited as ARSI).

33. Damen to Beckx, May 11, 1859, cited in Garraghan, *Jesuits*, 3:409; Damen to Druyts, June 1, 1859 and Damen to Beckx, June 14, 1859, MJA; Garraghan 3:399 identified Graham as granddaughter of millionaire John Mullanphy.

34. Daniel Bluestone, *Constructing Chicago* (New Haven and London:Yale University Press, 1991):65–67; "An Irish Relief Society," *CT*, November 23, 1857.

35. "John M. Van Osdel," in David Ward Wood, *Chicago and Its Distinguished Citizens* (Chicago: M. George & company, 1881): 46; "Death of Chicago's First Architect," *Inland Architect* (January 1892): 69-70; January 16, 1860 contract between Arnold Damen and Robert A. Carse, SICP Archives; Damen to Druyts, November 15, 1859, MJA;

36. "Brother Francis A. Heilers," *Woodstock Letters* (hereafter cited as *WL*, (March 1892): 123-5; Damen to Druyts, November 15, 1859, MJA.

37. Louise Callan, *The Society of the Sacred Heart in North America* (New York: Longmans, Green & Co., 1937): 625-632; Nikola Baumgarten, "Education and Democracy in Frontier St. Louis: The Society of the Sacred Heart," *History of Education Quarterly* 34, no. 2 (Summer 1994): 171–92; *CT*, January 4, 1860, July 17, 1860; *Chicago Daily Journal*, August 23, 1860.

38. The exterior of Holy Family was designed by the architectural firm of Dillenburg & Zucher and the interior was completed by John Van Osdel. See, "What our Builders are Doing," *CT*, July 17, 1860; *Chicago Daily Democrat*, August 11, 1860; "The Church of the Holy Family," *CT*, August 27, 1860. See also *Freeman's Journal* and *Record* accounts published in the *Baltimore Catholic Mirror*, September 15, 1860.

39. Damen to Druyts, November 7, 1859; December 28, 1859, MJA; Damen to Beckx, September 25, 1861 and June 12, 1863, quoted by Conroy, 216–19; 224–28; John Gilmary Shea to Peter DeSmet, S.J. quoted in Conroy, 233; account of New York mission, 233–34.

40. Damen statement on missions, n.d, MJA; Garraghan, *Jesuits*, 3:417.

41. "University of St. Mary's of the Lake," *CT*, May 26, 1863; Riordan, *Illinois Catholic Historical Review* (1919):149–53.

42. *CT*, May 11, 1864; June 13, 1864 contract between Arnold Damen and Robert S. Moss, SICP Archives; *CT*, January 2, 1865.

43. Damen to Beckx, September 25, 1861, quoted in Conroy, 218.

44. Arnold Damen, S.J., to T. J. Donaghoe, quoted in Mulkerins, *History of Holy Family*: 423.

45. For biographical sketches of Hurley and Kane see Skerrett, "The Irish of Chicago's Hull-House Neighborhood," in *New Perspectives on the Irish Diaspora*, ed. Charles Fanning (Carbondale: Southern Illinois University Press, 2000).

46. Ad for Mundelein College, in *NW*, August 8, 1930; Loyola University Commencement program, June 7, 1933, Loyola University Chicago Archives (hereafter cited as LUCA).

47. Charles J. Coppens,S.J., "Father Coppens' Recollections of Notable Pioneers," *Illinois Catholic Historical Review* (April 1920):393–94; quote from Sister Mary Scholastica McLaughlin, B.V.M., "Historical Notes of Our Missions in Chicago," Mount Carmel Archives of the Sisters of Charity of the Blessed Virgin Mary, Dubuque, Iowa.

48. Garraghan, 3:417–18; Keller to Beckx, September 24, 1867, Pr. Missouriani 1007 I 41v, ARSI.

49. 1871 Edwards' Annual Director [sic]; *1874-75 Lakeside Annual Directory*; Keller to Beckx, September 24, 1867, ARSI; Garraghan, *Jesuits*, 3:418.

50. Garraghan, *Jesuits*, 3:418-19; Keller to Beckx, February 16, 1868, Pr. Missouriani 1007 I 48, 1007 I 48v, ARSI; translation from Latin by Raymond J. Heisler, SICP; Coosemans to Beckx, February 20, 1868, Pr. Missouriani 1007 I 49, 1007 I 49v, ARSI, translation by Michael P. Barrett.

51. "Another Catholic College," *Chicago Evening Journal*, October 17, 1868.

52. *Chicago Times*, October 17, 1868; *Land Owner* (July 1869):17.

53. Joseph J. Roubik, S.J., "History of Loyola at Seventy," mss. LUCA; Garraghan, *Jesuits*, 2:128 and 3:419–20; Coosemans to Beckx, September 5, 1869, Pr. Missouriana 1007 I 74, 1007 I 74v, 1007 I 74vv, ARSI.

54. Coosemans to Beckx, January 8, 1870, Pr. Missouriana 1007,I 79v, ARSI; "Letter from Chicago," August 12, 1870, in *Baltimore Catholic Mirror*, August 20, 1870.

55. Damen to Druyts, June 15, 1870, MJA; "Common Council," *Chicago Times*, July 26, 1870; Mulkerins, *Holy Family*, 772–74.

56. On St. Louis philanthropists, Garraghan, *Jesuits*, 3:444, and William B. Faherty, S.J., *Better the Dream: Saint Louis University & Community* (St. Louis: St. Louis University, 1968): 153; "The Fair at St. Ignatius College," *CT*, August 26, 1870, August 30, 1870; *Chicago Republican*, September 2, 1870; William E. Rollo biography in A. N. Waterman, *Historical Review of Chicago and Cook County* (Chicago: Lewis Publishing Company, 1908), 3:1267–69; J. R. Payson biography, *CT*, November 23, 1871, April 27, 1872.

57. *CT*, "The New Jesuit College on West Twelfth Street," August 26, 1870. The *Catalog of St.Ignatius College, 1870-1871*, lists Charles Comiskey in the preparatory class, LUCA; April 19, 1872 entry on baseball, *Diarium St. Ignatius College*, 1870-1874 (hereafter cited as *Diarium*). "First Story of Life Told By Comiskey," *Chicago Daily News*, April 15, 1916.

58. September 5, 1870 and October 29, 1870, *Diarium*; ad for St. Ignatius College, *CT*, August 28, 1870; "The Jesuits," *Chicago Times*, September 4, 1870; "The New Jesuit College in Chicago, Illinois," reprinted from *Chicago Republican* in *New York Tablet*, September 17, 1870.

59. *Catalog,1870-1871*, LUCA.

60. James O'Toole, *Passing for White: Race Religion, and the Healy Family, 1820–1920* (Amherst and Boston: U of Massachusetts Press, 2002): 157; "First Annual Exhibition of St. Ignatius College, June 29, 1871," *Catalog,1870-1871*; Ambrose Goulet later founded St. Louis parish in Chicago.

61. Lester F. Goodchild table 3 "St. Ignatius College Spring Headcount Enrollment Data, 1870–1909," in "The Mission of the Catholic University in the Midwest, 1842-1980: A Comparative Case Study of the Effects of Strategic Policy Decisions Upon the Mission of the University of Notre Dame, Loyola University Chicago, and DePaul University," Ph.D. dissertation, University of Chicago (June 1986), 1:190–91; quote from *CT*, August 26, 1870.

62. Karen Sawislak, "Fire of 1871," *Encyclopedia of Chicago*, 297; "The Cradle and the Grave of the Fire," *New York Tribune*, October 17, 1871; Pulpit announcement, Holy Family Church, Feast of the Circumcision, January 1, 1872, LUCA.

63. "How It Originated," *CT*, October 20, 1871; "The Burning of Chicago," *London Graphic* (October 21, 1870): 390; Chicago in Ashes," *Harper's Weekly*, October 28, 1871.

64. *London Graphic* (December 2, 1871): 531;" Incendie De Chicago," *L'Illustration* (November 4, 1871): 304.

65. Henry Ward Beecher, "The Lecture-Room Talk," *Christian Union* (October 18, 1871): 245.

66. "The Sufferers in Chicago," *Baltimore Catholic Mirror* (October 21, 1871):4; "Catholic Contributions for Chicago Sufferers, *New York Times*, October 23, 1871.

67. "Mrs. O'Leary Is Dead," *CT*, July 4, 1895; "Mrs. O'Leary's Cow, *CT*, July 7, 1895; "Chicago: Death of a Benefactress of the Arts," *American Architect and Building*

News (July 27, 1895): 37; "Infamous Cow Gets a Shot at Absolution," *New York Times* (October 7, 1997).

68. "Relief Items," *CT*, December 14, 1871; *The Lettres Annuelles, 1869–1871*, Society of the Sacred Heart, National Archives, St. Louis, MO.; "The Church in Chicago, *Baltimore Catholic Mirror*, October 21, 1871.

69. Holy Family Parish pulpit announcement, October 22, 1871; "Special Protection of Our College and Parish During the 'Chicago Fire,'" *WL* (1872): 32, 34, 36.

70. "The Church in Chicago," *Baltimore Catholic Mirror*, (October 21, 1871): 4.

71. February 5, 1873, *Diarium*; Charles Coppens, S.J., "A Visit to Chicago," *WL* (September 1873): 207; April 1, 1873, *Diarium*; "Our Great Educational Institutions," *Land Owner* (April 1873): 65; August 26, 30, 1873; September 8, 1873, *Diarium*.

72. October 21, 1874, *Diarium*.

73. "Conferring of Degrees," June 28, 1876, *Catalog, 1875-1876*, LUCA. Enrollment at Northwestern University in 1875–76 was 1098; table 1-1, Harold F. Williamson and Payson S. Wild, *Northwestern University: A History*, 1850–75 (Evanston, Illinois: Northwestern University, 1976): 19; "Educational," *CT*, June 27, 1873; Coppens, 207-8; *Chicago Times*, June 22, 1873.

74. "Memorabilia," Carter H. Harrison Papers, series 8, box 16, Newberry Library; Carter Harrison, *Stormy Years* (Indianapolis and NY: Bobbs-Merrill Company, 1935): 29–33. The earliest use of "Loyola" is found in September 24, 1880 minutes of Chrysostomian Society, LUCA. See also Chrysostomian reports, box 3, June 11, 1879; January 24, 1880; and February 11, 1880.

75. "Captain Patrick Finn," *History of the Great Lakes* (Chicago: J. H. Beers & Co., 1899), 2: 312–13; "Mrs. Catherine Finn is Dead," *Chicago Tribune*, June 13, 1898; "Captain Patrick Finn," *CT*, May 27, 1907; "Father Thomas B. Finn," *Province News-Letter* (May 15, 1920): 32.

76. Testimony of Mayor Carter Harrison, I, August 2, 1886, in People of the State of Illinois vs. August Spies et al, in Carl Smith, *The Dramas of Haymarket*, http://www.chicagohistory.org/hadc/transcript/volume1/000-050/L026-052.htm

77. "The Bomb's Awful Work," *CT*, May 13, 1886; "A Dark Day for the Reds," *CT*, July 21, 1886; "Chicago's Wounded Policemen," *New York Times*, June 17, 1886.

78. Carter H. Harrison, "Proclamation to the People of Chicago," May 5, 1886, Chicago History Museum.

79. "Five Good Men Gone," *Chicago Inter Ocean*, May 10, 1886; "Another Victim Dead," *Chicago Times*, May 10, 1886; Cook County Coroner's Office, "Sheahan" entry by Rev. Florentine Boudreaux, S.J., sacramental record, Holy Family Church, May 12, 1886; "Officer Sheehan's Funeral, *CT*, May 13, 1886; "Certificate of Death of Michael Sheehan," May 14, 1886.

80. "Nooses for the Reds," *CT*, August 20, 1886; "Dropped to Eternity," *CT*, November 12, 1886.

81. "Case of the Anarchists Stated," *CT*, June 27, 1893.

82. "Heroism Commemorated," *CT*, May 31, 1889.

83. "Corner-Stone of the Anarchist Monument to be Laid at Waldheim," *CT*, November 6, 1892; "Unveil the Statue," *CT*, June 26, 1893.

84. Hal Dardick, "Haymarket riot not forgotten," *CT*, September 15, 2004.

85. Christopher Thale, "Haymarket and May Day," *Encyclopedia of Chicago*, 377.

86. May 5, 1886, *Diarium*; "Scientific Circle of St. Ignatius College," *Catalog, 1885-1886*.

87. "Prospectus of the Jesuit Collegiate School on the North Side," 1888, LUCA; "*Missouri Province*," *WL* (1888): 403; biographical information on Fitzgerald in Garraghan, *Jesuits*, 3:429-30.

88. *WL* (1890):441;E. A. Higgins to Joseph Grimmelsman, S.J., May 10, 1902, MJA.

89. "Father Damen's Golden Jubilee," *WL* (March 1888): 29-34; "Their Tongues Loosened," *CT*, November 20, 1887; "The Golden Jubilee," November 21, 1887; "Her Golden Jubilee," *CT*, December 14, 1894.

90. Damen Avenue Committee, "In Re Damen Avenue," SICP Archives.

91. "Aldermen Can't Decide Robey-Damen Argument," *Chicago Daily News*, July 12, 1927; "Implore Council to Restore Name of Robey Street," *CT*, July 13, 1927.

92. "Damen Avenue Got Its Name After Bitter Contest," *CT*, August 11, 1929; "Robey Street," *CT*, December 27, 1927; "Street Names and Traditions," *CT*, January 1, 1928; "Value in a Name," *CT*, December 2, 1927; "Proposals for a Jesuit College," *CT*, May 25, 1857; "P.O. Clerks Find Mail Still Sent to Robey Street," *CT*, December 28, 1927.

93. *Consultors' Meeting Minutes, 1891–1930* (hereafter cited as *CMM*), March 28, 1893; April 24, 1895; April 29, 1895.

94. *Chicago Inter Ocean*, June 24, 25, 1895; *CT*, June 23, 25, 1895; menu from Silver Jubilee of St. Ignatius College, June 25, 1895, Chicago History Museum.

Chapter 2

1. *Chicago Journal*, December 12, 1895.

2. *CT*, December 26, 1895; "Mobbed By Women," *Chicago Evening Journal*, December 26, 1895.

3. Residents of Hull-House, *Hull-House Maps and Papers* with a new introduction by Rima Lunin Schultz (Urbana: University of Illinois Press, 2007): 60; "Sacred Heart," *CT*, September 30, 1879.

4. "Exempt from Taxation," *Chicago Tribune*, May 11, 1890; Carroll D. Wright, *The Slums of Baltimore, Chicago, New York, and Philadelphia* (1894, repr. New York: Arno Press, 1970): Introduction, 13. *CT*, September 11, 1898; "Buy Much for a Penny," *CT*, September 20, 1896.

5. *Chicago Inter Ocean*, June 25, 1895. For biographical information on Thomas Brenan and Gen. George W. Smith see Suellen Hoy, *Good Hearts: Catholic Sisters in Chicago's Past* (Urbana: University of Illinois Press, 2006): 180 n. 61.

6. *The Bench and Bar of Chicago: Biographical Sketches* (Chicago: American Biographical Publishing Co.,n.d.): 605-6; *Chicago Journal*, August 17, 1899; *Chicago Record*, August 17, 1899; *CT*, August 18, 1899; *NW*, August 26, 1899.

7. "Gives One Million," *CT*, December 28, 1892; "New College Buildings, *Harper's Weekly* (July 28, 1894):711.

8. "Demonstration of X Ray's Powers," *CT*, February 24, 1896; "X Rays for Diamonds," *CT*, March 9, 1896; *NW*, February 29, 1896; R. A. Millikan, "Recent Discoveries in Radiation and Their Significance," *Popular Science Monthly* (April 1904): 481–99; Biography of Wilhelm Conrad Roentgen, http://nobelprize.org/nobel_prizes/physics/laureates/1901/rontgen-bio.html; Catalog, 1895–96; bio information on William N. Brown in Mulkerins, *Holy Family*, 187.

9. *Catalog, 1878-79*, LUCA.

10. "St. Ignatius College Notes," *NW*, December 14, 1895.

11. Chrysostomian Society, box 3, November 11, 1896; October 20, 1897, LUCA.

12. *Catalog, 1897–1898*:6; *Catalog, 1895-95*:14, LUCA.

13. "Educational Statistics," *Statistical Abstract of the United States, 1900* (Washington, D.C.: Government Printing Office, 1901): 411-412.

14. Sister Mary Innocenta Montay, C.S.S.F., "The History of Catholic Secondary Education in the Archdiocese of Chicago (Washington, D.C.: Catholic University of America Press, 1953): 85-87; James W. Sanders, *Education of An Urban Minority: Catholics in Chicago, 1833–1965* (New York: Oxford University Press, 1977): 130-38.

15. May 5, 1897, *Diarium*; George J. Zahringer, "Chats With our Alumni," *Loyola Magazine* (November 1912): 13–16. For information on SIC v Marquette game see *CT*, Nov. 20, 21, 1902.

16. For Philip J. Gleason's agreement with Midwest Jesuit historian Gilbert J. Garraghan see, *Contending With Modernity: Catholic Higher Education in the Twentieth Century* (NY: Oxford Press, 1995):54; See also suggestions on curriculum changes made by St. Ignatius College professors, May 8, 1887, MJA.

17. J. Haven Richards to Timothy Brosnahan, S.J., March 16, 1898, quoted in Kathleen Maloney, *Catholic Higher Education in Protestant America* (Baltimore: Johns Hopkins University Press, 2003): 76; Charles Eliot to W. G. Read Mullan, S.J., January 17, 1900, cited by Maloney, 81.

18. "Aims at Diploma Mills," *CT*, January 27, 1899; "McGoorty Opposes Measure," *CT*, January 28, 1899; "S.H. Harris Scores the Mayor," *CT*, February 8, 1899.

19. "Educators in Session," *Chicago Inter Ocean*, April 13, 1899; "For Uniform Study," *CT*, April 13, 1899; Austin O'Malley, "Catholic Higher Education in the United States," *Catholic World* 67 (June 1898): 289–304; "Ends With Big Meeting," *Chicago Chronicle*, April 14, 1899; "End College Talk," *Chicago Inter Ocean*, April 14, 1899; "Catholic Session Ends," *CT*, April 14, 1899.

20. "College Orators Are Heard," *CT*, April 15, 1899.

21. "St. Ignatius Gymnasium Dedicated," *CT*, March 21, 1902; statistics from *St. Ignatius Catalog, 1900–1901*: 81; "Students Present a Play," *CT*, December 29, 1899; Commencement program, June 27, 1900, *Catalog, 1899–1900*: 123; "Degree for the Mayor," *CT*, June 28, 1900; "To Stage 'The Black Arrow'," *CT*, December 16, 1900; Mary Agnes Amberg, *Madonna Center*, ed. George A. Lane, S.J. (Chicago: Loyola University Press, 1976):40-54.

22. "Class to Leave St. Ignatius," *CT*, June 25, 1900. Mac Veagh served as Secretary of the Treasury from 1909 to 1913; MacVeagh and Warvelle entries, *Who's Who in Chicago*, (Chicago: A. N. Marquis & Company, 1926): 554, 908.

23. Biographical information on Ponziglioni in Garraghan, *Jesuits*, 2:590-93.

24. "Priest Fifty Years," *CT*, March 20, 1898; "Rev. Paul M. Ponziglioni, S.J.," *Catalog, 1899–1900*: 60; *CMM*, February 3, 1892, March 10, 1892.

25. Madonna Center:48; Edmund M. Dunne, *Memoirs of Zi Pre'* (St. Louis: B. Herder, 1914).

26. "Will Build Mission Church," *CT*, October 23, 1898; "Catholic Work for Children in Little Italy," *NW*, October 8, 1915; See also Deborah A. Skok, *More than Neighbors: Catholic Settlements and Day Nurseries in Chicago, 1893-1930* (DeKalb,Ill.: Northern Illinois University Press, 2007): 65-90.

27. "Italian Church Dedicated," *NW*, December 2, 1899.

28. "Give a Play and Dance to Aid Italian Mission," *CT*, April 25, 1911; Mary Agnes Amberg honorary doctor of laws degree, June 6, 1928, William T. Kane, S.J. (hereafter cited as KANE), box 16,LUCA.

29. Florence Scala, "The New Site for the U. of I. Campus," *CT*, February 15, 1961; "Resume City Hall Sit-In; Daley and Women Clash," *CT*, October 16, 1962; "U. of I. Campus Site Gets O.K. of Plan Board," *CT*, April 7, 1961; Emma Graves Fitzsimmons, "'Heroine' led fight against City Hall in '60s," *CT*, August 29, 2007.

30. *CMM*, January 8, 1896, October 28, 1899, LUCA; *CT*, October 6, 1900; James Cardinal Gibbons' quote on banner schools of America, Mulkerins, *Holy Family*, 186.

31. *CMM*, August 29, 1899; Robert Hunter, *Tenement Conditions in Chicago* (Chicago: City Homes Association, 1901): 98, 94, 112, 114; "Tuberculosis in the Jewish District of Chicago," *Journal of the American Medical Association*, August 6, 1904.

32. E. A. Higgins, S.J. to Joseph Grimmelsman, S.J., May 10, 1902, MJA.

33. *CMM*, March 7, 1902; Julia Sniderman Bachrach, *The City in a Garden* (Santa Fe, New Mexico: The Center for American Places, Inc., 2001), Charles French, ed., *Biographical History of the American Irish in Chicago* (Chicago and New York: American Biographical Publishing Co., 1897): 687–689; "John F. Cremin," *CT*, January 7, 1899.

34. *CMM*, March 7, 1902.

35. John F. X. Tehan, S.J. to Grimmelsman, March 19, 1902, MJA; Edward Gleeson, S.J., to Grimmelsman, March 22, 1902, MJA.

36. Francis Cassilly, S.J. to Grimmelsman, March 23, 1902, MJA.

37. A. K. Meyer to Grimmelsman, April 5, 1902, MJA; J. F. Neenan, S.J., to Grimmelsman, April 6, 1902, MJA.

38. Henry J. Dumbach, S.J. to Grimmelsman, April 16, 1902, MJA; John P. Walsh, *"The Catholic Church in Chicago and Problems of an Urban Society: 1893–1915,"* Ph.D. diss., University of Chicago, 1948):11–13.

39. Marshall Boarman, S.J. to Grimmelsman, May 26, 1902 and Dumbach to Grimmelsman, May 27, 1902, MJA;

Biographical information on Francis S. Henneberry in *SIC* (November 1905):43.

40. "School Praised by Quigley," *CT*, March 25, 1903; *SIC* (April 1903):35–36; *CMM*, May 14, 1903, Dec. 10, 1903.

41. Draft of letter, March 21, 1904, in *CMM*.

42. Dumbach to Archbishop James E. Quigley, n.d., MJA.

43. Dumbach to Grimmelsman, August 26, 1904, MJA.

44. Dumbach to Archbishop Quigley, June 29, 1905,MJA.

45. Quigley to Dumbach, July 1, 1905, LUCA; Dumbach to Grimmelsman, July 10, 1905, MJA.

46. *CMM*, September 19, 1905, October 20, 1905.

47. *CMM*, October 20, 1905.

48. Archbishop Quigley to Dumbach, November 1, 1905, MJA; Dumbach to Grimmelsman, November 1, 1905, LUCA.

49. "Jesuits Plan School," *Chicago Record-Herald*, November 23, 1905; *CMM*, November 24, 1905, November 26, 1905.

50. Hauman G. Haugan to Dumbach, December 2, 1905, LUCA; Haugan bio in *Book of Chicago*, 1911 (Chicago: Chicago Evening Post, 1911):110; *CMM*, December 5, 1905; Morris St. Palais Thomas to Dumbach, December 11, 1905, LUCA; Dumbach to Haugan, January 27, 1906, LUCA; "Jesuits to Build School," *CT*, March 10, 1906.

51. Hagan to Dumbach, January 5, 1906, LUCA; St. Palais Thomas to Dumbach, December 11, 1905, LUCA; Dumbach to Joseph W. Cremin, May 11, 1907, LUCA.

52. Archbishop Quigley to Rev. William Barnswell, C.M., January 24, 1906, DePaul University DeAndreis-Rosati Memorial Archives; Rev. Msgr. Harry C. Koenig, ed., *A History of the Parishes of the Archdiocese of Chicago* (Chicago: The Archdiocese of Chicago, 1980): 2:961–965.

53. Circular, "St. Ignatius College, 1906," LUCA.

54. Ibid. See also *SIC* (July 1906): 36-37.

55. See Dillon and Kavanagh biographies in Charles F. French, ed., *Biographical History of the American Irish in Chicago* (Chicago and New York: American Biographical Publishing Co., 1897; Patrick H. O'Donnell to Dumbach, January 13, 1906, LUCA; *CT*, March 20, 1895; "First Annual Exhibition, June 28, 1871," LUCA; *CMM*, February 16, 1906.

56. See *Biograhical Sketches of the Leading Men of Chicago* (Chicago: Wilson, Peirce & Co., 1876); *Biographical History of the American Irish in Chicago*, 1897; and *Biographical Dictionary of American Architects (Deceased)*, ed. by Henry F.

Withey and Elsie Rathburn Withey (Los Angeles: Hennessy & Ingalls, Inc., 1970).

57. James J. Egan to Dumbach, September 7, October 15, November 16, December 3, 1906, LUCA; "New Jesuit Church," *NW*, March 9, 1907; *CMM*, May 16, 1907. See especially, Nancy Lennon, *Saint Ignatius Parish, Chicago: The First Century* (Virginia Beach, VA: The Donning Company Publishers, 2007).

58. Hotel St. Benedict Flats was designated a Chicago landmark on March 26, 1996. For background information, see "Hotel St. Benedict Flats," Commission on Chicago Historical and Architectural Landmarks, revised February 1986.

59. "One Curse of Great Cities," *CT*, April 8, 1881.

60. Quote from *Chicago Inter Ocean*, May 20, 1883, in "Hotel St. Benedict Flats."

61. "St. Joseph's German Catholic Church," *Chicago Republican*, December 25, 1865.

62. "Among Architects and Builders," *CT*, July 24, 1898; John V. Fox, "How One Man Views the North Shore," *CT*, December 25, 1904; Garvy home building permit, *American Contractor* (June 23, 1906); *Who's Who in Chicago*, 1936; "Dr. A. C. Garvy of Loyola Gets State Medical Post," *CT*, November 19, 1937; Mary Garvy obituary, *CT*, September 17, 1926; "Father Arnold J. Garvy, S.J.," *Lineage: A Biographical History of the Chicago Province* (Chicago: Loyola University Press, 1987):22–24; "Cleric in Area Observes 50th Year as Priest," *CT*, July 2, 1950.

63. *SIC* (November 1906): 24; *SIC* (July 1907): 46.

64. *SIC* (July 1906): 36; *SIC* (Nov. 1906): 43, 45–47; *SIC* (January 1907): 44-47. For World Series coverage see, *CT* and *Chicago Daily News*, October 15, 1906.

65. Patrick J. Mulhern, "The Rhodes Scholarship," *SIC* (Apr. 1907): 25-26; Thomas Q. Beesley, "The Rhodes Scholarship," *SIC* (April 1908): 10-12; *WL* (1907):174-75; "Pass Oxford Examinations," *NW*, March 9, 1907.

66. "Reception to the Vice President," *SIC* (April 1907): 22–24; *CT*, March 3, 18, 19, 1907; "Fairbanks Tastes of Roosevelt Rush," *Chicago Daily News*, March 18, 1907; "Fairbanks Lauds Heroes of Erin," *CT*, March 19, 1907.

67. *CMM*, October 23, 1907; November 11, 1907.

68. *CT*, November 11, 1907; *NW*, November 9, 16, 1907; Mulkerins, *Holy Family*, 301–305, 237–238; "Feast for the Infirm," *Chicago Record-Herald*, November 14, 1907.

69. "New Head for St. Ignatius," *CT*, February 11, 1908; "Change of College Rectors," *NW*, February 15, 1908; 49-51. According to the March 16, 1881 minutes of the Loyola Debating Society, A. J. Burrowes, S.J., professor of the Humanities Class, "read a paper on Washington Irving which was highly applauded by the society and for which he was rewarded with a degree of honorary membership," box 3, Chrysostomiam Society.

70. [John J. Steinbach] "Architect Blessed by Pope," *CT*, August 9,1908; Jennifer M. Masengarb, "Changing Face: The Architectural identities of two Polish immigrant churches in early twentieth-century Chicago," M.A. thesis (University of Virginia, 2000); John J. Steinbach obituary, *CT*, May 30, 1958; Henry Worthmann obituary, *Illinois Society of Architects Monthly Bulletin* (July-August 1946): 8; *Modern Buildings Designed by Worthmann & Steinbach* (Chicago, c. 1905), Concordia Historical Institute, St. Louis; the firm's office was located at what is now 1859 W. Chicago Avenue.

71. Original sketch of St. John Berchmans, *Modern Buildings*: 11; St. John Berchmans dedication book, Archdiocese of Chicago's Joseph Cardinal Bernardin Archives and Records Center. Jesuit colleges and universities in the United States began to celebrate the feast of St. John Berchmans following his canonization on January 15, 1888, *WL* (1888):103.

72. "Archbishop Dedicates Church," *NW*, December 21, 1907.

73. "To Erect New College," *Chicago Record-Herald*, June 25, 1908. The earliest description of "Loyola University," is by Thomas Quinn Beesley, *SIC* (July 1908): 35-37.

74. For biographical information on Burrowes see Thomas J. Jablonsky, *Milwaukee's Jesuit University: Marquette, 1881-1981* (Milwaukee: Marquette University Press, 2007); Burrowes's biographical file, MJA; "St. Louis-born Jesuit Becomes Head of St. Louis University," *Western Watchman* (February 8, 1912), MJA; "Father Alexander J. Burrowes," *WL* 57(1928): 86–91.

75. "'Fight to End' on Socialism," *CT*, February 12, 1908; ad for DePaul University, *NW* (February 15, 1908): 21; Burrowes to Meyer, Mar. 31, 1908, MJA, cited by Lester Goodchild 2:351; Rudolph J. Meyer, S.J. to Burrowes, May 14, 1908, LUCA.

76. "University for North Side," *CT*, June 24, 1908; *Chicago Record-Herald*, June 24,25, 1908. See also Carl Smith, *The Plan of Chicago: Daniel Burnham and the Remaking of the American City* (Chicago:University of Chicago Press, 2006).

Chapter 3

1. "New University Born in Chicago," *CT*, October 18, 1909.

2. *WL* (1909):298.

3. "Growth of Catholic Colleges," *NW*, October 23, 1909.

4. *SIC* (January 1910):17–19.

5. "Medical School to Merge with St. Ignatius College," *CT*, August 15, 1909; *SIC*, January 1910.

6. Arnold McMahon, "The Lincoln College of Law," *SIC*, July 1908; "Law Department," St. Ignatius Catalog, 1908–9; *SIC*, November 1908.

7. *SIC* (July 1909): 40; *CT*, April 27, 1909; "Father Alexander Burrowes," *WL* (1928): 90.

8. *CT*, March 1, 3, 1910; Alexander J. Burrowes, S.J., to Rudolph J. Meyer, S.J., March 11, 1910, LUCA.

9. Abraham Flexner, *Medical Education in the United States and Canada: A Report to the Carnegie Foundation for the Advancement of Teaching*; Bulletin No. 4. New York: Carnegie Foundation for the Advancement of Teaching, 1910: 207–20, LUCA; "Scores Chicago's Medical Schools," *CT*, June 6, 1910.

10. *CT*, June 6, 1910.

11. Henry S. Spalding. S.J., "The Beginning of the Loyola University Medical School and an Account of the School During the First Ten Years," n. d., LUCA. Over the years there has been disagreement about the founding date of Loyola's medical school. Some sources point to 1909, others to 1915 or to 1917. However, on October 23, 1909, Francis Xavier Wernz, S.J., Father General of the Society of Jesus, wrote to Alexander Burrowes, S.J. from Rome, praising him for "making your School of Medicine so closely associated with the College and with clear and specific agreements." The 1910 Catalog of the Missouri Jesuit Province identified Henry S. Spalding, S.J. as regent of the School of Medicine. See also Richard A. Matre, *Loyola University and its Medical Center: A Century of Courage and Turmoil* (Chicago: Department of Printing Services, Loyola University Chicago, 1995).

12. Burrowes to Meyer, January 25, 1910, MJA.

13. "Cudahy Aids Chicago School," *CT*, June 22, 1910.

14. "$135,000 Given to New University," *CT*, June 6, 1910; *SIC*, July 1910; Mrs. Barbara De Jonghe obituary, *CT*, July 11, 1911; Burrowes to Meyer, December 23, 1910, LUCA.

15. *WL* (1909): 299; *Georgetown College Journal* (October and November 1909); "Loyola Installs Seismograph," *Chicago Record-Herald*, September 7, 1912;

"Chicago Jarred by Earthquake," *CT*, October 1, 1912; "As the Earth Shakes, a Machine Below the Bronx Takes Note," *New York Times*, November 20, 2006.

16. "New Dean at Loyola University," *CT*, January 4, 1911; *WL* (1911): 258; *Catalog 1910–11*.

17. Floyd A. Harley, "Pharmacy," *Catalog, 1910–11*.

18. "Loyola University," *SIC*, July 1908; Burrowes to McMahon, September 21, 1911, LUCA.

19. *SIC*, March 1912, March 1911.

20. [R.T.Crane] *CT*, June 9, 1907; "Gives Last Blow to College Men," *CT*, January 9, 1912; *SIC*, May 1912; Burrowes, "Christian Education," reprint of his speech at the dedication of Cudahy Science Hall, April 28, 1912," in *SIC*, July 1912.

21. Frederic Siedenburg, S.J., to Meyer, March 7, 1912, MJA; Mathery to Meyer, March 5, 1912, MJA.

22. Paul M. Breen, S.J. to Meyer, March 27, 1912, LUCA; *Loyola University Magazine*, November 1912.

23. Sketch of engineering hall in *Loyola University Magazine* (March 1914); *NW*, February 17, 1914.

24. Westbrook Pegler to J. E. Cooper, S.J., October 20, 1949, James Westbrook Pegler Papers, Herbert Hoover Presidential Library, West Branch, Iowa; Westbrook Pegler, "Alumnus' Recalls When Loyola Played Football Just in Fun," *CT*, December 6, 1930.

25. "Splendid Tribune to Worthy Work," *NW*, January 9, 1914; "Catholic Women Honor Priest," *NW*, April 24, 1914.

26. *The Protectorate of the Catholic Woman's League Yearbook*, 1913-14, featured an ad for Loyola's School of Sociology; Rev. Gardner MacWhorter, "Loyola School of Sociology Showing Brisk Development," *CT*, December 5, 1920.

27. L. Frederick Happel, "Rev. Frederic Siedenburg, S.J.," *Loyola University Magazine*, March 1914.

28. "Alumni Notes," *SIC*, January 1912.

29. "A Catholic Lecture Bureau," *America*, October 12, 1912; "Catholic Lecture Bureaus," *America*, January 11, 1913; Paul Blakely, S.J., "Sociology," *America*, September 4, 1915; Loyola University Lecture Bureau, 1913–1914, LUCA.

30. Rev. W. B. Norton, "News of the Religious World," *CT*, March 14, 1915; Frederic Siedenburg, S.J., "Foreword—A Catholic Historical Society," *Illinois Catholic Historical Review*, July 1918.

31. *Chicago Herald Examiner*, March 14, 1924; "Varied Religious Views to Be Told at Hirsch Center," *CT*, October 11, 1928.

32. Invitation to August 9, 1932 dinner and request for donation for auto, Siedenburg scrapbook; Council on Social Agencies clipping, July 5, 1932, Siedenburg Scrapbook; Graham Taylor to Frederic Siedenburg, S.J., June 26, 1932, Ms Taylor, series 2, box 10, folder 408, The Newberry Library.

33. Gifford Ernest, "Father Siedenburg's Work Here on the Eve of Departure," *Chicago Daily News*, August 4, 1932; Hartnett to Charles Shanabruch, April 15, 1974, LUCA.

34. November 18, 1916 Loyola University Alumnae letter re. scholarship, LUCA; *Loyola University Magazine* (November 1920); "Woman Teacher to Quit Schoolroom for Law Practice," *CT*, August 4, 1922; Senior Class of Department of Law Loyola University Banquet, June 8, 1925, LUCA.

35. *Loyola University Magazine*, March 1916.

36. "Evasion of Entrance Requirements to Medical colleges," and "High School Credentials for Sale," *Journal of the American Medical Association* (February 7, 1914): 462, 477-81. "Credential Mill Used As Lure to Medical School," *CT*, February 7, 1914; "Call Upon Owens for Explanation," *CT*, February 8, 1914; "Loyola and the Bennett Medical," *NW*, April 10, 1914; *America* (December 5, 1914):205; "A Reply to the Charges of the American Medical Association Journal," KANE, box 8; Spalding, "The Beginning of the Loyola University Medical School and An Account of the School During the First Ten Years," c. 1929.,LUCA.

37. April 12, 1915 agreement between John D. Robertson, M.D. and John L. Mathery, S.J.,KANE, box 8; "Loyola Absorbs Bennett Medics," *CT*, Apr. 15, 1915; Spalding to G. M. Wells, August 26, 1915, LUCA; "Medical Commencement," Loyola University Magazine (July 1916); "Loyola Has Long Trained Doctors for War Service," *NW*, May 4, 1917. On July 27, 1934, T. H. Ahearn, S.J., regent of Loyola's School of Medicine, wrote the Cook County Assessor that, "In 1915, however Bennett was taken over and made the medical school of Loyola University," KANE, box 8.

38. Spalding to Burrowes, July 20, 1917, MJA.; J. B. Furay, S.J. Burrowes, July 23, 1917, LUCA; Furay to Burrowes, August 30, 1917, MJA; Spalding to students, September 15, 1917, LUCA; *Loyola University Magazine*, November 1917.

39. Spalding, "The Beginning of the Loyola University Medical School."

40. "State Board Statistics for 1919," in *Journal of the American Medical Association*, April 17, 1920: 1094; "Medical Education in the United States: Annual Presentation of the Educational Statistics by the Council on Medical Education and Hospitals of the American Medical Association, 1920." Reprinted from the Educational Number of the *Journal of the American Medical Association*, August 7, 1920; *Loyola University Magazine* (November 1920).

41. Bertha Van Hoosen, *Petticoat Surgeon* (Chicago: Pellegrini & Cudahy, 1947):198–99.

42. Van Hoosen, *Scopolamine-Morphine Anaesthesia* (Chicago: The House of Manz, 1915); "Twilight Sleep Aids 24 Mothers," *CT*, December 10, 1914).

43. John M. Warren, "The Medical School Progress," *Loyola Quarterly*, November 1921; *Province News-Letter* (December 1920):20.

44. Louis D. Moorhead, *Loyola University Magazine*, July 1917; *WL* (1922): 295; *Province News-Letter* (November 1921): 20; John B. Furay, S.J., to Edward F. Hoban., July 26, 1921, LUCA; Hoban to Furay, S.J., September 9, 1921, LUCA; R. M. Kelley, S.J., diary entry, September 11, 1928.

45. "Loyola Mothercraft Lectures, October–December 20, 1920, Loyola University School of Medicine," Siedenburg scrapbook, LUCA; "The Stork's New Palace," *CT*, February 3, 1921; "University Chronicle," *Loyola University Magazine*, March 1921.

46. "Loyola Roll of Honor," *Loyola Magazine* (July 1917); "Tierney and Zvetina Leave for O.T.C.," *Loyola News* (hereafter cited as *LN*), November 2, 1918; remarks by John A. Zvetina on June 19, 1974, LUCA.

47. "Fr. Furay and Geo. Mulligan Address Unit," *LN*, November 2, 1918.

48. "Loyola Marches to Loop on Victory Day," *LN*, November 16, 1918; November 11, 1918, *Diarium*; biographical material on John A. Zvetina, LUCA; "Mass for War Heroes," *CT*, January 25, 1919; "5,000 to Enact Foreign Group Festival Today," *CT*, August 23, 1941.

49. "'Outer Chicago' Grows Rapidly," *CT*, June 30, 1912; "3 New Stations on North Side 'L' Ready Jan. 1," *CT*, December 1, 1920.

50. "Address at the Dedication of the New Church of St. Ignatius Loyola, Chicago, September 16, 1917," in *Two Crowded Years* (Chicago: Extension Press, 1918): 216–219; George A. Lane, S.J., *Chicago Churches and Synagogues: An Architectural Pilgrimage* (Chicago: Loyola University Press, 1981): 144–145.

51. St. Ignatius parish bulletin (June 1921): 23; *Province News-Letter* (June 1921): 68.

52. Edward R. Kantowicz, "Cardinal Mundelein and the Shaping of Twentieth-Century American Catholicism," in *Catholicism, Chicago Style*, eds.

S.J. to John C. Hayes, March 23, 1960 and Hayes to Mulligan, April 1, 1960, Committee on Religious Welfare: retreat, 1953-1966.

27. http://www.macfound.org; Jim Ritter, "Chicago writer wins genius grant," *Chicago Sun-Times*, September 25, 2007; Robert K. Elder, "Stuart Dybek: We knew he was a genius all along," *CT*, September 25, 2007.

28. Dybek interview with Elizabeth Nolan, Chicago History Museum, December 10, 2007.

29. Ibid.

30. Dybek e-mail to Ellen Skerrett, June 25, 2007; Stuart Dybek, "Notes on a 'Time Passing' Retreat," *LN*, May 2, 1963; "Sea Sonnet," *LN*, May 7, 1964.

31. "The Long Thoughts," from *Cadence*, December 1962, revised, appeared in Dybek's first collection of fiction, *Childhood and Other Neighborhoods* (Chicago: University of Chicago Press, 1980).

32. "Mandatory Mass: Forced Religion or Obligation," *LN*, April 12, 1962; "Fr. Maguire Outlines LU Problems and Prospects," *LN*, May 3, 1962; Peter Gilmour, "Required Mass A Mess?" *LN*, May 2, 1963; John C. Hayes memo, March 3, 1966, Committee on Religious Welfare, 1953-1966.

33. Hartnett memo, August 10, 1962, LUCA.

34. Ibid.

35. "Basketball, 1958 *Loyolan*: 240; ESPN feature on Loyola's 1963 NCAA men's basketball championship team aired on February 7, 2003; John Husar, "Ireland's Loyola champions triumphed over racism," *CT*, March 25, 1979; "Ron Fimrite, "It Was More Than Just a Game," *Sports Illustrated* (Nov. 18, 1987): 106–14; Gene Frenette, "Before Texas Western, Loyola Traveled 'Glory Road'," *Florida Times-Union*, January 17, 2006; Neil Milbert, "Praise for a forgotten foe," *CT*, December 14, 2007.

36. ESPN feature; *CT*, March 25, 30, 1963. On March 25, 1963, Marilynn Gayda asked Father Maguire to "lodge a protest against the use of the canine corps" after the NCAA win, March 25, 1963. Maguire responded that the matter "has been brought to the attention of Mayor Daley and will also be discussed with the Superintendent of Police, Mr. O.W. Wilson," MAGUIRE, box 25 folder 4. Richard A. Barry e-mail to Ellen Skerrett, February 6, 2007. As director of Loyola public relations, Barry "designed and had placed on the west wall of the Alumni Gym" the 1963 NCAA championship sign; "Basketball Banquet Honors Ramblers," *LN*, May 2, 1963.

37. Baumhart to Maguire, March 24, 1963, MAGUIRE, box 28 folder 5.

38. The nuns' moving story of how they decided to participate in the demonstration appeared in *Community* (Summer 1963), a Friendship House publication, and became the basis for the account in Suellen Hoy, *Good Hearts: Catholic Sisters in Chicago's Past*, University of Illinois Press, 2006. See also John T. McGreevy, *Parish Boundaries: The Catholic Encounter with Race in the Twentieth-Century Urban North*, University of Chicago Press, 1996.

39. Who are we? Margaret O'Brien Steinfels and Barry Hillenbrand wrote this story with close attention from Peter Steinfels; his 3,500-word article, "The Students and Mrs. Lewis," was published in *New City*, July 15, 1963; Nancy Amidei recollected her part in various e-mails to us; Micki (G. Marie Leaner) answered a query from us via e-mail. James Masek, Richard McGlynn, and David Fishman helped clarify facts and events. Ellen Skerrett, who invited this essay, provided reams of archival material.

40. The entire May 9, 1963 issue of the *Loyola News* is missing from the microfilm of the newspaper in the university's archives; Professor Richard McGlynn of Texas Tech provided a copy. Warren Bracy graduated from Loyola in 1964. After serving as an army lieutenant and intelligence officer in Vietnam, he received a master's degree in political science from Rutgers and a law degree from Cornell. At the time of his death in May 1996, Bracy was a law professor at North Carolina Central University. Nancy Amidei is project director, The Civic Engagement Project, and Senior Lecturer, University of Washington School of Social Work, Seattle, WA.

41. Dr. David Fishman recalls that the group spontaneously formed itself, and may have had some logistical help from the Catholic Interracial Council.

42. The marchers included Sister Angelica Seng, Sister Andrina Miller, Sister Austin Doherty, Sister Edgar Woefel, Sister Cecilia Marie Day, and Sister Marita Joseph Kanaly, all members of the School Sisters of St. Francis (Milwaukee); also Sister Anthony Claret Sparks of the Sisters of St. Francis of Mary Immaculate (Joliet); and Rev. Daniel J. Mallette of St. Agatha parish.

43. The papers of the Catholic Interracial Council and Friendship House are available at the Chicago History Museum.

44. Mrs. Frank J. Lewis, "The President's Message," the *Triune*, June 1963.

45. "Mrs. F. J. Lewis Acts in Loyola Picketing," *CT*, July 10, 1963; news release, Illinois Club for Catholic Women, July 9, 1963.

46. "Change of Policy," *America*, (July 20, 1963): 72; ; "Catholic Club Pool Still 'Off Limits,'" *Chicago American*, October 11, 1963; Marciniak to Rev. John J. Egan, April 23, 1965, Marciniak papers, Archives of Archdiocese.

47. "Enrollment in Baccalaureate Degree Programs in Nursing in Catholic Institutions, 1960–1961," MAGUIRE, box 23, folder 11; "Loyola University Background and History," includes projected enrollments for nursing school, 1962–72.

48. Mulligan to Sister Ann Ida Gannon, B.V.M., March 2, 1961, WLA.

49. Joan Frances Crowley, "Remembering 1962–1969," *Mundelein Voices*: 153-80; information on Northland Apartment building and Sullivan Center, WLA.

50. Robert Markus, "O'Hara Sets World Indoor Mile Mark," *CT*, March 7, 1964; Bill Jauss, "More Stadium Lore: O'Hara's mighty mile," *CT*, May 6, 1994; "Report of a Visit to Loyola University, Chicago, Illinois, May 16–20, 1965 for the Commission on Colleges and Universities of the North Central Association of Colleges and Secondary Schools, School of Nursing/Dean Kiniery, box 5 folder 23; enrollment and financial figures in "The Loyola Story," presented to Most Rev. John P. Cody, Archbishop of Chicago, MAGUIRE, box 25 folder 8.

51. "Call Class Building Unique," *CT*, July 8, 1965; "Architect Tells Why the Chicago Style Commands Respect Without Using Fads," *CT*, July 3, 1966; "Loyola Tops Off Building of 10 Stories," *CT*, January 7, 1966; "Dedication Ceremonies Arnold J. Damen Hall, December 4, 1966, LUCA.

52. "Construction Set for February," *CT*, June 30, 1966; "Earth Flies for Loyola," *Chicago Sun-Times*, March 6, 1967; "Suggested Remarks by John F. Smith," MAGUIRE, box 14 folder 3.

53. Baumhart, "Loyola's Medical Center, A Small Miracle: How It Happened," talk LUMC, November 8, 2007; *I Remember It Clearly*: 84.

54. "College Tutoring for Slum Youths in Poverty War," *Chicago American*, May 17, 1966; "Motivation and a Helping Hand," *Chicago Booster*, June 26, 1966.

55. David F. Freeman to Dean Gladys Kiniery, May 27, 1966, and LU School of Nursing, Advisory Committee of the Sealantic Project, May 16, 1968, School of Nursing, Dean Kiniery, box 5 folder 4; Fred E. Crossland to F. Virgil Boyd, Dean, School of Business Administration, March 25, 1969, Niehoff School of Nursing, box 5 folder 2; Maguire to Wayne Tinkle, January 27, 1969 on Jesuit colleges and the admission of Upward Bound students, BAUMHART, university relations, 1966-1985.

56. "Minutes of Ad Hoc Committee Afro-American Requests, July 26, 1968; Walter P. Krolikowski, S.J. to Maguire, February 25, 1969, MAGUIRE, box 14, folder 2; Wayne F. Tinkle to Maguire, memo on Black Students, April 1, 1969, BAUMHART, box 2 folder 8; Final Report of Sealantic Project LUC School of Nursing, May 23, 1969, Kiniery, box 5 folder 6; James F. Maguire to Dr. Frank Cassaretto, February 17, 1969; "Black Conference Report" [April 29, 1969], BAUMHART, box 2 folder 8; Walter P. Krolikowski to Maguire, February 25, 1969; Wayne F. Tinkel to Maguire, April 1, 1969 re. space for black students; Rich Norman, "Housing: But Not for Blacks," *Phoenix*, October 20, 1969; [Committee Without Name] CNW to Maguire, January 30, 1969; A. E. Albini, "Background Data on Committee Without a Name," CWN, March 25, 1969, MAGUIRE, box 19 folder 13.

Chapter 6

1. James F. Maguire, "Progress for Loyola University in the Seventies," LUMC *Profile*, April 1972; "Ideas to be covered by Joseph Lanterman," LUCA; statistics quoted in Smith press release, January 15, 1971, LUCA.

2. Baumhart, *I Remember It Clearly*; biography, LUCA; Father Baumhart received three degrees from Loyola University: a bachelor of arts in 1950; a licentiate in philosophy, cum laude, in 1952; and a licentiate in theology in 1958.

3. "Loyola University Appoints John F. Smith, Jr. First Lay Chairman of the Board of Trustees," press release, January 15, 1971, LUCA.

4. Philip A. Doyle to Maguire, July 2, 1969 on problems facing Maywood; Edward Bobinchak, S.J, "Report on Activities in Maywood and East Proviso," January to June 1969, LUCA; "Report of the Survey Visit to Stritch School of Medicine Loyola University," January 11–14, 1971, BAUMHART; Gail Danks Welter, "Maywood" in *Local Community Fact Book: Chicago Metropolitan Area* (Chicago: Chicago Fact Book Consortium, 1984): 257–258; and Jean Louise Guarino, "Maywood," in *Encyclopedia of Chicago*: 513. Located in unincorporated Cook County, Loyola University Hospital's postal address is Maywood, IL.

5. Baumhart, "Loyola's Medical Center, A Small Miracle: How It Happened," talk at LUMC, November 8, 2007; *I Remember It Clearly*, 84.

6. "Freeark, Dunne Clash on County Hospital," *CT*, March 13, 1969; Ronald Kotulak, "Freeark Acts to Save Hospital in County's Crowding Crisis," *CT*, March 23,

1969; Kotulak, "Freeark Quits Hospital Post," *CT*, May 16, 1970; "Report of the Survey Visit to Stritch School of Medicine Loyola University," January 11–14, 1971, BAUMHART.

7. Visiting committee report, 17, 9, 23; "History and Current Status of Loyola University Stritch School of Medicine" 1972; Matre: 199–200.

8. Harvey W. Zorbaugh, *The Gold Coast and the Slum* (Chicago: University of Chicago Press, 1929): 115–16; Richard Nelson and Associates report on Washington Square Development, February 6, 1968, MAGUIRE, box 23.

9. "Facts About Speedway," *CT*, July 26, 1915; Floyd Gibbons, "Resta Wins; Sets World Record," *CT*, June 27, 1915.

10. "Loyola Med School on the Move," *NW*, February 2, 1968; "Open House Set at Loyola Hospital," *CT*, May 18, 1969; "McGaws to Receive '73 Sword of Loyola," *NW*, October 26, 1973; "Loyola expands medical center," *CT*, May 10, 1983; "Outpatient Center named for Mulcahys," *Loyola Magazine*, Winter 1984-85.

11. Gary Wisby,"Loyola Unveils Center for Cancer, Care," *Chicago Sun-Times*, September 17, 1994; "Bernardin stands as a beacon of hope for cancer patients," *CT*, May 30, 1996; Joseph Cardinal Bernardin Remarks at LUMC, May 31, 1996; Joseph Cardinal Bernardin, "Cardinal's call to embrace life," *CT*, June 2, 1996.

12. Joseph Cardinal Bernardin and Dr. Anthony Barbato remarks at naming of Cardinal Bernardin Cancer Center, May 31, 1996; Daniel J. Lehmann, "Loyola's cancer center renamed for Bernardin," *Chicago Sun Times*, October 30, 1996; See also, *CT*, November 21, 1996.

13. Amanda Barrett, "One-sword salute—nun who authored 'Dead Man Walking' honored by Stritch School of Medicine," *CT*, November 28, 1996. See also John T. McGreevy, *Catholicism and American Freedom* (New York: W. W. Norton & Company, 2003):282-87.

14. "Ronald McDonald House Charities donates $10 million to support children's hospital," *Loyola World*, October 17, 1996; John Gorman, "McDonald's Fast-Rising Burger King," *CT*, October 13, 1986.

15. June 1966 report, "Date Supporting a Proposal for Urban Renewal Action Submitted by Henrotin Hospital and Loyola University," cited by Richard Lawrence Nelson, February 6, 1968 in his "Report on Actions Which Now Need to be Taken on the Washington Square Development Program"; "Robert Deshon, "Loyola, Henrotin Ask City Help

for Expansion," *Chicago Daily News*, September 28, 1966; Maguire to Robert Harvanek, S.J., March 28, 1968; see also correspondence relating to Washington Square Project in MAGUIRE, box 23, folder 2.

16. "The Loyola Story," MAGUIRE, box 25, folder 2.

17. John J. Cullerton to Ellen Skerrett, December 21, 2007.

18. Robert T. McAllister (BA 1971, JD 1974),a former U.S. Attorney, now practices law in Denver, CO.

19. Thomas V. McCauley, JD, 1975, received Loyola's St. Robert Bellarmine Award in 1989. He is now a partner at Niesen & Elliott.

20. May 15, 1974 minutes of the meeting of the Executive Committee of the Loyola University Board of Trustees; "Law School Resolution," *Blackacre* (April 1, 1977).

21. May 27, 1980 dedication brochure, James F. Maguire, S.J. Hall; Maggie Daly, "Loyola pays off new law building," *CT*, November 8, 1979.

22. Baumhart to class of 1950 at twenty-fifth reunion, September 13, 1975.

23. Roy Damer, "New Loyola gym 'in wind:' Ireland," *CT*, December 15, 1976; Baumhart statement on Coach Ireland, January 20, 1975.

24. "Building Bridges: A Survey of Minorities Studies and Services at Loyola University of Chicago," n.d., LUCA.

25. Milton A. Gordon, "A Survey of Black Undergraduates," August 1, 1974; Charles W. Murdock to James P. White, April 25, 1979, LUCA.

26. Biographical data on [Agnes] Mary Griffin, WLA; Griffin, *The Courage to Choose: An American Nun's Story* (Boston: Little, Brown and Company, 1975): 40–41; 45; Meg McSherry Breslin, "Mary Griffin, 81, educator, author, feminist, *CT*, April 11, 1998.

27. Griffin, "Reinventing Mundelein: Birthing the Weekend College, 1974," in *Mundelein Voices*: 215–24; "General Statistics—Mundelein College—1931–1991," WLA.

28. Baumhart memo April 7, 1977 announcing the "Project WALK-TO-WORK;" Edgewater Community Council, "Operation Winthrop-Kenmore," May 1, 1979; "Slum turned into residence," *Lerner News*, December 8, 1982.

29. M. W. Newman, "Marciniak: Peacemaker in a Storm," *Chicago Daily News*, August 6, 1963; Edward Marciniak, "Chicago and civil rights—2 'We are making headway,'" *Christian Science Monitor*, March 15, 1967; Edward Marciniak, "The Racial Attitudes of Students in the Catholic Colleges of the Chicago Area," M.A.

Loyola University, 1942; Megs Langdon to Sister Susan Rink, B.V.M., November 18, 1980, WLA.

30. Katie Drews, "Bears president was a Loyola alumnus (sic)," *LN*, January 31, 2007.

31. Steve Daley, "Pete Rozelle's tale of tough times," *CT*, September 3, 1982.

32. Baumhart to Donald A. Smirniotis, July 24, 1986, BAUMHART.

33. "A Proposed Plan for Lake Shore and Water Tower Campuses: Loyola University of Chicago in the 1990's," (draft plan), November 18, 1986: 6, 7.

34. Draft report, November 18, 1986, 8, 10, 17.

35. Cynthia R. Field, "Burnham Plan," *Encyclopedia of Chicago*, 108–9; Thomas S. Hines, *Burnham of Chicago: Architect and Planner* (Chicago: University of Chicago Press (Phoenix edition), 1979; Timothy J. Gilfoyle, *Millennium Park: Creating a Chicago Landmark* (Chicago: University of Chicago Press, 2006); Carl S. Smith, *The Plan of Chicago: Daniel Burnham and the Remaking of the American City* (Chicago: University of Chicago Press, 2006).

36. Williamson and Wild, *Northwestern University*: 252–253.

37. "Clear the Way for Loyola's Landfill," *CT*, April 13, 1988; "Loyola landfill benefits Chicago," *Crain's Chicago Business*, May 16, 1988; James Warren, "City watchdog calling it quits," *CT*, January 3, 1989.

38. Loyola University of Chicago, "Lake Shore Protection: Private Initiative Yields Public Benefits," May 1988, BAUMHART.

39. Baumhart to William Bartholomay, Chicago Park District, January 6, 1989; Charles Nicodemus, "Suit seeks to block Loyola lakefill," *Chicago Sun-Times*, May 17, 1990; according to his online biography, http://www.ilnd.uscourts.gov/judge/ASPEN/MEABio.htm Judge Marvin Aspen received a B.S. degree in Sociology from Loyola University (no date given) and a J.D. from Northwestern University in 1958.

40. "Loyola discontinues Rogers Park/Edgewater lakefill," with Baumhart handwritten comments, BAUMHART; Stevenson Swanson, "Loyola ends controversial lakefill plan," *CT*, July 12, 1990; *CT* editorial, "An empty victory for Lake Michigan," July 16, 1990; Glenda L. Daniel, "Refusal to compromise killed Loyola lakefill," *Chicago Sun-Times*, July 28, 1990; Baumhart to Reuben Hedlund, Chicago Plan Commission, July 31, 1990.

41. LU news release, February 16, 1976, "Loyola Strengthens Administration: Karl Zeisler Named V. P.–Finance"; Laurie Cohen, "Loyola to offer fast-buck, tax exempt bonds," *CT*, June 18, 1980; "Senior VP Kasbeer wraps up a satisfying Loyola career," *Loyola World*, May 5, 1994.

42. Janice Stockwell, "Mallinckrodt Campus: Loyola's new foothold on the North Shore," *Loyola Magazine*, Winter, 1991; Carol Jouzaitis, "Tiny college is reborn by merger with Loyola," *CT*, April 3, 1991.

43. "Mallinckrodt College of the North Shore approved as the Mallinckrodt Campus of Loyola University Chicago," news release, August 9, 1990; "Wilmette trustees clear the way for MCNS to join Loyola," *Loyola World*, August 16, 1990; "Mallinckrodt now part of LUC," *Loyola World*, January 17, 1991. Minnette McGhee, "Loyola expands its program at Mallinckrodt in Wilmette," *Chicago Sun-Times*, March 5, 1991. Dr. Marjorie Noterman Beane began her tenure at Loyola on January 1, 1991 when Mallinckrodt College became a campus of Loyola. At the time of her retirement on April 29, 2005, she was vice president for planning and administration. On May 11, 2006, Father Garanzini dedicated the Marjorie L. Beane Hall in Lewis Towers in recognition of "her extraordinary administrative service and commitment to Loyola students, faculty, and staff."

44. "War, seized cargo, and the King of England: history paves the halls at Mallinckrodt," *Loyola World*, April 22, 1993.

45. "Mundelein Graduates Who Earned the Ph.D. Degree in the 50 Years from 1935 through 1984," WLA; "Mundelein, Loyola announce merger," *CT*, April 17, 1991.

46. Mundelein Sisters on the Coordinating Committee for Affiliation with Loyola," April 3, 1991; bio on Sr. Carol Frances Jegen, B.V.M., WLA.

47. Victoria Higgins, "Q and A with Mundelein's new President," *Features*, March 8, 1991, WLA.

48. Loyola University, Mundelein College discuss affiliation," *Loyola World*, March 28, 1991; Tom Seibel, "Mundelein women back tradition," *Chicago Sun-Times*, April 5, 1991; Carol Jouzaitis, "Mundelein students protest merger talk," *Chicago Tribune*, April 5, 1991.

49. Figures provided by Raymond Baumhart, S.J. to Ellen Skerrett, February 28, 2008.

50. Margery Frisbie, "Mundelein merger is city's loss," *Chicago Sun-Times*, June 15, 1991; Statistics, "Mundelein at Loyola," October 1991, in WLA file; "Mundelein Affiliates With Loyola," *Mundelein Now*, Summer 1991.

51. Griffin, *Mundelein Voices*, 282–85.

52. RB to Dental Alumni, box 10; RB draft essay, "Dental School Closing."

53. John J. Piderit, S.J. bio, LUCA.

54. Frank James, "Loyola Taps Marquette Vice President to Be Chief," *CT*, June 6, 1993; Frank James, "Loyola Has Its Man of Vision," *CT*, June 6, 1993; Bill Jauss,

"Forward Steps—Loyola President Has A Plan to Get the School Moving Toward Renewed Athletic Prowess," *CT*, March 6, 1994; Piderit to "Friends of Loyola" June 1995.

55. Kristina Marlow, "Loyola Inaugurates New Traditions, New Leader," *CT*, April 8, 1994; *Chicago Tribune*, April 10, 1994. A convert to Catholicism in 1940, Cardinal Lustiger advised Pope John Paul II on issues of Jewish-Catholic relations; his mother had been deported from France and died in Auschwitz.

56. "Building New Traditions: The Strategic Plan for the Lakeside Campuses—Loyola University Chicago, 1995–2000," 10–11.

57. Jauss, *CT*, March 6, 1994; Piderit, "Friends of Loyola," 1995; Jauss, "Loyola Seeks 'Glory Days' in New Gym," *CT*, August 28, 1996.

58. Beth McMurtrie, "An Ambitious Catholic University Flexes Its Muscle in Chicago," *Chronicle of Higher Education*, July 12, 2002.

59. William Grady, "Law school takes aim at child abuse," *CT*, September 15, 1993; Bob Greene, "Help is on the way for children in need," *CT*, September 21, 1993; Stephania H. Davis, "Graduates to focus on abused kids," *CT*, May 9, 1996.

60. "LUC President's Coordinating Council," April 12, 1994.

61. Piderit, "Changing Loyola," *CT*, April 7, 2001; "Notes from December 3, 1993 Board of Trustees meeting," LUCA; March 15, 1994 discussion regarding separate incorporation, LUCA; J. Linn Allen, "Plummeting Loyola Enrollment Leaves School Scrambling," *CT*, November 15, 2000.

62. Cindy Schreuder, "Faculty's Vote on Loyola Chief Inconclusive," *CT*, March 9, 1999; Patrice M. Jones, "At the Crossroads—Clouds of Doubt Hover as Loyola Begins Changes," *CT*, September 19, 1999.

63. J. Linn Allen, "Protesters Call for Loyola President's Ouster," *CT*, March 3, 2000.

64. Piderit to members of President's Advisory council and major benefactors, May 9, 2000; Msgr. John J. Egan to Piderit, May 23, 2000.

65. Piderit State of the University Address, November 7, 2000.

66. "Classic Mistakes at Loyola," *CT*, March 30, 2001; Martin van der Werf, "Loyola of Chicago May Eliminate Classics Dept.," *Chronicle of Higher Education*, March 30, 2001. For a discussion of the challenges of leadership and governance see John J. Piderit, S.J. and Melanie M. Morey, *Catholic Higher Education: A Culture in Crisis* (New York: Oxford University Press, 2006).

Chapter 7

1. In announcing the appointment of Michael J. Garanzini, S.J. on January 19, 2001, board of trustees chairman Michael R. Quinlan noted that: "the Board of Trustees and the Presidential Search Committee were impressed with Father Garanzini's strengths in consensus building, communication and problem solving, qualities that will enable him to move easily among groups both inside and outside the community." For a collage of graduation and installation see *Loyola World*, February 13, 2002; Meg Mc Sherry Breslin, "Loyola spirits rise with enrollment," *CT*, September 3, 2001.

2. Bill Noblitt, "Face-to-Face with Loyola's New Leader," *Loyola Magazine* (Summer 2001); "President's Biography," http://www.luc.edu/president/biography.shtml; Kathy Catrambone, "Reverend Michael J. Garanzini President of Loyola University Chicago," www.amiciorgit.net

3. J. Linn Allen, "Plummeting Loyola Enrollment Leaves School Scrambling," *CT*, November 15, 2000; Robert Becker, "Loyola's endowment shrinks—University used reserves in '90s," *CT*, November 5, 2002.

4. *Chronicle of Higher Education* reported on March 9, 2001 that Herta and John Cuneo had donated $14 million to Loyola University's school of medicine.

5. "Loyola grows upbeat as troubles subside," *CT*, December 28, 2003; "Loyola Again Sets New Enrollment Records," University News, http://www2.luc.edu.news/media/releases//enrollment.shtml; Garanzini, "State of the University Address," September 2004, LUCA; enrollment figures from John P. Pelissero, PhD, vice provost, Division of Academic Affairs, to Ellen Skerrett, April 21, 2008.

6. Christine Wiseman, J.D. is the first permanently appointed female chief academic officer at LUC http://www.luc.edu/academicaffairs.bio_wiseman.shtml; according to "Loyola University Chicago Unveils 2007-08 Enrollment Figures," news release, November 1, 2007: "Currently, Loyola is the largest Jesuit, Catholic university in the United States, the nation's third-largest Catholic university overall, and the nation's largest Catholic comprehensive doctoral institution." Loyola's total enrollment of 15,545 in 2007 included 2,035 new freshmen and 740 transfers.

7. Ann Keeton, "Priest Turns Around Chicago's Loyola," *Wall Street Journal*, December 14, 2005; March 1, 2005 draft, "Loyola University Chicago Comprehensive Campaign White Paper," LUCA.

8. Chris Kopacz and Blair Brown, "Mallinckrodt campus for sale," *Phoenix*, September 26, 2001; Susan Dodge, "Loyola plans to sell Wilmette campus," *Chicago Sun-Times*, October 4, 2001; Wayne Magdziarz statement on Mallinckrodt Campus Property, January 8, 2002; Monica Patankar, Mallinckrodt developers announced," *Phoenix*, February 6, 2002.

9. Mary A. Healey, B.V.M., "Mundelein/Loyola's Piper Hall Begins a New Chapter in a Storied Life," http://www.bvmcong.org/Salt/salt/fall2005/healey.htm. For information on Carolyn Farrell, B.V.M. endowed chair, see Susan Ross, "Greetings from the Director," *Linkage: The Spirit of Mundelein* (Spring 2008):1.

10. Charles Storch, "New Loyola museum of art to unveil its hidden jewel," *CT*, November 22, 2004.

11. Maudlyne Ihejirika, "Loyola University gets its biggest gift ever: $20 million," *Chicago Sun-Times*, December 7, 2005; Jodi S. Cohen, "Loyola schools given 2 big gifts," *CT*, December 7, 2005. Since the announcement of the Hank gift, the MacNeal Foundation has been renamed the Arthur Foundation.

12. *Madonna della Strada Chapel: Jubilee Celebration 2007-2008*, LUCA. Michelle Martin, "Loyola reopens lakefront chapel," *Catholic New World*, October 14-27, 2007.

13. Meltem Aktas, "My vision for Madonna della Strada," LUCA. Shannon McEntee, "Divine Inspiration," *Echo* (Winter 2002): 28-29; Amy E. Nevala, "Artist puts face on native saints," *CT*, January 10, 2003.

14. Lucien Roy quoted in *Madonna della Strada Chapel*: 31.

15. Patrice M. Jones, "The miracle along the lake," *Chicago Tribune Magazine*, March 26, 2006. On March 27, 2006, the university launched its "Loyola Values" campaign, created and executed entirely by Loyola's Division of Marketing and Communications department, headed by Kelly L. Shannon. Michael Garanzini to Ellen Skerrett, November 20, 2007, and April 10, 2008.

16. Frederic Siedenburg, S.J., "A Plea for Old Age Pensions," *Catholic Charities Review* (January 1930): 38-40. The Loyola University Chicago Board of Trustees announced the new School of Communication on December 13, 2007.

17. Jodi S. Cohen, "Couple's love benefits Loyola," *CT*, September 5, 2006; Terese Terry quote from DVD recording by John Hillman, September 7, 2006, LUCA.

18. Raymond C. Bauhmart quote, September 7, 2006 dedication; Alyssa Przybyl, "Block Party Takes over East Pearson," *Phoenix*, September 13, 2006.

19. Robert A. Seal, "Remarks," at opening of Information Commons, December 7, 2007, LUCA.

20. "SCB Wins 2007 LEAF Award," Solomon Cordwell Buenz, http://www.scb.com; Russell Fortmeyer, "Getting Aggressive About Passive Design," *Architectural Record*, May 2007; Brendan Keating, "Learning on the Lake," *Loyola Magazine* (Spring 2008): 10-13.

21. "New University Born in Chicago," *CT*, October 18, 1909.

22. "About TIF/FAQS," http://www.luc.edu/tif/about.shtml See also *Phoenix*, February 13, 2006.

23. Fran Spielman, "Police to retire star: 1st line of duty death of '06," *Chicago Sun-Times*, February 14, 2006; "Officer's Badge Retired," *CT*, September 8, 2006.

24. Michael J. Garanzini, S.J., "State of the University Address," February 2002, praised Wayne Magdziarz's diligent efforts to "sell the Mallinckrodt campus in order to secure for us the resources we need to do some of the work on this [Water Tower] campus." For information on Loyola Station, see Michael Brosko, *Loyola Magazine*, Fall 2008.

25. Garanzini quote from "State of the University Address," Lake Shore Campus, April 8, 2008. See also articles by Caitlin Smith and Ahad Syed, *Phoenix*, April 9, 2008.

26. "Tulane doctor to lead Loyola Health System," *CT*, December 14, 2006; "Loyola hospital opens its high-tech tower," *CT*, April 7, 2008; Bruce Japsen, "Loyola hospitals chief making a mark in a hurry," *CT*, April 27, 2008. For an announcement of the Gottlieb merger, see "Loyola to take over Gottlieb," *CT*, January 30, 2008. The Gottlieb merger was pending state approval as this publication went to press.

27. Garanzini to Skerrett, November 20, 2007.

Index

Acknowledgments

In researching and writing the history of Loyola University Chicago, I am indebted to many individuals. Foremost is President Michael J. Garanzini, S.J. Not only did he support my vision for a book that would be substantive—and beautiful—but he selected a title that captured the spirit of the university, *Born in Chicago*.

Robert F. Ward's enthusiasm for this book has been maintained by his successor, Nicole LeDuc Meehan, Director of Alumni Relations. Martin J. Lane, assistant director, shared his extensive knowledge of Loyola, and I am grateful for his keen attention to detail.

As the manuscript moved into production, Lorraine G. Snyder, special assistant to the president, provided invaluable help. I also appreciate the assistance of Jonathan R. Heintzelman, Wayne Magdziarz, Kelly Shannon, Maeve Kiley, Katie Hession, Carla Beecher, and proofreading by Anastasia Busiek.

I thank Kathryn Young, university archivist, for providing hundreds of Xeroxes and appreciate the scans made by Rebecca Hyman, assistant archivist. I remain grateful for the research assistance of Dr. Elizabeth A. Myers, now director of Loyola's Women and Leadership Archives.

As I began my work, Candace O'Connor shared her wisdom about writing the 2003 history of Washington University in St. Louis. Thomas J. Jablonsky also generously sent me information from his fine history of Marquette University. I am particularly indebted to Suellen Hoy, Ann Durkin Keating, Timothy B. Neary, Malachy R. McCarthy, John C. O'Malley, Joan A. Radtke, and Rima Lunin Schultz, who read the entire manuscript and offered valuable advice. My gratitude extends as well to Raymond C. Baumhart, S.J., and Dr. Marjorie Beane for sharing documentation on Loyola's development.

Born in Chicago has benefited significantly from the vivid recollections of Margaret O'Brien Steinfels, Peter Steinfels, Barry Hillenbrand, James Masek, Richard McGlynn, Stuart Dybek, John J. Cullerton, Dr. Anthony Barbato, Heather Accurso, and Andre Zielinski. Finding rare documents and images to tell the Loyola story was an adventure that succeeded because of so many generous souls, among them Timothy Appel; Michael P. Barrett; Richard D. Barrett; Mary Jo Collins Barry; Richard A. Barry; Timothy V. Barton; Bill Behrns; John Belmonte, S.J.; Lyle Benedict; Sonia Birocheau; Rev. Jeremiah Boland; Heather Bourk; Monique and John Brinkman; John D. Burke; Laura Carroll; Rev. Dr. Elaine S. Caldbeck; Ann Caron; John P. Chalmers; Lynn Conway; James M. Corboy; John E. Corrigan; Frank Covey; Sister Joella Cunnane, R.S.M.; Martha Curry, R.S.C.J.; Marguerite (Peg) Cusick; William Cuthbertson; Kathryn DeGraff; Mary A. Dempsey; Brian S. Donovan; Charles Fanning; Sarah J. Fleming; John Fiedler; Ann Fritzsche; Ray Gadke; Gerald Gems; Frances Gimber, R.S.C.J.; Tom Gnidovic; Monica Grayless; Tom Guerra; David Hagen; Alvin Hayashi; Anita Therese Hayes, B.V.M.; Raymond J. Heisler; Kevin B. Herbert; Dr. Philip M. Hillmer; Morgen MacIntosh Hodgetts; Donald Hoffman; Frank Hogan III; Harry Hoit; Richard Holland; Donald Hubert; Michael D. Jacobs; Carol Frances Jegen, B.V.M.; Joy Kingsolver; Elaine Kreuz; John J. Lane; Paul Lane; Robert C. Lane; Leo Latz II; Peggy Lavelle; Mary Lesch; Lauranne Lifka, B.V.M.; John C. Lillig; Dolores Madlener; Jackie Maman; Lesley Martin; Michelle Martin; Jennifer Masengarb; Robert Medina; David P. Miros; Bryan McDaniel; Thomas McElligott; John T. McGreevy; David P. McGuire; Frank Morrissey; Elizabeth Nolan; Emmett Nolan; Margaret O'Gara; Monica O'Gara; Janet Olson; Lori Osborne; Brian Paulson, S.J.; David Pavelich; William Cremin Perlitz; John Planek; Wendy Plotkin; Daniel Pogorzelski; Robert Pruter; Ralph Pugh; Charles Purcell; Patrick M. Quinn; Rick Rann; Charles S. Rollings; Sharon Roth; Maureen E. Ryan; Julie Satzik; Richard Seidel; Robert A. Sideman; Mary Cassaretto Simon; Deborah Simpkins; Linda Stahnke; Martin Steinfels; Michelle Sweetser; Scott Taylor; Erin Tikovitsch; Debbie Vaughan; Timothy Walch; Richard Williams; Harold T. Wolff; Dr. John Wozniak; Teresa Yoder; and Florence and John Zvetina.

The design of Beth Herman Adler and Carrie Bruggers on *Born in Chicago* is unmistakable, as are Mark Beane's stunning photographs. Collaborating with Sylvia B. Bace, editor extraordinaire, has been a pleasure. But my deepest debt is to the O'Malleys for their abiding love and faith—John, Mary, Ellen, and Maisie.

Ellen Skerrett

Credits

Heather Accurso, 247

American Medical Association, 67; JAMA, August 6, 1904: 391 c American Medical Association. All rights reserved.

Antunovich & Associates, Architects, 275 bottom

Archdiocese of Chicago's Joseph Cardinal Bernardin Archives and Records Center, 72 top, 81 middle, 87 top, 117 top

Archivum Romanum Societatis Iesu, Rome (ARSI), 26 top

Art Institute of Chicago, 238 bottom; Jules Guerin, delineator, Edward Herbert Bennett, architect; Plan of Chicago, Plate 87: View Looking West Over the City, Showing the Proposed Civic Center, the Grand Axis, Grant Park, and the Harbor, 1907, Watercolor and graphite on paper, approx. 140 x 230 cm, Gift of Patrick Shaw, 1991.1381.

Author's collection, 5 left, 6, 8, 11, 13, 19 top, 20, 25, 26 bottom, 32 top, 33 top, 35, 38, 42, 49 top, 51 bottom left, 54, 60, 73 top, 75 middle, 76 top, 76 bottom, 78 middle, 82 top, 83 bottom, 84, 86 right, 88 top, 93, 97 top, 98 bottom, 106 top, 115 top, 123 middle, 129 top, 151, 152, 157, 183, 196, 238 top

Timothy V. Barton, 29, 50, 69, 71, 74 bottom

Mark Beane, LUC, cover photo, inside cover photo, 2-3, 15, 16, 17 top, 81 bottom, 85 top, 90-91, 95 top, 134-35, 168 bottom left, 216-217, 242, 256-57, 258 bottom, 261 left, 265 right, 266 top, 267 top right, 268 top right, 269 top left, 269 bottom, 270 right, 271, 272, 273, 274, 276, 277, back cover

Boston Athanaeum, 58

John D. Burke, 112 top

Catholic New World, 202

Chicago History Museum, 4-5 bottom, ICHi-05654; 28, ICHi-39670; 39, ICHi-31336; 45, ICHi-50284; 73 bottom, DN-0000488; 78 top, DN-0008367, 79 top, ICHi-50675; 86 left, DN-0006550; 99, ICHi-51645; 164, ICHi-51664; 182 bottom, ICHi-18886; 204, 205 top, Catholic Interracial Council collection

Chicago Public Library Municipal Reference Collection, 70, 74 top, 115 bottom

Chicago Public Library Special Collections and Preservation Division, 5 right, Hesler view from *The Story of Chicago* (1894); 21, CCW 4.15-Jesuite Church, 1866; 31 left, CCW 4.31-Chicago University, 1866; 33 bottom, GP-SMITH 891-137 DeKoven Street

Chicago Tribune, 163 bottom, 166, 199 top, 259 top, photo by Nancy Stone

Concordia Historical Institute, St. Louis, 87 bottom

James M. Corboy, 162 bottom

John J. Cullerton, 227 top

Charles W. Cushman Collection, Indiana University Archives, 226 (P15365)

DePaul University Library Special Collections and Archives, 77 top left, 131 bottom

Evanston History Center, 31 top right, stereopticon card of University Hall, Northwestern University, accession #1963.11.24

Sarah J. Fleming, 46-47, 167 top

Franciscan Sisters of Chicago Service Corporation/Jack Simmerling, 270 left

Georgetown University Archives, 12, "Earliest View of the College, 1863;" 192, Clare Boothe Luce Photographic Collection, 1962, box 9 folder 24

William and Joan Hank, 267 bottom, courtesy William J. and Joan Hank

Bart Harris for Loyola University Chicago, 137, 268 bottom, 269 top right, 269 middle

Alvin Hayashi, Loyola University Health System, 176-77, 223 bottom, 260 right

Dr. Philip M. Hillmer, 96

Herbert Hoover Presidential Library & Museum, 105 bottom

Illinois Institute of Technology Archives (Chicago), 128 middle

Lucy A. Kennedy/Kennedy Photography, 259 bottom, 260 left

George Lane, S.J., 65 bottom

John J. Lane, 156 top, photo by Jacques Lowe for *The Sign*, November 1955

Leo Latz, II, 158, 159

Library of Congress, 30

Loyola Athletics Department/Bud Bertog, 237 bottom

Loyola University Chicago Archives (LUCA), 32 bottom, 34, 37 bottom left, 40, 44, 51 top left, 52, 53, 56, 57, 61, 62, 63, 64 top right, 68, 72 bottom, 75 bottom, 76 middle, 77 top right, 77 bottom, 78 bottom, 79 bottom, 83 top left, 83 top right, 85 bottom, 88 bottom, 89, 92, 94, 95 bottom, 98 top, 101, 102, 103, 104 top, 105 top, 106 bottom, 107, 108, 109, 110, 111,112 bottom, 113 top, 114 middle, 116, 117 middle, 118, 119, 121, 122, 123 top, 123 bottom, 124, 125, 126, 127, 129 bottom, 130, 131 top, 132, 133, 136, 140, 141, 146, 147, 148, 149, 153, 154, 155, 156 bottom, 161 middle, 162 top, 165, 167 middle, 168 top, 168 bottom right, 169 top, 169 middle gift Joan Smith O'Gara, 170, 171, 172, 173, 174, 175, 178, 181, 182 top, 184, 185, 186, 187, 188, 190, 191, 193 bottom gift Kathleen Richards, 194 gift Kate Felice, 195, 197, 199 bottom photo by Thomas J. Dyba, 200, 201 right, 205 bottom, 206, 207, 208, 209, 210, 211, 212, 214-215 bottom photos by Thomas M. Haney, 215 top, 218, 219, 220, 225 middle, 227 bottom, 228, 229 photo by James F. Pelka, 230, 231, 234, 235,

236, 237 top, 239, 240, 243, 248, 249, 250, 251, 252, 253, 255, 258 top photo by Bruce Powell, 266 bottom, 268 top left

Loyola University Chicago Marketing & Communications, 261 right, 262, 263, 264, 265 left

Loyola University Health System (LUHS), 222, 223 top, 224, 225 top, 225 bottom

David P. McGuire, 193 top

Marquette University Department of Special Collections and University Archives, 59 left, 64 bottom

Midwest Jesuit Archives, St. Louis, 9,10, 14, 17 bottom, 36, 37 bottom right, 41, 80, 104 bottom, 161 top

Mary C. O'Malley, 258 middle

Mount Carmel Archives of the Sisters of Charity of the Blessed Virgin Mary, Dubuque, Iowa, 24, 43, 55, 66,

NCAA Photos, 198

Newberry Library, 37 top, Harrison portrait, Midwest MSS Harrison Box 17 folder 826

New York Public Library, 7, I. N. Phelps Stokes Collection, Miriam and Ira D. Wallach Division of Art, Prints and Photographs, The New York Public Library, Astor, Lenox and Tilden Foundations

Northwestern University Special Collections, 128

William Cremin Perlitz, 75 top

Picador, 196 top

Polish Museum of America, 100

John Reilly Photography, 266 middle

Rogers Park/ West Ridge Historical Society, 163 top

Rush University Medical Center Archives, 82 middle

David Seide/Defined Space, 267 top left

St. Ignatius College Prep, 19, 23

St. Louis University Archives, 59 right

Sisters of Mercy, Regional Community of Chicago Archives, 113 bottom

Spertus Museum, 65 top

University of Chicago Library, Special Collections Research Center, 51 bottom General Campus Views. Henry Ives Cobb Plan, 1893. Image #1. "Study [dated] 1893 of the University of Chicago." (apf2-02712)

University of Illinois at Chicago Special Collections, 48, 49 middle

Vanderbilt University Medical Center, Historical Collection, Eskind Biomedical Library, 97

Jeff Williams/Lewis Communications, 275 top

Women and Leadership Archives (WLA), Loyola University Chicago, 120, 138, 139, 142, 143, 144, 145, 179, 201 left, 213, 232, 233, 244, 245

Andre Zielinski, 246

John Zvetina, 114 bottom